Posthumanism

ALSO AVAILABLE FROM BLOOMSBURY

Anatomy of Failure, Oliver Feltham
Beyond Human, edited by Charlie Blake, Claire Molloy and Steven Shakespeare
Invasive Technification, Gernot Böhme
Philosophy and Simulation, Manuel DeLanda

Posthumanism

A critical analysis

STEFAN HERBRECHTER

BLOOMSBURY
LONDON • NEW DELHI • NEW YORK • SYDNEY

Bloomsbury Academic
An imprint of Bloomsbury Publishing Plc

<table>
<tr><td>50 Bedford Square
London
WC1B 3DP
UK</td><td>1385 Broadway
New York
NY 10018
USA</td></tr>
</table>

www.bloomsbury.com

First published 2013

This English translation © Stefan Herbrechter, 2013

© Original edition *Posthumanismus. Eine kritische Einführung*, 2009 by WBG (Wissenschaftliche Buchgesellschaft), Darmstadt.

The translation of this work was funded by Geisteswissenschaften International – Translation Funding for Humanities and Social Sciences from Germany, a joint initiative of the Fritz Thyssen Foundation, the German Federal Foreign Office, the collecting society of VG WORT and the Börsenverein des Deutschen Buchhandels (German Publishers & Booksellers Association).

All rights reserved. No part of this publication may be reproduced or transmitted in any form or by any means, electronic or mechanical, including photocopying, recording, or any information storage or retrieval system, without prior permission in writing from the publishers.

Stefan Herbrechter has asserted his right under the Copyright, Designs and Patents Act, 1988, to be identified as Author of this work.

No responsibility for loss caused to any individual or organization acting on or refraining from action as a result of the material in this publication can be accepted by Bloomsbury Academic or the author.

British Library Cataloguing-in-Publication Data
A catalogue record for this book is available from the British Library.

ISBN: HB: 978-1-7809-3837-0
PB: 978-1-7809-3606-2
ePub: 978-1-7809-3622-2
ePDF: 978-1-7809-3690-1

Library of Congress Cataloging-in-Publication Data
Herbrechter, Stefan.
[Posthumanismus. English]
Posthumanism : a critical analysis / Stefan Herbrechter.
pages cm
Includes bibliographical references and index.
ISBN 978-1-78093-606-2 (pbk.)-- ISBN 978-1-78093-837-0--
ISBN 978-1-78093-622-2 (epub)--
ISBN 978-1-78093-690-1 (pdf)
1. Human beings. 2. Technology–Social aspects. 3. Technology in literature.
I. Title.
BD450.H467813 2013
149–dc23
2013005642

Typeset by Fakenham Prepress Solutions, Fakenham, Norfolk NR21 8NN
Printed and bound in India

Contents

Acknowledgements vi
Preface vii

1 Towards a critical posthumanism 1
2 A genealogy of posthumanism 31
3 Our posthuman humanity and the multiplicity of its forms 75
4 Posthumanism and science fiction 107
5 Interdisciplinarity and the posthumanities 135
6 Posthumanism, digitalization and new media 179
7 Posthumanity – subject and system 195

Afterword: The other side of life 207
Bibliography 214
Index 228

Acknowledgements

Parts of Chapter 2 ('A Genealogy of Posthumanism') previously appeared as '"A passion so strange, outrageous, and so variable": The Invention of the Inhuman in *The Merchant of Venice*', Stefan Herbrechter, in *Posthumanist Shakespeares*, eds Stefan Herbrechter and Ivan Callus, 2012 Palgrave Macmillan, reprinted with permission of the publisher (Palgrave Macmillan, www.palgrave.com).

Parts of Chapter 4 ('Posthumanism and Science Fiction') previously appeared as 'What Is a Posthumanist Reading?', Stefan Herbrechter and Ivan Callus, *Angelaki*, 2008 volume 13, number 1, reprinted by permission of the publisher (Taylor & Francis Ltd, http://www.tandfonline.com).

Preface

What is 'man'? This age-old question is being asked again everywhere today and with increased urgency, given the current technological developments levering out 'our' traditional humanist reflexes. What this development also shows, however, is that the current and intensified attack on the idea of a 'human nature' is only the latest phase of a crisis which, in fact, has always existed at the centre of the humanist idea of the human. The present critical study thus produces a genealogy of the contemporary posthumanist scenario of the 'end of man' and places it within the context of theoretical and philosophical developments and ways of thinking within modernity.

Even though terms like 'posthuman', 'posthumanist' or 'posthumanism' have a surprisingly long history, they have only really started to receive attention in contemporary theory and philosophy in the last two decades where they have produced an entire new way of thinking and theorizing. Only in the last ten years or so, posthumanism has established itself – mainly in the Anglo-American sphere – as an autonomous field of study with its own theoretical approach (especially within the so-called 'theoretical humanities'). The first academic publications that deal systematically with the idea of the posthuman and posthumanism appeared at the end of the 1990s and the early 2000s (these are, in particular, works by N. Katherine Hayles, Cary Wolfe, Neil Badmington and Elaine L. Graham). In conjunction with this theoretical debate, Francis Fukuyama's book *Our Posthuman Future* (1999) about the importance of new biotechnologies for a return to the debate on eugenics opened up a more general philosophical and political discussion. Ever since, a much wider public has shown growing interest in the proliferating ideas and visions of 'our posthumanity'. Many anxieties but also utopian hopes are projected onto new bio-, nano-, neuro- and infotechnologies. These are circulating in the traditional mass media and increasingly, of course, in the so-called 'new', 'digital' and 'social media'. Whereas Fukuyama's contribution to the discussion about the future of the human had been motivated by rather conservative and moralistic motives based on the apparent opposition between technological development and human nature, there has been sheer delight in 'transhumanist' circles at the prospect that these new technoscientific developments might transform us in a not too distant future into a new digital species with fantastic new potential (cf. Hans Moravec, Max Moore, Vernor Vinge and their followers).

The present volume understands itself as a mediating force between these two extreme positions. The kind of critical approach that is being promoted here first attempts to relativize the apparent radical novelty of the 'posthumanist' phenomenon. While the current context might indeed be new and singular, the idea of posthumanism relies on questions and problems that have a long history and are therefore closely connected to other past and present contexts. On the other hand, it is also important to show the truly innovative potential of a *critical* posthumanism. Most welcome is, for example, the new and extensive possibilities for co-operation between sciences (and the new bio- or life sciences in particular) and the humanities and social sciences. In this respect, the question of the relationship between humans and technics, or to be more precise, the role of technology for human (and nonhuman) evolution, is of particular importance. In addition, one should not underestimate the fact that the current developments and thus also the discussion about posthumanism are taking place within the context of radical changes affecting the material economic base. This change constitutes a radical transformation within increasingly globalized late capitalism from an 'analog' (humanist, literate, book or text-based) to a 'digital' (posthumanist, code, data or information-based) social, cultural and economic system.

The present volume hopes to do justice to all of these complex connections by dealing with posthumanism as a 'discourse', or as a combination of material, symbolic and political changes which are 'constructed' within knowledge production and information politics. As with every critical analysis, the questions that are most prominent in this respect are: Who is the main beneficiary of this discourse? What does the discourse presuppose? What does it exclude? What alternatives are thinkable?

Stefan Herbrechter
Heidelberg and Coventry 5 November 2012

1

Towards a critical posthumanism

In some remote corner of the universe, poured out and glittering in innumerable solar systems, there once was a star on which clever animals invented knowledge. That was the haughtiest and most mendacious minute of "world history" – yet only a minute. After nature had drawn a few breaths the star grew cold, and the clever animals had to die.

One might invent such a fable and still not have illustrated sufficiently how wretched, how shadowy and flighty, how aimless and arbitrary, the human intellect appears in nature. There have been eternities when it did not exist; and when it is done for again, nothing will have happened. For this intellect has no further mission that would lead beyond human life. It is human, rather, and only its owner and producer gives it such importance, as if the world pivoted around it. But if we could communicate with the mosquito, then we would learn that it floats through the air with the same self-importance, feeling within itself the flying center of the world. There is nothing in nature so despicable or insignificant that it cannot immediately be blown up like a bag by a slight breath of this power of knowledge; and just as every porter wants an admirer, the proudest human being, the philosopher, thinks that he sees on the eyes of the universe telescopically focused from all sides on his actions and thoughts.

(NIETZSCHE, 1982 [1873]: 42)

This well-known passage from Nietzsche's 'On Truth and Lie in an Extra-Moral Sense' (1873, §1) may serve as a starting point for, but also as an anticipated summary of, the notion of 'posthumanism' this volume wishes to investigate. Nietzsche's nihilistic, relativist and provocative challenge to 'man', the 'clever animal', is directed against the pettiness of humanism inspired by Christian values and his/its self-inflicted state of godlessness. At the same time, Nietzsche's critique prepares the ground for the supposedly liberating, life-affirming coming of the 'overman'. It appears that Nietzsche's 'revaluation of all values', which dismisses the traditional distinction between truth and falsehood in a moralist and humanist sense, and instead aims to describe a radically new, non-moralist and posthumanist situation, is within reach today. Whereas Nietzsche's nihilism mocks the arrogance of the human species along with its self-proclaimed anthropocentric view of 'world history', some humans, inspired by the vision of a technologically induced self-surpassing, thanks to new cogno-, bio-, nano- and information technologies, are pushing the hubris of their species to new extremes. It is likely therefore that even though Nietzsche has repeatedly been proclaimed as a proto-posthumanist thinker, he would probably not be particularly impressed with the current widespread posthumanist techno-euphoria. To project the 'missionary' aspect of the 'human intellect' purely onto the machine-prosthesis is certainly not enough to produce the desired coming of Nietzsche's overman, who, on the one hand, would be humble enough to communicate with a 'mosquito', to learn from it, and, on the other hand, would be powerful enough to overcome humanism's narcissistic pathos.

Yet how exactly is the philosopher to tilt his 'telescope' in order to avoid recognizing humanity as already everywhere at work, either in its glory or its deprivation? This could prove to be the most difficult and therefore most important, most urgent and most 'critical' role of a 'postanthropocentric' and thus truly posthumanist philosophy. There are many approaches to this idea. However, a particularly powerful one lies in so-called poststructuralism and deconstruction, with their apparent radically 'antihumanist' critiques. This volume therefore addresses the current technology-centred discussion about the potential transformation of humans into something else (a process that might be called 'posthumanization') as merely the latest symptom of a cultural malaise that inhabits humanism itself – humanism in the sense of an ideology and a specific discourse. To perform a critique of the widespread idea of a supposedly inevitable passing of the human species with its associated apocalyptic or euphoric scenarios, it is important to again confront current forms of (techno)cultural criticism with the 'antihumanism' of theory in the 1970s and 1980s. While some prophets of a coming post- or transhumanity joyfully proclaim (once again) the 'end of man', the kind of critical posthumanism advocated in this volume seeks to investigate the possible crisis and end of a certain *conception* of the human, namely the humanist notion of the human, and, if possible, contribute to the accelerated transformation of the latter. Or, in other words, the underlying rationale of this volume could be: whoever cares about humans and their past, present and future might want to critically engage with humanism's anthropocentric ideology.

This could indeed be regarded as a preliminary definition of posthumanism: it is the cultural malaise or euphoria that is caused by the feeling that arises once you start taking the idea of 'postanthropocentrism' seriously. To be able to think the 'end of the human' without giving in to apocalyptic mysticism or to new forms of spirituality and transcendence – this would correspond to the attitude that the phrase 'critical posthumanism' wishes to describe. The word 'critical' here has a double function: it combines, on the one hand, openness to the radical nature of technocultural change, and, on the other hand, it emphasizes a certain continuity with traditions of thought that have critically engaged with humanism, and which, in part, have evolved out of the humanist tradition itself. The task is, therefore, to re-evaluate established forms of antihumanist critique, to adapt them to the current, changed conditions, and, where possible, to radicalize them.

An interesting starting point can be found in Jean-François Lyotard's essay 'A Postmodern Fable', which takes up Nietzsche's fable motif again. Its opening gambit runs like this: 'What a Human and his/her Brain – or rather the Brain and its Human – would resemble at the moment when they leave the planet forever, before its destruction; that, the story does not tell' (Lyotard 2001: 12). Lyotard plays here with the possibility of a 'disembodied' narrative. Should there still be any humans by the time our solar system is dying they will have to have completely transformed themselves technologically and evolutionarily in order to survive the explosion of the sun. Should there be a sequel to the narrative after this most extreme of all ends, some narrating species inevitably has to escape the inferno. For Lyotard therefore some form of posthumanization seems an inevitable transformation process to enable humans to face the conditions that would have to be met in order to send some (quasi-)human form onto future intergalactic travels.

From a cosmic point of view, the prehistory to this fable is a narrative that explains how the energy that was unleashed during the big bang spread out according to the laws of entropy, and how, under very specific and highly unlikely circumstances, at a local level, systems and forms of life could emerge, despite entropy, among them planet Earth and humans. The system called 'human' further displays highly improbable evolutionary characteristics like bodily and symbolic techniques (cf. tools, language). These techniques, moreover, are 'self-referential', which makes them adaptable and transferable to future generations. They are conducive to the creation of communities and social systems. Among these social systems, eventually, a particularly successful form gains the upper hand, namely a system called 'liberal democracy', against other socio-political economic organisations of society, thanks to its ability to subordinate its authoritarian control mechanisms to the idea of free creativity, which allows for self-optimization. As a by-product, this system also creates the eschatological device of 'progress'. The only obstacle that remains for this system is the aging of its solar system and with it the required self-transformation of its humans, who will have to survive under radically altered conditions:

> At the time this story was told, all research in progress was directed to this aim, that is, in a big lump: logic, econometrics, and

monetary theory, information theory, the physics of conductors, astrophysics and astronautics, genetic and dietetic biology and medicine, catastrophe theory, chaos theory, linguistics and potential literature. All of this research turns out, in fact, to be dedicated, closely or from afar, to testing and remodeling the so-called human body, or to replacing it, in such a way that the brain remains able to function with the aid only of the energy resources available in the cosmos. And so was prepared the final exodus of the negentropic system far from the Earth.

(Lyotard 2001: 16)

Despite its apparent 'realism' this narrative is in fact no longer entirely 'realist' in the humanist, literary and stylistic sense, since it is not the human who is the real hero of the story but the struggle between entropy and negentropy. Humans are merely a by-product of the story so to speak. It is thus a story without 'subject':

> The human species is not the hero of the fable. It is a complex form of organizing energy. Like the other forms, it is undoubtedly transitory. Other, more complex forms may appear that will win out over it. Perhaps one of these forms is preparing itself through techno-scientific development right from the time when the fable was being recounted.

(17)

Who (or what) will represent the complex system – humans, cyborgs or an entirely different form of organization – remains unpredictable. In any case, it will have to be a more complex form of life which will need to be able to survive the conditions that will reign as soon as the sun turns into a supernova. This is why the fable does not literally presuppose a 'survivor', since it is questionable whether the required form of a system of negentropic organization can still be a recognizable life form at all. It is this uncertainty, however, which propels the narrative and represents the necessity of 'fabulation', and which guarantees the inventiveness on which technological progress depends. And technological progress, in turn, is what is needed for survival. Lyotard terms this fable 'postmodern', because it is situated 'after it has succumbed to the contagion of modernity and has tried to cure itself of it' (18). At the same time, however, one could argue that this narrative is 'posthumanist' if, like Lyotard, we see modernity as coterminous with Christianity, Augustine and Neoplatonism, and understand it foremost as a form of 'eschatology':

> It is essential for the modern imaginary to project its legitimacy forward while founding it in a lost origin. Eschatology calls for an archaeology. This circle, which is also the hermeneutic circle, characterizes *historicity* as the modern imaginary of time.
>
> (19–20)

In contrast, the postmodern (or posthumanist) fable referred to is neither eschatological nor historical in the strict sense, but merely diachronic. Rather than circular in a hermeneutic sense, it is circular in the sense of a 'cybernetic loop' (20). The fable also does not correspond to a 'new', final or ultimate, humanist-anthropocentric 'grand narrative' of modernity the kind of which Lyotard described in *The Postmodern Condition* (1984) by referring to the 'Enlightenment', 'Marxism' and 'Liberalism'. Instead, it is rather 'inhuman' (Lyotard 1991), in that it expresses at once the unlikelihood of the energetic system 'human/brain' as well as its necessary finality:

> The Human, or his/her brain, is a highly unlikely material (that is, energetic) formation. This formation is necessarily transitory since it is dependent on the conditions of terrestrial life, which are not eternal. The formation called Human or Brain will have been nothing more than an episode in the conflict between differentiation and entropy. The pursuit of greater complexity asks not for the perfecting of the Human, but its mutation or its defeat for the benefit of a better performing system. Humans are very mistaken in their presuming to be the motors of development and in confusing development with the progress of consciousness and civilization.
>
> (Lyotard 2001: 20)

As such, this fable is neither explanatory nor critical in a moral sense, but represents pure postmodern (or posthumanist) melancholia, after the end of the modern and humanistic principle of hope. It has to be understood in merely 'poetic-aesthetic' terms, as a postmodern and posthumanist affect and as the expression of the ultimate humiliation of anthropocentrism (after Galilei, Darwin and Freud). It is not even pessimistic because the idea of pessimism would still imply an anthropomorphic perspective according to which a distinction between good and evil would still be thinkable (21).

What Lyotard's sequel to Nietzsche's fable shows is that, on the one hand, there is no point in denying the ongoing technologization of the human species, and, on the other hand, that a purely technology-centred idea of posthumanization is not enough to escape the humanist paradigm. While popular ideas of posthuman humanity augmented by technology often continue to be influenced by ideologically naïve humanist values, traditional approaches in cultural theory and in the humanities usually remain too anthropocentric in their defense of a notion of the 'human' that is not sufficiently historicized or grounded in a quasi-mystical notion of 'human nature'. Required is thus an approach which takes seriously both the technological challenge as well as the radical critique of anthropocentrism. A posthumanism, therefore, which understands the human species as a historical 'effect', with humanism as its ideological 'affect', while distancing itself from both – a 'critical posthumanism', which does not, from the start, position itself 'after' a humanism, which always remains to be defined (from the point of view of a superior stage of technological development, for example), but which inhabits humanism deconstructively, and for which technology and Lyotard's principle of the 'inhuman' are merely a means and not an end in themselves. A posthumanism which, precisely, is not post-*human* but *post*-human(ist).

This also seems to be Lyotard's intention in the collection entitled *The Inhuman* (1991), with its subtitle 'Reflections on Time'. The essays in this collection are aimed at humanism's arrogance and they critique the idea that humanism might still be able to teach 'us' a lesson. Instead, humanism's authority, which strictly speaking is based on the resistance to analyse the 'human' as such, is on the wane. Exposing humanism as a form of 'prejudice' Lyotard asks: 'what if human beings, in humanism's sense, were in the process of, constrained into, becoming inhuman …, what if what is "proper" to humankind were to be inhabited by the inhuman?' (Lyotard 1991: 2). The inhuman *in* the human takes two forms: on the one hand, the inhumanity of the 'system', which only uses humanism as its ideology, and, on the other hand, the inhuman which inhabits the human as its 'secret' core, and to which 'the soul is hostage' (2). This is opposed to the idea of an essential humanity on which humanism is traditionally based, for example, wherever there is reference to 'humanitarian action'. But where exactly would this essential humanity be? In its 'savageness' (or the 'initial misery' of childhood)? Or in its capability of speech, its culture or social drives ('their capacity to acquire a "second" nature which, thanks to language, makes them fit to share in communal life, adult consciousness and reason')? Is the human in fact human because of its 'nature' or its 'culture'? Of course, this is not about a simple opposition between nature and culture – nobody has ever really contested their interdependence. For Lyotard and a way of thinking which is 'not-quite-humanist-anymore' it is rather a question of what the dialectic between nature and culture excludes, of the remainder, the 'other', the inhuman, which always presupposes the human and its properties and, at the same time, posits the human as its goal, as an unattained ideal, as original *and* copy, etc. The 'essence' or true being of the human is in fact its 'absence' [*Ab-wesen-heit*]: 'In short, our contemporaries find it adequate to remind us that what is proper to humankind is its absence of defining property, its nothingness, or its transcendence, to display the sign "no vacancy"' (Lyotard 2001: 4).

It seems that today this inhumanity of the system has thoroughly embraced the 'absence of an essence' and the endless 'plasticity' of the human with its secret inhuman core. Lyotard does not refer to 'plasticity', which has become a fashionable word especially for cognitive science in recent times (cf. Malabou 2008), but simply to 'development'. The meaning, however, is quite clear: at stake is the accelerated liberalization, flexibilization, virtualization, etc. of modernity whose internal dynamics and metaphysics corresponds precisely to the 'ideology of development'. This ideology of development and (self-)transformation has become automated and no longer needs any grand narratives which used to promise humanity's emancipation. Instead it is now threatening to become the embodiment of the inhuman or even the posthuman, because, for the complex system, humans are merely a means to an end: 'The interest of humans is subordinate in this to that of the survival of complexity' (Lyotard 2001: 7), which is part of the continuing cosmic struggle between entropy and complexity over the allocation of 'energy'. Against this radically inhuman logic of the (cosmic) system, one has to revert to the other inhuman (the secret 'remainder' of the human, which cannot be explained by either the opposition between nature and culture, or the scheme of cosmic evolution) to obtain a starting point for a critical posthumanism:

> And what else is left to resist with but the debt which each soul has contracted with the miserable and admirable indetermination from which it was born and does not cease to be born? – which is to say, with the other inhuman?
>
> (Lyotard 2001: 7)

It is clear that this double inhumanity requires a parallel approach in terms of analysis: a rigorously historical materialist, and a more metaphysical deconstructive approach. The first reinvents a broadly cultural materialist methodology, however, without falling prey to its typically anthropocentric perspectives. Humans and their humanity are historical and cultural constructs rather than transcendental concepts free from ideology and they therefore have to be placed within larger contexts like ecosystems, technics or evolution. This approach only becomes posthumanist when the human is no longer seen as the sole hero of a history of emancipation, but as a (rather improbable but important) stage within the evolution of complex life forms. The second approach cares about the other inhuman, about the 'other' inhabiting the human, which constitutes its singularity but also its indeterminacy. This could indeed be called a psychoanalysis of humanness, a kind of anamnesis aimed at working through the represseds which were lost on the way towards becoming human. Posthuman and posthumanist therefore also means this: to acknowledge all those ghosts, all those human others that have been repressed during the process of humanization: animals, gods, demons, monsters of all kinds (cf. Graham 2002). Both approaches share the conviction that a traditional humanist world view and understanding of the human have become untenable if not irrelevant, either because of external, mostly technological, economic or ecological influences, or because of internal metaphysical and ethical reasons. The external forces can be seen as either enabling or threatening, or as both at the same time. The internal forces might best be understood as benevolent or 'strategic' misanthropy (cf. Cottom 2006), which for the love of the human species opposes human *hybris* and instead demands a self-critical but not necessarily self-pitying *humilitas*.

From time immemorial [*seit Menschengedenken*] – this wonderfully romantic and nostalgic expression, which captures the tragic undertone of greatness regarding everything human within the discourse of humanism – thus receives an entirely new meaning within critical and cultural theory at the beginning of the twenty-first century. For one, it points to the fact that there was a time before humans (and humanity), and therefore a history without the human, and, on the other hand, it hints at the possibility of a time after the human (and humanity). This is no evolutionary platitude or mere apocalyptism, as Michel Foucault's approach in *The Order of Things* (1970) demonstrates. Instead, this is where the critique of 'representation' which has become so influential in the past decades within theory takes its point of departure. Anthropocentric humanism is first and foremost of course human self-representation (cf. Kant's 'What is man?' as the starting point of a (neo)humanist philosophical anthropology). The regime of knowledge which accompanies the rise of the humanist paradigm (or 'episteme') within modernity is called 'realism'. Realism is based on the fundamental principles of similarity, the transparency of the medium and on meaningful identity – which means that a situation that was once present or still is can, without major loss, endlessly and 'realistically' (that is, true to its reality and originality) be reproduced and thus made present again (re-*present*-ation). Moreover, this can be reproduced within any 'subject' who feels individually addressed and who identifies with the reproduced situation, by which it comes into its own so to speak, and by which it also countersigns the truth of the representation as such. This means that a crisis of realism is also a crisis of its concept of subjectivity. By detracting the subject as 'decentred' – since it is defined both as interchangeable and as uniquely and individually identifiable (i.e. supposed to underwrite the idea of self-identity) – the notion of transparency on which the principle of representation relies also loses its legitimation. Instead, the medium of representation, including symbolic language of course, develops a dynamic of its own. This, in an extremely simplified form, is the point of departure for so-called poststructuralism: on the one hand, the impossible identity of the subject with itself, on the other hand, Derridean *'différance'* at work in symbolic representation, which always promises truth but constantly defers it (*'différer'*, to defer) and therefore always differs from itself (*'différer'*, to differ). The result is a constantly promised but structurally unattainable form of self-identity which conceals or attempts to repress its own difference. Its main 'agent' – the free universal and at the same time singular and unique individual – thus exposed or undone, 'liberal humanism' itself becomes incredible as a grand narrative (cf. Lyotard), as ideology (cf. Althusser), as myth (cf. Barthes), or as historical and political discourse (cf. Foucault).

The most important lever of a poststructuralist critique of humanism is the primacy of language (or the medium, or 'technics', in general) over subjectivity and thus over identity. Catherine Belsey's influential manifesto, *Critical Practice* (1980) can be seen as representative of this critique of 'liberal humanism':

> Common sense proposes a *humanism* based on an *empiricist-idealist* interpretation of the world. In other words, common sense urges that "man" is the origin and source of meaning, of action, and of history (*humanism*). Our concepts and our knowledge are held to be the product of experience (*empiricism*), and this experience is preceded and interpreted by the mind, reason or thought, the property of a transcendent human nature whose essence is the attribute of each individual (*idealism*).
>
> (Belsey 1980: 7)

This humanism of common sense transposed onto art, literature and aesthetics and ultimately onto all forms of cultural production represents the basis for realism's hegemony as far as reading is concerned: '[The theory of expressive realism] is the theory that literature reflects the reality of experience as it is perceived by one (especially gifted) individual, who *expresses* it in a discourse which enables other individuals to recognize it as true', as Belsey explains (7).

In this sense, humanism is the idea by which constant identification with a quasi-mystical universal human 'nature' produces great cultural achievements, which serve to promote the cohesion of humanity in general. Consequently, it is precisely this idea which has been attacked by postmodernism and poststructuralism in their respective critiques of humanism. In terms of ideology and politics this humanism is termed 'liberal' in the sense that it presupposes a bourgeois capitalist subject who promotes 'tolerance' in the face of seemingly 'superficial' difference (like gender, race, culture, location, history) in the name of the universal principle of 'humanity'. This strategy serves as a politics of appeasement which protects the values humanism has declared as universally valid, by calling any attack on these values 'extremism', 'intolerance' or simply 'regression'. The cultural politics of humanism's ideology thus remains the target for any posthumanist critique inspired by postmodernist and poststructuralist principles, which, instead, have been stressing alternative values like 'particularity', 'difference', 'multiplicity' and 'plurality' as much as the 'singularity' of cultures (in the plural) and nonhuman forms. Accordingly, a poststructuralist and postmodernist critique emphasizes the radically local and temporal context-specificity, negates the immanence of signification and instead stresses the politically conflictual construction of meaning. It also criticizes the supposed transparency of mediality (realism in language, painting, media and any image-based technology) and instead emphasizes the fact that any medium has its own dynamic, its own power to construct identities and to 'position' subjects. It also stresses the changeabilty and relativity of human nature and individuality as well as the relativity of values. But it also turns against any idealistic form of transcendence, accentuates the inseparability of form and content, the radically determining function of context and an understanding of truth as process. Instead, it insists on the 'materiality' of thinking and the importance of 'embodiment' in agency.

As seen in Belsey, freedom, universality and the principle of individuality of the humanist subject are being questioned, as much as its notion of truth and representation. A critical posthumanism is consequently the only logical theoretical and philosophical radicalization of this position, since it is not likely that humans can do without representation, nor without identity. The entire effort of posthumanist critical and cultural theory therefore goes into the construction of a post-realist and post-phenomenological form of hermeneutics and a post-subjective form of agency.

In this way, Foucault's often cited phrase of the 'end of man' can be seen in an historical, discursively critical and not necessarily jubilant apocalyptic sense:

> One thing in any case is certain: man is neither the oldest nor the most constant problem that has been posed for human knowledge ... man is an invention of recent date. And one perhaps nearing its end. If those arrangements were to disappear as they appeared, if some event of which we can at the moment do no more than sense the possibility – without knowing either what its form will be or what it promises – were to cause them to crumble, as the ground of Classical thought did, at the end of the eighteenth century, then one can certainly wager that man would be erased, like a face drawn in sand at the edge of the sea.
>
> (Foucault 1970: 386–7)

This disenchantment has two immediate implications: first, the historicization of the human as an object of investigation is likely to exceed the framework of philosophical anthropology and the so-called 'humanities'. Secondly, according to many cultural theorists, philosophers but also scientists, the scenario depicted by Foucault has in a sense already become reality, for example, in the form of an evolutionary transition towards 'posthumanity' (understood as a replacing of the species *homo sapiens* by a representative of a superior but possibly merely intermediate stage within further 'human' development, i.e. the so-called 'robo sapiens', or cyborg, or in the ultimate form of a transhumanity or, basically, 'artificial intelligence').

More will have to be said about the ways in which contemporary institutions concerned with human knowledge or knowledge about humans will have to adapt to this situation, or to what extent they might already have done so. However, it seems likely that the 'humanities' will have to transform themselves into what could be called 'posthumanities', in connection with the posthumanizing trends described above, if they want to continue posing the question of 'What is human?' with some authority. Lyotard's twofold notion of the inhuman, Foucault's notion of 'man and his doubles' (1970: 303–43), and the whole variety of interdisciplinary challenges described by Derrida as part of the 'university without condition' (Derrida 2001a), as well as the demand for a new postanthopocentric or 'post-speciesist' approach (cf. Wolfe 2003, 2010) are pointing towards the current transformation of what is arguably the most humanist of institutions, namely the university.

So, is the 'time of the human' (cf. Zons 2001) definitely gone? And how could this be 'humanly' possible, i.e. recognizable for humans themselves? In fact, the distinction that can be drawn between 'man' and 'human' shows that the end of one of these concepts in no way automatically entails the end of the other. This becomes very clear if one recalls one of the high points of the poststructuralist critique of humanism, namely the *Colloque de Cerisy* organized by Jean-Luc Nancy and Philippe Lacoue-Labarthe, between 23 July and 2 August 1980, called *Les Fins de l'homme: à partir du travail de Jacques Derrida* (Nancy and Lacoue-Labarthe 1981). The point of departure for this conference was Derrida's eponymous essay in *Margins of Philosophy* (1990), 'The Ends of Man' (originally given as a speech in 1968), in which Derrida, through a reading of Heidegger and Sartre, plays on the double meaning contained in the word 'end' – in the sense of 'purpose' and of 'finality'. Derrida moves on to deconstruct the 'phenomenological ontology' at work in Sartrean existentialism and its reliance on 'human reality' and Heideggerian 'being-there [*Dasein*]'. Already Heidegger's 'On Humanism' (1978 [1949]) mentions the 'destruction' of the metaphysical foundation [*Grund*] on which every humanism with its question of the 'essence of man' is based. Consequently, Derrida takes up the challenge to think the idea of the 'end of man' outside the framework of a Hegelian dialectic [*Aufhebung*] and metaphysical teleology:

> The challenge for thinking today is an end of man not structured according to a dialectic of truth and negativity, an end of man that does not represent a teleology in the first person plural.
>
> (Derrida, in Nancy and Lacoue-Labarthe 1981: 144; *my translation*)

Derrida could be said to be already arguing here for a posthumanism which uses neither 'I' nor 'we', which neither uses the finality of the singular human (e.g. in the idea of a 'being-towards-death', in existentialism) nor the teleology of any notion of humanity (idealism) to 'anthropocentre' the human so to speak. Instead, Derrida uses a notion of the human as a singularity that is radically open towards the nonhuman other of futurity, beyond any metaphysical horizon and any determinedness. Neither dialectic, completion, surpassing, nor renewal, nor disappearance, nor any question regarding the 'essence' of the human, but the move from the question 'What is man?' to 'Who is man?' thus becomes the new focus:

> This is exactly the question our epoch has forgotten. The epoch of the complete domination ... of anthropology, which continues to pursue, in blind and indefatigable fashion, the question of 'What is man?', and whose most extreme advance, as we are gradually becoming aware, lies in the age of technology.
>
> (Nancy, in Nancy and Lacoue-Labarthe 1981: 13; *my translation*)

It is thus becoming clear that the intensification of technologization, understood as the engine of posthumanization and greeted enthusiastically by some proponents of post- or rather transhumanism, while condemned by technosceptics, cannot itself escape humanist metaphysics or anthropocentrism. This remains the case at least as long as our understanding of technology forces us to ask the question 'What is man?' at a metaphysical-ontological level – a level that even the negation or the apparent surpassing of the question is unable to achieve. Only a deconstruction of the 'human' and 'technology' promises a change with regard to the metaphysics that is at work in the idea of the 'disappearance of man'. A *critical* posthumanism therefore has to question humanism even in the form of its own critique, as Lacoue-Labarthe and Nancy have already pointed out in *Les Fins de l'homme*:

> Between a 'disappearance of man' that today is so well known that it again threatens to be misunderstood, and a general critique of humanism, which has been embraced so enthusiastically that it itself has become questionable in turn, and the abominable,

naïve and reactionary forms of humanism, which so many other discourses embrace for lack of alternatives or mere spitefulness, it could well be that the question concerning 'man' has to be asked in entirely new philosophical, literary, as well as ethical and political terms, namely in the form of a question concerning the end.

(1981: 20; *my translation*)

After the end of man, therefore, is also before man, but in between finality and renewal there might be a possibility to think 'man' or rather, the human, otherwise. This is the ambiguity which inhabits every 'post-'.

The claim that something is reaching or has reached its end is of course not a claim like any other, and especially not, where such a venerable tradition as humanism is at stake, and, with it, that which is held to be the essence of our species, namely 'our' humanity. There is no question, however, that the notion of humanity itself has a concrete history and that, in fact, it is the effect of a combination of humanism as an ideological discourse and modernity as a socio-historical formation. The radical critique of humanism and the humanist tradition (at least since the Renaissance and its rediscovery of Greek and Roman Antiquity and Neoplatonic Christianity), from a posthumanist point of view, thus takes precedence over the question 'What is man?' To 'position' oneself 'after' such a tradition – posthumanism – means (in strict analogy with postmodernism and the idea of postmodernity) to embrace a conscious ambiguity that lies in two possible forms of accentuation: the undeniable experience that a certain humanism has reached its end (*post*-humanism); and the certainty that this humanism because of its own plurality and slipperiness cannot just be classified without remainders and repressions but needs to be 'worked through' in a critical deconstructive sense (hence, post-*humanism*).

A third, much more 'descriptive', form of accentuation, however, is also thinkable: posthumanism is all this and more, namely the entire discourse, critical or less critical, enthusiastic or sensationalist, ironic or alarmed, which embraces the 'posthuman' as a possibility and thus brings it to life, so to speak, as a discursive object: *posthuman*-ism. This angle, nevertheless, is precisely the one that seems predominantly driven by technology. It also seems to increasingly correspond to the public face of a 'popular' posthumanism, a more or less sensationalist mixture of the arts and culture sections in newspapers, popular science magazines, futurologists, the wider intelligentsia, marketing gurus, and other lobbyists, everything, in short, that might be termed 'third culture', as Slavoj Žižek maintains, in recollection of C. P. Snow's 'two cultures' debate (science *versus* literature and the arts or the humanities), namely as a product of 'cognitivist popularizers of "hard" sciences':

> The Third Culture comprises the vast field that reaches from the debaters of evolutionary theory (Dawkins and Daniel Dennett versus Gould) through physicists dealing with quantum physics and cosmology (Stephen Hawking, Steven Weinberg, Fritjof Capra), cognitive scientists (Dennett again, Marvin Minsky), neurologists (Oliver Sacks), and the theorists of chaos (Benoit Mandelbrot, Ian Stewart) – authors dealing with the cognitive and general social impact of the digitalization of our daily lives – up to the theorists of an autopoetic system who endeavor to develop a universal formal notion of self-organizing emerging systems that can be applied to 'natural' living organisms and species and social 'organisms' (the behavior of the markets and other large groups of interacting social agents).
>
> (Žižek 2002: 20)

Even if Žižek's list of names is somewhat one-sided and no longer quite up-to-date it nevertheless explains that for the public or in the 'cultural imaginary' the consequences of technological interventions in the human and human nature today are everywhere to be seen. Žižek also demonstrates that many cultural theorists or proponents of cultural studies are so fascinated by technological phenomena that they tend to forget to question the authority of scientistic metaphors and to verify their truthfulness. While the cognitive science approach can often be shown to be searching for 'ultimate answers' and 'true natures' in fairly naïve metaphysical ways, the predominant institutionalized relativism of values, cultures and histories may be stopping cultural studies scholars from providing a convincing alternative explanation of the relationship between humans, nature, culture and word 'critical' in 'critical posthumanism' names precisely this: the task of analysing the process of technologization, based on the idea of a radical interdependence or mutual interpenetration between the human, the posthuman and the inhuman. This interpenetration happens at a political, economic, philosophical, technoscientific as well as a cultural level. However, critical and cultural theory, and cultural studies, will not of course be in a position to define what constitutes human 'being' either. A more serious and intensified form of interdisciplinarity between human, social, natural, cognititive and bio- or life sciences thus forms a major imperative for the future posthumanities – or whatever name will be given to the institutional framework in which the new forms of critical knowledge production about posthuman and anthropodecentred humans and their environments will take place.

Without doubt contemporary breakthroughs in bio-, nano-, cogno- and infotechnologies have pushed the influence of technology on (techno)culture under the current political and economic conditions of technoscientific capitalism to a level never witnessed before. There are new 'phenomena' like a completely new, digital (as opposed to an analog, 'material') culture or 'cyberculture', the progressing prosthesization of the human, the emerging autonomy of artificial intelligence, which may be about to move beyond human control or even beyond human comprehension. Welcome, therefore, to the radicalized, autopoietic information society governed by complexity? Aronowitz and Menser proposed a three-dimensional analytical framework for questioning the 'technocultural': first, at an ontological level – What 'is' technology? At a pragmatic level – What does technology 'do'? And, at a phenomenological level – What 'effects' does technology have? (1996: 15). Seen from an ontological point of view posthumanization shows that human beings have always been 'technological' through and through, whether as a result of tool use or of the 'recursivity' of symbolic language as ultimate, 'ontologizing' tool (language would thus have to be understood as the ineluctable human 'prosthesis'), or as the contemporary physical amalgamation of technological object and human subject (cyborgization) – hence, there would be no humanity without technics (i.e. the ontological involvement between humans, techniques and technologies). This is what allows Bruno Latour to see the social not as opposite but as in relation to the object world and 'nonhuman' actors, and which thus calls for a combination of social theory and the history of technology. It is the interaction between human and nonhuman actors which really constitutes the social, while technology plays the role of a 'stabilizer' in this process, which connects actors and observers within social 'assemblages'. In this sense, technology can be understood, according to Latour, as 'society made durable' – or, social organization can be seen to last only because of its technologies (Latour 1991). Seen pragmatically, technology is also always part of a process of material embodied adaptation, a kind of 'biopower' in the Foucauldian sense – a process which starts long before modernity. In addition, technology has always formed either a bridge across or a breach of the boundaries between 'nature' and 'culture'. In the age of complete mutual interpenetration of these two there is no nature and culture thinkable anymore (if there ever was) but only 'nature(s)culture(s)', so much so that being a 'subject' means being 'natural-cultural-technological', and being a 'social animal' means being a 'techno-social animal' (Aronowitz and Menser 1996: 21). Phenomenologically, technology triggers a process of 'mediation' between humans and their environment. In the same measure as technology 'understood as tool' changes and constitutes social realities it also makes social reality accessible. At the same time, through feedback processes, technology also provokes transformations within the understanding of the self as a user. However, as with all media, be they social, technological, communicative, image-based, etc. (a differentiation which is almost impossible to maintain today), the poststructuralist critique of realism referred to above applies. On the one hand, the medium is its own message (following McLuhan) – which means that automatic self-legitimation is built into every medium (a medium is first of all always keen to portray itself as inevitable and at the same time as transparent and value neutral); on the other hand, a medium creates exactly that kind of reality which it subsequently pretends to 'merely' and 'faithfully' depict. The same is the case with technologies – they tend to make themselves inevitable and invisible at the same time. What technologies therefore produce at a phenomenological level is in the Marxist sense a form of (self-)alienation; in a deconstructive or post-Marxist sense, however, it is an alienation process from a self that has always been an illusion and thus has always (already) been alienated from itself. An alienation of alienation, or *différance*, or a, paradoxically, absolutely necessary supplement – in this sense technology represents a privileged form of the (Lyotardian notion of the) 'inhuman' which has always already inhabited the core of the human.

There is another important aspect to a critical (deconstructive) posthumanism: many people working within the history and philosophy of technology (technics), critical and cultural theory, sociology and critical science studies see posthumanism, either in parallel with or as opposed to postmodernism, as the next big challenge and therefore as the next wave of intellectual 'fashion' that one needs to be seen to catch. There is without doubt a fashionable and popular posthumanism, but there is also a serious and philosophical one. In analogy to the debate about postmodernism the present critical introduction aims to investigate both aspects of posthumanist discourse. Similar to Wolfgang Welsch's approach in *Unsere postmoderne Moderne* [Our Postmodern Modernity] (1991) one could refer to our current situation as an investigation into 'our posthuman humanity'. Comparing postmodernism to posthumanism one notices significant similarities but of course also differences. Both have their intellectual roots in a critique of modernity and the Enlightenment. Both take advantage of a certain liberation of thinking as the result of a critique of reason, a return to speculative philosophy and the relativization, localization and contextualization of a perspective that is conscious of its own arbitrariness and contingency. Both presuppose a radical openness and plurality of meaning as a precondition for any singularity (e.g. an event or a subject) to achieve its full meaning. And just as for postmodernism, there is a populist or 'diffuse' posthumanism alongside a conceptually rigorous one. Posthumanism in fact partly takes over from postmodernism, but it also undoes some radical postmodernist aspects. And there is of course also a partial temporal overlap between the two and a parallel co-existence. This is why this study proposes an approach where both postmodernism and posthumanism are placed side by side, as a reading of each other. The idea that posthumanism functions merely as postmodernism's successor would indeed be too simplistic. This is not to deny that there have been signs of a turning away from postmodernism, but precisely in order to avoid a simple 'backlash' and political regression after the supposed end of postmodernism, the move towards posthumanism should be made with as much vigilance as possible. There is for example a danger that after the presumed end of grand narratives (cf. Lyotard 1984) – which was, after all, one of the cornerstones of the postmodern world view – the ongoing discussion around human nature and the role of technology in its transformation might be in the process of turning into a new hegemonic narrative – a new narrative ever more capable of portraying itself as inevitable, indispensable and credible. This, of course, goes against the postmodern ethos, which is based on radical plurality and the democratic co-existence of heterogeneous visions or 'language games'. While posthumanism can be seen as an acceleration and accentuation of some aspects of modernity, these aspects nevertheless are mostly on the side of a rationalization process emerging from the Enlightenment and coinciding with the accelerating process of capitalization. In opposition to this, a return to some postmodernist readings could lead to a much needed deceleration and demystification (cf. Barthes), which would lead to more variety and plurality within posthumanist approaches. Welsch's concept of 'transversal reason', or Lyotard's 'paralogic', which are trying to do justice to the idea of a plural form of rationalities, could thus be used to counteract the current threat of predominant technoscientific reason. One could even argue, from a cynical point of view, that the postmodernization (in the sense of a move towards hypercapitalism, neoliberalism and postindustrial society) of the economic base is being intensified by current processes of globalization, virtualization and further technologization, and might thus merely be using the ideological superstructure of a 'posthuman scenario' to detract from the consequences of an ever-increasing gap between rich and poor and the further concentration of power and capital. This does not mean that there is no actual posthumanizing process occurring, but it would be the task for a critical posthumanism to develop alternative, more egalitarian, democratic and just models for a future posthuman(ist) society.

One could start, for example, by differentiating – as Paul Marie Rosenau (1992) did for postmodernism – between an 'affirmative' and a 'sceptic' posthumanist position. Within the affirmative spectrum of posthumanisms or group of posthumanists there would be, in turn, positions ranging from unreflected euphoria to technocultural pragmatism, while the variety within posthumanist sceptics would range from catastrophists to, precisely, critical deconstructive posthumanists. Already in Welsch there is an awareness of the tension between postmodernism and what he calls the 'technological age' as competing diagnoses of the present (1991: 215ff.). Welsch sees three possible relations between postmodernism and the 'technological age': negative, positive or critical. The connection is negative if seen mainly within the German debate about postmodernism. For Habermas, for example, who equated the postmodern with 'unrestricted affirmation of technological development', this position would correspond to 'neoconservatism' seen from the point of view of a socially and culturally radically transformational 'project of modernity'. A positive view of the relationship between postmodernism and technological age dominates large parts of the Anglo-American debate, especially where influenced by Lyotard's notion of the postmodern. An exception, however, may already be found in Fredric Jameson who is rather ambivalent in his attitude towards postmodernism, including postmodernism's relationship with technology. Welsch is right of course in pointing out that postmodernism's own fundamental experience is technologically induced (cf. postindustrialism, virtuality, Baudrillard's idea of the 'simulacrum' and 'teleontology', as well as McLuhan's 'global village', and Lyotard's information society). On the other hand, already in Lyotard we find a critique of the homogenizing effects of new informational media in terms of the production of and access to knowledge. For us therefore both Welsch and Lyotard can be seen as allies for a critical posthumanism, which takes technological change seriously both at an ontological and epistemological level, but questions the claim towards exclusivity of such an explanation in order to resist any 'automation of techno-logic' (Welsch 1991: 224).

What has changed, however, since this classic moment of postmodern debate, or since the 'postapocalyptic' 1980s and 1990s, is that a new 'ghost' announcing the 'end of time' has started haunting popular and intellectual circles alike, namely the figure of the posthuman in all its forms. This time it really seems the 'end of all ends', not – as during the Cold War – the self-annihilation of some more or less abstract notion of 'humanity', but the end of humans as biological species and the dissolution of human 'nature' from the inside so to speak. Symptoms of this phenomenon of dissolution and species anxiety abound and examples concerning the technologies of virtualization and digitalization, or 'new and social media', or the general transformation of data into electronically storable digital 'information' can easily be found. Whether it is the question of how many 'bytes' a human brain can store and compute, or what exactly the relationship is between virtual, 'actual' and 'factual' reality (e.g. in the case of 'virtual rape'), or to what extent the 'digital revolution' represents social progress or merely another instrument of global surveillance, there is hardly any aspect of life and its daily routines that is not affected by these technological developments. What all these technocultural practices with their new possibilities of inter-activity, self-representation, communication and 'identity work' have in common, however, is that they produce new forms of subjectivity, which at least in part are dissociated from material forms of embodiment. They constitute not only an additional dimension to life, but the new digital virtuality has tangible effects on and transforms 'actual' reality – which means, as will be argued in the subsequent chapters, that the very notion of materiality and the associated ontology of our humanist world view is being questioned.

The new image of the human painted by the neuro- and cognitive sciences can be summarized in the provocative phrase: 'the mind as machine', which is beginning to change the way humans see themselves, even where this does not automatically entail a sudden change in daily life practices. Popular science magazines, however, are busy spreading the word and the new ideology of the 'plasticity' of the human brain and the human self and thus prepare humans for the required intensified plasticity of 'global capital flows'. Global virtual hypercapitalism needs an equally plastic and flexible individual subject. Thus, for example, *The Economist* (23 December 2006) in a special issue with the title 'Who do you think you are? A survey of the brain', informed its readers of the latest neuroscientific insights into the human brain and its extreme 'adaptability'. The *New Scientist* (7 October 2006) speaks of 'Mind fiction: your brain just can't help telling tales'. The French newspaper *Le Monde* a few years ago introduced a regular feature called '*futures*' in their Sunday–Monday edition, which analysed the effects of technologically induced social change with articles by prominent scientists, cultural critics, artists and experts in technopractice. For example, in the 11–12 November 2006 edition, there is an article entitled 'Training one's brain at will?', which explains how implanting electrodes or the use of new neuromedical substances help so-called 'brainbuilding' and augments intelligence. The German weekly *Die Zeit* published an entire series on the topic 'The Search for the Ego', which presented the new understanding of what it means to be human today. On 16 August 2007 for example, Ulrich Bahnsen asks (29): 'Components of the soul: doctors repair psychological illnesses by inserting micro chips and probes directly into the brain. Is mind just biology?' The trend has been continuing and intensifying ever since. Here are some recent examples: the *New Scientist* (15 October 2011) promotes a more holistic approach in 'The Thinking Body: There's more to your mind than the brain'; in a special issue, the *New Scientist* also proposes 'The deep future: A guide to humanity's next 100,000 years' (3 March 2012), while the *Scientific American* (September 2012) attempts to go 'Beyond the limits of science: how we will transcend today's barriers to get smarter, live longer and expand the power of human innovation'. The connection between posthumanizing technologies and politics is made explicit in a recent issue of *Foreign Policy* (September–October 2011), with a special report on 'The Future is now', while the connection to the economy is the focus of *Marketing Week* (20 October 2011) with its title 'Brain teaser: How twenty-first century technology is causing "brain change" and why it matters to marketers'. Many more examples could be listed to show the extent to which this popular form of posthumanism has been developing, intensifying and has become an intrinsic part of globalization – an aspect which is only beginning to receive the appropriate attention in academic circles (cf. Monique Atlan and Roger-Pol Droit 2012).

However, not only the human brain as the supposed seat of the human 'mind' is self-transforming under the microscope of neuromedicine, cognitive science and biotechnology, but other cornerstones of 'human nature' have been eroded. Parts of the biosciences or 'life sciences' have been producing anorganic, artificial life forms on the basis of a new 'postbiological' notion of life. This amounts to an entirely different understanding of cyborgization than the one usually promoted in popular film versions in which Arnold Schwarzenegger stars as the hypermasculine human-machine terminator. It is not only that these new forms of knowledge question the fact that humans are located at the end of Darwinian evolution, but in connection with new gene technology they also enable entirely new forms of (de-essentializing) 'hybridity' within human 'nature'. Not only does the spectre of cloned humans arise with increased force but entirely different possibilities also emerge through new forms of genetic engineering and gene splicing: chimeras, 'nanovisions' of artificial life (nanobots), which can function constructively – preserving life – or destructively – should they become uncontrollable and turn the entire world into chaotic 'grey goo'. But also artificially created viruses are thinkable, which can be used to benefit medicine but might also be used as biological warfare and for new forms of bioterrorism – a possibility hinted at in the *Times Higher Education* (17 May 2012): 'Bio-Luddites square up to friends of Frankenstein' (16–17). The article discusses the 'designer baby' question and the kind of biologically induced futures which are pictured in Francis Fukuyama's influential book *Our Posthuman Future* (2002), or in Jürgen Habermas's *The Future of Human Nature* (2003). On the other hand, creating a microorganism that will help to produce new forms of bio-fuel promises to solve humanity's energy problem. The extent of popular unease about the ambivalence of technological developments involving 'eugenics' can be seen in the discussion about genetically modified foods. Detracted as 'Frankenstein food', on the one hand, while seen as a cure of world poverty and hunger, gene technology symbolizes the crisis of humanism and the radical posthuman underdetermination of the 'new human' to come. As one of the gurus of the gene technology scene, Craig Venter, explained in his speech at the BBC's annual Richard Dimbleby lecture (2007):

> I have called this lecture *A DNA-Driven World*, because I believe that the future of our society relies at least in part on our understanding of biology and the molecules of life – DNA. Every era is defined by its technologies. The last century could be termed the

nuclear age, and I propose that the century ahead will be fundamentally shaped by advances in biology and my field of genomics, which is the study of the complete genetic make-up of a species.

(Venter 2007)

The century of the gene, therefore, but also the century of neuro- and cognitive science and thus equally the century of the brain. The particular challenge for science currently is to connect the diverse strands of innovative technologies, namely digital, and nanotechnologies, neuro-cognitive medicine, robotics and digital mechanics and genetics in order to make the new image of the human more palatable for the public and for potential investors and for politics; and there is no lack of initiatives.

Bionic hands, implants for epileptics, 'smart drugs' – these are signs that human prosthesization and cyborgization have been advancing. They coincide with the digitalization and virtualization of the cultural environment and the life practices of humans and their others. The anxious question is whether the next step of human evolution on its supposed way to posthumanity will create new forms of injustice, discrimination, exploitation and repression, or whether the stage of posthumanity will in turn lead to the complete disappearance of the human species. Maybe in embracing technology too enthusiastically we have already created our own successor species? Maybe the 'machine' is only waiting for our definitive demise? Is the cyborg merely one but an irreversible stage within this handover of power? These questions all concern the issue of co-existence. If one takes the phrase 'artificial intelligence' literally there is indeed no intrinsic necessity for AI to continue to function according to humanist or even human principles. How to behave therefore towards artificial intelligence once it appears or indeed becomes 'autopoietic'? Ethical as well as political questions arise: should there be rights (and responsibilities) for 'machines'? Do machines have identity, culture or their own aesthetic? This discussion also becomes inevitable because the 'machine' is merely one form of the traditional way humans have been differentiating themselves from their 'other' or rather 'others'. New technologies not only pose the question of the human anew and with increased urgency, but they challenge the entire humanist system of categorization and exclusion. The moment the human 'disappears' its repressed 'mirror images' of identity return to haunt it and the entire history of anthropocentrism has to be rewritten: the 'object' world, the 'animal' world, the entire 'cosmos' (cf. for example Richard Dawkins' approach, or also Martin Rees (2003), the eminent astronomer, who suggests that the twenty-first century might well be 'our last'). The entire ghostly ontology (or *hauntology*, following Derrida, 1994b) suddenly visualizes how 'teratology' – the creation of monsters, the representation of monstrosity, inhumanity, animality, objectification, fetishization but also spiritualization and religion – can be used to inscribe and uphold a system of differences and hierarchies, supported by a mystical notion of human 'nature' with its insistence on uniqueness and exceptionalism – a 'device' which sanctions and perpetuates processes of inclusion and exclusion. This alone should be a reason for any critical posthumanism not to underestimate the aspect of technological change. However, it should also prevent it from idealizing it. The fragmentation and pluralization of the human principle (as a result of the dissolution of traditional boundaries between human and animal, or between superhuman, subhuman and inhuman) energizes a critical rereading of humanist history. At the same time it demands a new way of aesthetic engagement with the *conditio humana* or indeed the *conditio posthumana*, which opposes the simple ideologization that prevails within the public debate on eugenics, for fear or desire (or indeed euphoria), of a coming transhumanity (used here and throughout this volume in opposition to the notion of 'posthumanity').

2

A genealogy of posthumanism

[W]e need a critique *of moral values, the value of these values is for the first time to be called into question – and for this purpose a knowledge is necessary of the conditions and circumstances out of which these values grew, and under which they experienced their evolution and their distortion (morality as a result, as a symptom, as a mask, as Tartuffism, as disease, as a misunderstanding; but also morality as a cause, as a remedy, as a stimulant, as a fetter, as a drug), especially as such a knowledge has neither existed up to the present time nor is even now generally desired.*

(NIETZSCHE 1918: IX [1887 *VORREDE* §6])

In many ways posthumanism is a reply to Nietzsche's demand for a critique of morality in his preface (§6) to *The Genealogy of Morals* (1887). Man alongside his hated *and* idealized morality is seen as an effect, symptom, mask, hypocrisy, corruption, misunderstanding as well as a cause, cure, inhibition and poison. It would indeed be difficult to overestimate the Nietzschean influence on posthumanism. There are, however, at least two Nietzsches and differentiating between them will be helpful for a critical analysis of posthumanism. There is first of all the 'critical' Nietzsche, who with his philosophical hammer is intent on breaking up traditional and venerable but ossified knowledge without any respect and whose refreshing tone and radicalness forces a break with a stifling, established and moralizing doctrine. This Nietzsche is against any form of retreating behind some taboo or transcendence and understands the death of God as first of all a new responsibility for which nothing remains out of bounds or sacred. This Nietzschean ethos is exactly what has been informing so-called 'French Theory', or poststructuralism and deconstruction (i.e. Derrida, Foucault, Barthes, Lacan, etc.). This Nietzsche and the kind of antihumanist thinking that follows him, which no longer accepts any final forms of truth and no longer sees the morality of philosophical anthropology and humanist anthropocentrism as self-explanatory, is in fact the last and most radical inheritor of Enlightenment philosophy. This 'hermeneutics of suspicion' is still aimed at a renewal and a liberation of 'man' from 'his self-imposed immaturity', and thus, in turn, needs to be inherited but also questioned by a critical posthumanism.

How about the other Nietzsche, then? This is the 'prophetic' vitalist, craving the coming of the overman (or the posthuman), and who despises sickness, glorifies strength, will and power and plays with nihilistic fire while giving over to his unbridled megalomaniac instincts to provoke the 'weak' into making moralistic judgements about him. A metaphysician who seems to blindly follow an absolute 'will', similar to Lacan's imperative (generalized by Žižek): 'enjoy your symptom!' – avoid repression at all cost! However, in conjunction with the contemporary omnipresent trust in the 'will to technology' as a rebirth of the 'will to power', especially in the form of transhumanist futurology, the words of this other Nietzsche continue to sound highly problematic, as the memory and experience of European fascism and its messianic cult of power and strength have shown:

> This man of the future, who in this wise will redeem us from the old ideal, as he will from that ideal's necessary corollary of great nausea, will to nothingness, and Nihilism; this tocsin of noon and of the great verdict, which renders the will again free, who gives back to the world its goal and to man his hope, this Antichrist and

Antinihilist, this conqueror of God and of Nothingness – *he must one day come.*
(Nietzsche 1918: 93–4 [1887, 2. *Abhandlung* §24])

Is it possible to face this Nietzschean challenge without being captured by both the despair and the fascination with the overman? Is there a way to think 'posthumanistically' without losing sight of (actual) humans and to understand the human without any 'guarantees', the human in its radical 'incommensurability', so to speak?

The lack of orientation at the moment of a posthumanist transvaluation of all values demands the reformulation of the anthropological question 'after the human'. This is to avoid committing old and new forms of humanist errors. What Nietzsche called the transvaluation of all values does not necessarily imply a devaluation or destruction of values, but in fact points towards an invention of an 'other' human. The specific challenge remains thus to, on the one hand, radicalize Nietzsche's critique in the face of a continuation of the 'all-too-human' under new technological conditions, in order to, on the other hand, create entirely new foundations for defining the human 'as such', namely outside humanist tradition. This implies an idea of being-human as something that has not (yet) been achieved and which instead is to be understood as a 'singularity' that might in fact be obscured by technological augmentation, rather than brought to light. Nietzsche with all his dangers and fascinations will therefore remain posthumanism's uneasy companion since what is at stake is a radical break and a 'post-positioning'. This position may provide a critical commentary on a looming end, by anticipating, accelerating, reinterpreting or even preventing it from happening. A 'genealogy' of posthumanism must take the form of an investigation of the desire that informs this process.

Obviously, however, a genealogy also demands a genealogy of the concept of 'posthumanism' as such. Oliver Krüger, for example, quotes the *Oxford English Dictionary* which indicates Thomas Blount's *Glossographia* (1656) as the first use of the word 'posthumain' (Krüger 2004: 107). Neil Badmington cites the theosophist H. P. Blavatsky as the first commentator on the 'post-Human' (1888; in

Badmington 2006b: 240). Both, however, locate the first *critical* use of 'post-humanism' in Ihab Hassan (1977). Hassan's 'Prometheus as Performer: Toward a Posthumanist Culture? A University Masque in Five Scenes' is a parody of the contemporary state of postmodernity in the form of a medieval disputation. In it a character called 'Pretext' mentions an 'emergent ... posthumanist culture' (831). 'Text' – another character – finishes the same scene with the words: 'There is nothing supernatural in the process leading us to a posthumanist culture. That process depends mainly on the growing intrusion of the human mind into nature and history, on the dematerialization of life and the conceptualization of existence' (835). Accordingly, the posthumanization of human culture is nothing but a natural effect of Western metaphysics and thus the progressive penetration of the Hegelian 'spirit'. In this sense, as the character 'Pretext' adds, posthumanism is not a sudden change but rather a process based on a combination of the imagination, science, myth and technology; a process which began with Prometheus or the discovery of fire by prehistoric 'man'. However, this combination of imagination and science has transformative powers: 'their interplay may now be the vital performing principle in culture and consciousness – a key to posthumanism' (838). A later chapter in this study will take up these very thoughts and relate them to the genre of science fiction – understood in its literal sense, namely as fiction *of* science and science *as* fiction.

It thus seems that the current stage of human *logos* demands that new connections between art and science become possible, especially as far as 'performance' or the aesthetic 'experiment' or installation is concerned – a trend furthered by the thematic and formal-aesthetic integration of technology within contemporary art. However, long before the new, posthumanist 'futurism' (cf. for example contemporary artists like Stelarc, Orlan or Kac) Ihab Hassan, already in 1977, asked: 'Where will Marinetti's Futurism finally lead us?' (841). He continues by speculating on the question whether as a result of this development there is going to be an existential search for a 'unified sensibility' (839) or whether it might be possible to say that 'technology may be transforming human consciousness itself, so as to make art as we have known it gradually obsolete' (841). Even if posthumanism at present appears merely to be a 'dubious neologism' or just another image of human self-loathing (843), there is a chance that it might be more than just a trend, for as Hassan remarks: 'the human form – including human desire and all its external representations – may be changing radically, and thus must be re-visioned. We need to understand that five hundred years of humanism may be coming to an end, as humanism transforms itself into something that we must helplessly call posthumanism' (843). The result is an expansion of human consciousness to 'cosmic dimensions', with philosophical, psychological as well as biological and technological implications and challenges. The first task of a 'posthuman philosophy', Hassan explains, in 1977, it is worth stressing again, is tackling the conundrum of artificial intelligence (Hassan specifically refers to Stanley Kubrick's film *2001 – A Space Odyssey* and its omnipotent computer HAL), and thus the question: 'Will artificial intelligences supersede the human brain, rectify it, or simply extend our powers?' (846). Thus Hassan already understands posthumanization as the technologization and cyborgization of the human and its immersion within an expanding technoculture: 'artificial intelligences ... help to transform the image of man, the concept of the human. They are agents of a new posthumanism ...' (846). Towards the end of this 'university masque', as Hassan calls it, his character 'Text' formulates a dilemma that still accurately describes the current state of any discussion of posthumanism. On the one hand, there are the Cassandras who keep warning against the 'future shock'; 'of cloning, parthenogenesis, transplants, prosthesis, of alteration of memory, intelligence, and behavior; of the creation of chimeras, androids and cyborgs' (848). This view understands any tendency towards posthumanization as the kind of dehumanizing that Marx had already seen as the final goal of capitalist alienation, and which is now in the process of being achieved through rampant technologization. Heidegger, too, in his famous interview with *Der Spiegel* (1966, 1993) had already warned against the fact that 'technology is in its essence something which man cannot master by himself' (105), and that 'we still have no way to respond to the essence of technology' (105). The question concerning the 'essence of technology' will be dealt with in more detail in a later chapter on 'technoculture'. In the meantime it is worth stressing, however, that Hassan also deeply distrusts the euphoric prophets who proclaim the 'transhumanization' of the human as the next stage of 'natural' evolution.

Hassan's rather careful announcement has in the meantime given way to much louder and more alarmist proclamations like, for example, those by Arthur and Marilouise Kroker who claim that we have, in fact, already entered the 'era of the posthuman' (cited in Krüger 2004: 103). It becomes obvious that a change may have occurred in the intellectual climate during the 1990s, which made the use of terms like 'posthumanism' and 'posthuman' widely acceptable. The real breakthrough, however, undoubtedly comes with N. Katherine Hayles' *How We Became Posthuman* (1999). The storm that was brewing in the 1990s, however, was a combination of accelerated technological change driven by information, cognitive, bio- and nanotechnologies, as well as a public discussion about the implications of these new technologies in popular science fora, magazines and websites. This process formed, on the one hand, the beginning of a political and cultural critical interest in these phenomena, and, on the other hand, also provoked the use of artistic forms of processing these new 'posthumanist' tendencies. Therefore, the entire 'phenomenon' of this development invites a description, understanding and analysis of posthumanism as a 'discourse' in the Foucauldian sense.

A discourse is in fact the entirety of the statements and practices that relate to an 'object', which in this case would be the 'posthuman', 'posthumanity' and 'posthumanization', etc. – objects which are constituted 'discursively'. Whether this discourse is describing a reality or not and whether it does so 'realistically', is of course of great importance but it is not the only aspect. Since a discourse can weave itself around a real or fictive discursive object over a long period of time, by insisting, repeating and emphasizing information, this object might eventually become the centre of cultural politics, fascination and power within people's imagination and in a sense ends up 'constructing' its own 'reality'. On the other hand, a discourse usually also describes something that 'actually' exists, but which only now can be described discursively, for the first time so to speak. Whether the posthuman actually exists, or whether it only lives in the imagination of some cultural critics, popular scientists, prophets of technological change or marketing managers, becomes more or less irrelevant as soon as a broad public opinion starts embracing it as plausible and *believes* that something like the posthuman either already exists, that it might be in the process of emerging, or that it might have become somehow 'inevitable'. In a similar move, all the statements about posthumanist practices whether positive or negative contribute in some form to the emergence and existence of the posthuman and posthumanity. And this is precisely the starting point for the present study (which of course needs to be aware of its own implication within the construction of the very discourse it critically analyses), because in the same process by which the posthuman is beginning to take shape, a power struggle arises between different positions and interests regarding the nature of the posthuman, be they religious, economic, military, scientific or humanist/moral in orientation. At this moment in time, the posthuman discursive object has already become the plaything of diverse institutions, which in their strategic statements about factual or possible forms of posthumanity, produce specific and competent 'knowledge', the dissemination of which serves to consolidate the legitimation of these institutions, whether these be scientific, as for example the MIT lab, or ideological apparatuses of transhumanism, as for example the Extropian Institute, or even cultural criticism itself, which aims to show – in studies like the present one – that the construction of a critical posthumanism may lead to 'true' or at least more adequate statements about a discursive object. In doing so cultural criticism's expressive force may also serve to publicly legitimate its role and increase its own social capital. The following characterization of social discourses, adapted from Parker (1992), can be applied to the emergence of posthumanism (in the multiplicity of its forms). According to Parker, discourses manifest themselves in 'texts', with text being understood in its widest sense, namely as symbolic statements and representations of any kind. All the statements about the posthuman taken together (understood as the inhuman, nonhuman, all-too-human, etc.), even including the ones that negate its existence, constitute posthumanist discourse. The texts are linked with each other and share at least one goal and one effect, namely that they presuppose a discursive object called the 'posthuman'. Even a statement like: 'any talk about posthumanity is nonsense', within the context of the discourse, paradoxically, contributes to the legitimation of its object, 'posthumanity'. Through its discursive creation the object eventually reaches a certain 'reality'. One could thus argue that discourses are inherently teleological – which means that, ultimately, any subject that is part of the human species somehow might be affected by this posthuman object. Even 'subjects' who are or would not be members of the human species contribute to this process as soon as they become participants of the discussion and thus to the legitimation of the discourse, which, in turn, 'invents' them as subjects by 'positioning' or 'addressing' them. Even ignorance can be a discursive positioning. Discourse 'contains' its own subjects because it offers prefabricated positions from which the discursive object can be 'observed' and statements can be uttered about it. The positions can be rejected, contested, negotiated or accepted but only after they have been inhabited or taken up even if playfully. Louis Althusser famously called this process 'interpellation': posthumanism and the posthuman (which in this case play the Althusserian role of ideology) interpellate me as 'human' but in the form of a question, namely: Do you really know what it means to be human? Posthumanist discourse thus creates, on the one hand, subject positions 'within' humanism even while questioning its traditional values, on the other hand, it also creates (hypothetical and, increasingly, factual) 'posthumanist' or 'posthuman' subject positions from which subjects may articulate their newly found posthuman(ist) knowledge. In this case, they would already embody posthumanism and understand themselves as posthumans. In most cases, however, these kinds of statements are (still) placed in the mouths of fictional subjects. Classic examples are Hollywood science fiction films in which, for example, Arnold Schwarzenegger disguised as a posthuman cyborg is giving lectures to humanity. Another example which is often referred to in this context is Kevin Warwick, professor of cybernetics at Reading, who in a number of self-experiments had microchips implanted into his body only to see what living and feeling as a 'cyborg' might feel like. Warwick kept referring to his newly developed 'friendship' (or rather 'friendchip') with the chip. Also, 'posthuman' performance artists like Stelarc who inflict the most radical mutations onto their own bodies so that they might act as interfaces with diverse technologies and who speak as (proto)posthuman subjects about their work, express an 'existential' content of truth which is to exemplify the 'reality' of posthumanity and 'impress' the public. One therefore needs to insist on the fact that within a discourse there are always two kinds of subjects – more or less passive addressees, and addressers, who often inhabit a privileged, for example 'expert', position. If one wishes to refute the knowledge and the ideology, and maybe even the entire world view that comes with a discourse, or whether, as in our case, one wishes to analyse the discourse of the posthuman in the form of a critical posthumanism, one inevitably has to become an addressee first, before one can start to construct a position within that very discourse and thus become an addresser in turn. It is clear that there are always many contradictions and conflicts at work within a discourse – for example between transhumanists and defenders of some form of human 'nature' – but in general a discourse tends to aim for coherence. The smallest common denominator in our case is that there is a posthuman, at least in the form of an illusion, even if it may be uncalled for. Which means that within a discourse there is nothing but a power struggle about knowledge and force of expression, marginal or central positions, or, expressed in Foucauldian terms, 'subjugated knowledge' versus 'common sense'. Of course, a discourse like posthumanism does not exist in isolation from other, more general and more specific discourses. Radical constructivists see all of social reality as a constant process of negotiation between a great number of discourses. Reality here is the sum of all discourses with all their contradictions. Posthumanism in this sense is the plaything of the most diverse discussions which means that it enters into theological, philosophical, political, technological, economic and scientific discourses. This 'interdiscursivity' finds its expression in conflicts, agreements or somewhere in between the two. There is, for example, a rather close 'co-operation' between science fiction, the film industry and its lobbies and the discourse on posthumanity in general, while many groups of religious or moral persuasion of course find it hard to accept any notion of posthumanity. However, since a discourse aims at some minimal coherence there is also a certain level of self-selection, self-reflection and 'etiquette', even if this may only be visible in the existence of a jargon or special vocabulary. Within posthumanism, it is the vocabulary of the 'new sciences and technologies', as well as the vocabulary of critical and cultural theory, which play an important role. In addition, the entire traditional canon of humanist values with all its open or hidden symbolism and its metaphors is being dissected. The choice of words and metaphors in this context as with all discourses has to be seen as selective in a political sense, namely in close connection with the aforementioned power struggle, which prevails in every discourse. Even if discursive self-legitimation usually aims for universal validity, a discourse is always located historically and culturally. This means that the emergence of a discourse always raises questions like 'Why now?' and 'Why here?', and it is these two questions that a critical posthumanism will constantly have to bear in mind. It is worth adding, however, that a discourse may be locatable within history in its entirety, but the discourse itself will also attempt to legitimate itself historically, namely by constructing its own genealogy. A discourse is a product of history and it also represents itself within history. Apart from that, a discourse creates institutions and also underscores the legitimacy of other discourses. In the case of posthumanism there is the (by now disbanded) Extropy Institute (founded by Max More, with its goal of developing an adequate 'transhumanist philosophy' for the technological improvement of the *conditio humana*), and the support for diverse scientific laboratories and educational institutions like 'Singularity University' (co-founded by Ray Kurzweil, and based at the NASA Research Park in Silicon Valley), but also some cultural studies and theory centres, aimed at making cyborgizing practices palatable and acceptable at a social level. At the same time these also help create new markets and new technological solutions for perceived 'deficits' within human 'design' of course. In this sense, posthumanism supports a number of scientific, medical but also economic and military institutions and their discourses. Finally, the power relations within a discourse (e.g. transhumanists versus neohumanists) and between different discourses (e.g. religious moralists versus neo-Darwinists) produce ideological effects based on different 'regimes of truth' (in Foucault's terms). These power relations demonstrate to what extent some narratives have become dominant and thus are working as legitimating forces, while others have become marginalized. These forces are not necessarily based on visibility: military and economic intentions and finance streams are usually kept secret, while cultural or medical breakthroughs are pushed into the media foreground.

Take all these discursive effects together and it becomes clear that posthumanism has definitely 'arrived', including within the discourse of critical and cultural theory. The inclusion of the term within standard dictionaries and textbooks within the field testifies to this. There is, for example, an entry by Adrian Franklin on 'posthumanism' in the *Blackwell Encyclopedia of Sociology* (2007, edited by George Ritzer) which sees it as a fast growing area of 'ontological debate' that developed out of poststructuralism (Franklin, 3548). With particular reference to the work of Donna Haraway, Bruno Latour, N. Katherine Hayles, John Law, Andrew Pickering and Nigel Thrift it can thus be said that a new paradigm of thought has been emerging which is characterized by its opposition to and its transcendence of humanism. This paradigm, Franklin writes, opposes the separation between human and nonhuman environments and, instead, emphasizes the complexity and interrelatedness of human and nonhuman forms of agency (3548). The renewed interest in human-environment-networks (cf. Latour's actor network theory, ANT) needs to be placed within the old debate on C. P. Snow's 'two cultures' and their two forms of knowledge production (by the sciences and the humanities) with their irreconcilable differences. However, what appeared insurmountable in the 1950s returns today as a much more urgent demand for new forms of interdisciplinarity within the context of the interconnectedness between the human and the nonhuman. Franklin cites Pickering, who sees his own area, 'science and technology studies', as a complement to both, humanism and antihumanism. Usually, the humanities define the human and its environment and are thus inevitably humanist, while the sciences, consequently, are 'antihumanist' in their approach because they investigate a material world from which humans are largely absent. 'Posthuman' sciences, according to Pickering, are those sciences which are developing a 'de-centred perspective', in which humanity and the material world are interwoven symmetrically, while neither represents a controlling centre (Franklin 2007: 3549).

In a similar vein, Nicholas Gane in his definition of the 'posthuman' (2006: 2–3) locates a starting point for the concept of posthumanism in the cybernetic movement of the 1940s around Norbert Wiener's work. However, Gane also cites Haraway and the 1990s as the breakthrough for posthumanism and its reaching a wider public audience. The transgression and erasure of boundaries between humans and animals, the organic and inorganic, and between human and machine, which are represented by Haraway's 'cyborg' have undermined the inviolability of the human and have thereby opened up new, posthuman, perspectives. Together with a transvaluation of technological power ('the age of high technology') these are currently producing a 'transversal culture' for which the 'purity' of human nature is being replaced by new forms of creation and evolution which no longer rely on a strict separation between different species or between humans and machines. The central point of controversy here becomes the body, or rather embodiment, and the extent to which embodiment is affected by the new 'metaphor' of information. This is precisely where Gane locates a critical posthumanism, namely in the call for an embodied understanding of information and technology, regardless of whether such bodies can still strictly speaking be considered human (432).

The critique of a posthuman separation between information and matter and between mind and body is also Hayles' starting point (1999). She characterizes posthumanism as based on the following premises:

> First, the posthuman privileges informational pattern over material instantiation, so that embodiment in a biological substrate is seen as an accident of history rather than an inevitability of life. Second, the posthuman view considers consciousness, regarded as the seat of human identity in the Western tradition long before Descartes thought he was a mind thinking, as an epiphenomenon, as an evolutionary upstart trying to claim that it is the whole show when in actuality it is only a minor sideshow. Third, the posthuman view thinks of the body as the original prosthesis we all learn to manipulate, so that extending or replacing the body with other prostheses becomes a continuation of a process that began before we were born. Fourth, and most important, by these and other means, the posthuman view configures human being so that it can be seamlessly articulated with intelligent machines. In the posthuman, there are no essential differences or absolute demarcations between bodily existence and computer simulation, cybernetic mechanism and biological organism, robot teleology and human goals.
>
> (Hayles 1999: 2–3)

This explains the posthumanist fascination with the 'interface' – the seamless articulation between human and machine, technology and *bios*. Against this dematerialized information technology and information ideology Hayles – and, arguably, critical posthumanism in general – promotes the idea of an 'embodied virtuality' and emphasizes available new forms of subjectivity. As opposed to the dream of a disembodied informational reality Hayles wishes to develop a new form of 'posthuman realism':

> My dream is a version of the posthuman that embraces the possibilities of information technologies without being seduced by fantasies of unlimited power and disembodied immortality, that recognizes and celebrates finitude as a condition of human being, and that understands human life is embodied in a material world of great complexity, one on which we depend for our continued survival.
>
> (Hayles 1999: 5)

Another aspect that arises frequently is the question of the political implications of posthumanization. In this context there are conservative protectors of 'human nature' (Fukuyana, but also Habermas), as well as proponents of a new set of norms, laws and values that remain to be defined (cf. for example Chris Hables Gray's 'cyborg citizen', 2001). For Fukuyama, biotechnology represents the greatest political challenge for liberal democracy, which (after the 'end of history' thesis previously promoted by Fukuyama, following Hegel and Kojève) having witnessed the end of ideological struggles, now, as a result of the prospect of genetically engineered differences, is threatened by the advent of a new class society based on the distinction between the 'genetically poor' and the 'genetically rich'. The lack of equality in terms of access to genetic augmentation could thus lead to new instability and social conflict. It is in this same context that Jürgen Habermas speaks of the 'end of liberal eugenics'. In the end, however, it is not so much a question of maintaining law and order or protecting some more or less well-defined human nature or essence but a discussion about how these new technologies – beyond metaphysical taboos or naïve futurology – can be used for the benefit of everyone in a socially just way, as Hayles explains:

> What it means to be human finally is not so much about intelligent machines as it is about how to create just societies in a transnational global world that may include in its purview both carbon and silicon citizens.
>
> (Hayles 2005a: 148)

It is not so much human 'nature' but humanist values, human rights and human dignity that are at the centre of change, which is above all provoked by biotechnology, but which also raises deeper and more far-reaching questions concerning the reinvention and transformation of the human as such.

In this context it is worth emphasizing again that the current crisis of humanism has a long history which, most recently, has been extensively theorized by poststructuralism. The intellectual alignment between posthumanists and the 'antihumanists' of the 1970s and 1980s cannot be ignored, because it connects the current state of posthumanization to the longer history of 'hominization', or with that which we proposed to call a 'posthumanism without technology' (Herbrechter and Callus 2007). This is also in agreement with Neil Badmington's definition of 'posthumanism':

> While posthumanism owes many debts to antihumanist thinkers such as Michel Foucault, Jacques Lacan and Louis Althusser, it tends to differ from antihumanism in one principal respect: while the antihumanists actively set out to overturn the hegemony of anthropocentrism, posthumanists begin with the recognition that "Man" is (always) already a falling or fallen figure. What this means is that posthumanism often tends to take humanism's waning or disappearance as something of a given.
>
> (Badmington 2006b: 240–1)

In contrast to this, a critical posthumanism is aware that humanism as a grand narrative (to once again refer to Lyotard's expression) might have stalled but that it will continue to be available and that only persistent deconstruction will eventually change or undo humanism and prevent it from reinscribing itself in new forms within posthumanist and, in particular, transhumanist discourses. A starting point for this understanding of posthumanism as humanism's ongoing deconstruction, which understands itself as a continued and radicalized critique of humanism in the age of accelerated technologization, can be found in: 'a shared and growing recognition that humanism now (and perhaps always) finds itself in a state of profound crisis. "Man" is not all that "he" claims to be' (Badmington 2006b: 241).

What a critical posthumanism has to bear in mind is thus a technologically induced posthumanizing process, which needs to be taken seriously, and which needs to be radically thought through with all its potential, as well as an entirely other form of posthumanization, which is much 'older' but just as radical and which needs to be articulated by focusing on the 'inhuman' as the initial crisis within humanism itself – a posthumanism 'without' technology, which has always existed in a more or less latent form. Contributions to this latter approach to posthumanism can be found in Badmington's work, published from 2000 onwards. In 'Approaching Posthumanism', the introduction to his anthology *Posthumanism* (2000), Badmington explains that the ambiguity towards the notion of posthumanism is already at work in the radical plurality of meaning in humanism itself. While the 'antihumanism' dominating the second half of the twentieth century portrayed humanism as a conservative and old-fashioned ideology of Western 'common sense', there is also a humanism (especially in the Anglo-American context) which is identified with secular and scientific traditions and thus seen as progressive (cf. Richard Dawkins' version for example). It is therefore no surprise that a context which is already tuned towards a critical understanding of humanism will be quite reserved regarding the idea of posthumanism. It will thus tend to read posthumanism with an accent placed on its humanist component – i.e. post-*humanism* – while stressing more or less the intentional continuity between the two. On the other hand, in pro-humanist secularist circles there will be opposition to posthumanism and thus an accentuation of the 'post' in posthumanism – *post*-humanism – to emphasize the aspect of an (unwanted) break with a cultural tradition that is itself seen as progressive and radical and for which any kind of posthumanism would thus constitute something of a 'backlash' or even regression. The call for a critical posthumanism has to take into account this dynamic. On the one hand, it needs to show that humanism despite all its accompanying undeniable cultural progress, as an ideology, has always been (and today is more and more openly so) criticized for its merely apparent universality and the underlying specificity of its (Western, liberal, bourgeois) subject. One might say, therefore, that humanism was never as progressive as it made itself out to be, and it is now increasingly met with opposition, in a globalized, multicultural and multipolar world. On the other hand, if one really is to break with such a venerable tradition as humanism that is at least 500 years old, one has to be sure to protect and if possible appropriate and continue to make accessible the radical potential that already exists within this tradition in order to avoid giving in to naïve utopian claims towards 'revolutionary' change. Which means that a critical posthumanism requires an extremely intricate political and ethical positioning, namely one which signals to the technoprophets that their attitude despite all apparent utopian radicalism has a long history that needs to be remembered; and a position which reminds the sceptics that humanism never was as humanist as it claimed to be and that the current technological challenge merely represents the next logical step within a posthumanization process with which humanism has always been complicit and which it itself helped to create. The task of this kind of tightrope walk is, as we would agree with Badmington, to look both back and forward, and assist humanism in its own self-deconstruction, so that it will not be forced to repeat itself in new forms of old excesses. At the same time, new and overenthusiastic posthumanisms will have to be constantly reminded of their roots.

All this explains why Cartesianism with its humanist idea of 'man' as *animal rationale* has become the main battlefield for the discussion about posthumanism. If it is reason alone that makes the human human and serves to differentiate the human from all other beings and things in this world one can easily understand both the fascination and the anxiety that arises when a machine with artificial intelligence is beginning to contest this unique status of the human. Descartes, in this sense, reads, according to Badmington, like science fiction *avant la lettre* (2000: 3) when he declares that should machines (or animals) have reason, no *essential* difference would exist between them and humans. It is this risky partitioning-off of an essential difference which, on the one hand, creates the desire for the inhuman and its fascination (what if...), and which, on the other hand, produces a more and more frantic process of exclusion. If 'we' humans are no longer the sole masters and possessors of reason or consciousness, 'we' might also be no longer unique in our use of symbolic language, in the anatomy of our hand, in our awareness of our own mortality and so on. In each of these cases boundaries have been constructed which are supposed to create a community of humans based on their 'humanity' ('we' as a species). On the other hand, these boundaries are supposed to protect 'us' in our essence from more or less concrete and threatening forms of 'otherness'. The side effect – and this is where the true criticism of humanism's essentialist approach lies – is that the constructions of these boundaries which are always portrayed as absolute, inviolable and universally valid for all times are in fact concealing a perfect permeability – a permeability that becomes visible every time the threatening and inhuman 'otherness' is projected onto a concrete target, for example, when the inhumanity of a certain behaviour is depicted or some other form of 'dehumanization' is carried out. The fear of the machine and of the animal is in truth a fear that the radical difference between 'us' and these other beings might not be as radical as humanism claims. Moreover, under certain circumstances, humanism never shied away from using these purportedly radical differences to consolidate a 'speciesist' hierarchy by representing threatening 'others' as 'inhuman' (a phenomenon one might call humanism's politics of (dehumanizing) representation).

Humanism's 'deficit' therefore lies in its ideological belief in an essential humanity that might stand outside historical change and might exist in political and social relationships that are universal and always available. This alone would be enough to justify the idea of a critical posthumanism, as a continuation of a Marxist or post-Marxist critique of ideology so to speak. Contemporary technological development assists this critique in the sense that it helps question the existence of 'essential' humanity. The idea of a 'free and autonomous consciousness' is being questioned by neuroscientists, for example; the uniqueness of the human species is contested by biotechnology and genetics; the singularity of the human mind is queried by informatics, robotics and artificial intelligence. In attacking the humanist idea of human exceptionalism these developments continue a series of previous 'humiliations' of the human: Darwinism which put an end to the idea of a resemblance between 'Man' and God and to the idea of a spiritual form of 'human nature'; Marxism which attacked the liberal humanist idea of a free and conscious individual and replaced it with socialization processes and transformations of the material conditions as the only promise for human 'emancipation'; psychoanalysis which suspended the Cartesian *ego cogito ergo sum* by positing an unconscious self at the heart of human consciousness; geleological 'deep time', the proliferating discoveries of other hominid species and the recent environmentalist focus on the 'anthropocene' and human extinction (cf. Colebrook 2012), which all relativize anthropocentrism, together with 'posthumanist' science, which threatens to dethrone the human and the idea of human uniqueness from a biological, informational, cybernetic and cognitive perspective.

These humiliations are so far-reaching that popular culture seems to have thoroughly embraced the posthuman phenomenon. Not only is science fiction full of cyborgs today but posthumanization seems to have become an intrinsic part of the cultural imaginary of our time. Again, critical posthumanism has to act as a warning against this development, for as Jacques Derrida already foresaw in *Les Fins de l'homme* (in Nancy and Lacoue-Labarthe 1981), the end of man 'inevitably will be written in the language of man', which, in Badmington's words means that:

> 'each transgressive gesture re-encloses us' because every such gesture will have been unconsciously choreographed by humanism. There is no pure outside to which 'we' can leap. To oppose humanism by claiming to have left it behind is to overlook the very way that opposition is articulated.
>
> (Badmington 2000: 9)

The prefix 'post' therefore does not signify a radical break with humanism but a continued deconstructive-*cum*-psychoanalytical 'working through', as Lyotard (1992) suggested for the 'post' in 'postmodern'. That alone should make it clear that simply equating posthumanism with technoculture would be too narrow an understanding. Humanism was always inhabited by diverse posthumanisms, which mostly referred to the ghosts of post- or nonhumanity, the end of man, designed to lead to a renewal of the humanist principle. Posthumanism is thus related to the repressed of humanist tradition, which constantly haunts humans in uncanny ways (cf. Chambers 2001). The current sense of inevitability surrounding the idea of technological apocalypse and the techno-evolutionary supersession of the human species might therefore merely constitute the latest moment within the history of humanism's repression of the inhuman or posthuman within itself, just before it might rotate once again in established fashion around itself, compelled to repeat itself once again. Both, the fascination with and the negation of the inhuman are an intrinsic part of humanism and its repertoire, since the binary opposition between human and inhuman constitutes its very foundation. A direct confrontation with the idea of posthumanity will therefore not be enough, but rather a finely attuned ear that listens out for 'the deconstruction of the binary opposition between the human and the inhuman that is forever happening *within* humanism itself' (Badmington 2001: 16) is needed, because 'anthropocentrism always already contains the conditions of its own transcendence' (Badmington 2003: 19).

As these different examples of definitions show, posthumanization itself may fast be turning into a new 'grand narrative' in the Lyotardian sense. A good summary of this narrativization can be found in Steven Best and Douglas Kellner's *The Postmodern Adventure*, in a section called 'On the Road to the Posthuman' (Best and Kellner 2001: 92–204). Following three epigraphs from Ovid, Marinetti and Thomas Hine, all stressing the mutability and constant transformation of everything human, Best and Kellner dwell on the interpenetration of science fiction and technological realization which leads to a synthesis of human and technology and to an exchange between subject and object world. What leaves the MIT lab and is propagated by technoprophets like Ray Kurzweil and Hans Moravec has, meanwhile, by far surpassed the imagination of science fiction and has led to fundamental 'mutations' within human culture, so much so that evolution has to be redefined because: 'human beings do not evolve through an innate telos that unfolds in an evolutionary process, but instead in and through relations with the complex world of objects, technologies, institutions, and norms they create' (Best and Kellner 2001: 192). The interconnection between human and technology (already stressed by McLuhan) coincides with the intensified prosthesization of humans and their bodies and with their environment, which, in the end, becomes 'internalized'. While humans act on and transform 'their' environments through technology, technics, in turn, through 'its' technologies is acting on and transforming the human. While McLuhan still believed that the last stage of this development would be increasing mediatization leading towards a 'global electric village' with a giant wired brain network, which would produce a new human understood as a communicating being with a fully electronic sensorium, it is becoming increasingly clear in our time that even McLuhan's radical analysis might still have been too anthropocentric. It underestimates the extent to which technologization is changing us as a species: 'the human-technology dialectic has progressed to the point of a posthuman condition where subjects are imbricated in, penetrated by, and reconstructed through objects and technologies' (Best and Kellner 2001: 193). It is mainly the cybernetic interaction between humans and computers and 'Moore's Law', which predicts that, through constant doubling of the speed of data processing, computer intelligence will grow exponentially. This development is set to continue until, by the middle of the twenty-first century at the latest, computer intelligence will be superior to human brains in every respect and will thus lead to the 'emergence' of a new, artificial form of life, as Ray Kurzweil explains in *The Age of Spiritual Machines* (1999):

> The emergence in the early twenty-first century of a new form of intelligence on Earth that can compete with, and ultimately significantly exceed, human intelligence will be a development of greater import than any of the events that have shaped human history. It will be no less important than the creation of the intelligence that created it, and will have profound implications for all aspects of human endeavor, including the nature of work, human learning, government, warfare, the arts, and our concept of ourselves.
>
> (Kurzweil 1999: 5)

The resulting 'ideology' thus logically takes on transhumanist (as opposed to merely posthumanist) forms and foresees a kind of midwife function for humans (and cyborgized ones in particular) assisting the birth of the intelligent machine, the robot or artificial intelligence as their own evolutionary successor. In McLuhan's words: 'Man becomes, as it were, the sex organs of the machine world, as the bee of the plant world, enabling it to fecundate and to evolve ever new forms' (McLuhan 2001: 56). What many techno-utopian and transhumanist narratives thus share with prehumanist ones is that they subordinate the human and human autonomy to some kind of 'superior' and transcendental being, whether this be a god or a machine – or, in the worst case, a 'machine-god'. What many science fiction films preempt (but usually, then go on to foreclose), namely that the loss of control over our 'genotype' under posthuman conditions will also inevitably lead to the loss of control over our 'phenotype' and thus what usually constitutes our 'identity', is increasingly threatening to become reality in the twenty-first century. And this process is accompanied by the general symptoms of humanism's dissolution. Kellner and Best's posthumanist narrative thus culminates in the following definition:

> While 'posthumanism' is a vague term used in various ways, it is a marker for a number of critical mutations unfolding in the Third Millennium. If the time before the sixteenth and seventeenth centuries was our prehumanist history, an era before individualism, secular values, and capitalist markets, and the Renaissance and Enlightenment were the classical period of humanistic values that had roots in Greco-Roman culture, then the period since 1945 can be considered the beginning of a transition to a posthuman epoch. From this perspective, humanity is now in a liminal zone where individuals are forced to confront the meaning and future of the human.
>
> (Best and Kellner 2001: 195)

These posthumanist developments in many ways build onto the so-called 'postmodern condition' as their socio-economic base. However, there are also changes within the superstructure:

> Posthumanism stems from philosophical, technological, and historical shifts. Classical humanism articulates a notion of the self as an ahistorical given, whose timeless essence and nature is that of a rational mind, ontologically distinct from its body, in possession of free will and timeless truths. By contrast, posthumanism – in the form of poststructuralism and postmodern theory – immerses the self in history, social relations and institutions, and embodied reality. Reason is seen as epiphenomenal to the will, the unconscious, affective, and sociohistorical reality. Posthumanism dismantles the dualistic opposition between mind and body and makes the 'truths' available to reason partial, limited, and context-bound.
>
> (195)

For Best and Kellner there is thus continuity between the poststructuralist and the cybernetic attack on the 'liberal humanist self'. This, however, as shown above, in the context of a critical posthumanism, cannot be easily squared with the critique of technology one already finds in poststructuralism. In addition, it is often precisely this liberal humanist self which survives in transhumanist philosophy, but merely in a technologized form – as a new version of Descartes' 'ghost in the machine', so to speak.

The crisis of humanism and the Enlightenment intensified during and after the two world wars, in the first half of the twentieth century, when the irrational core within rational-enlightened modernity became visible in the light of the systematic extinction of Jews by the Nazis and the possibility of humanity's nuclear self-destruction. Kellner and Best call this 'a watershed for posthumanism' (196). Ever since, the impression has been further consolidated that 'we might not have any control over our technoprogeny' (196). As a result of the development towards a mass and consumer society and the omnipresence of mass media, the West has become ever more dependent on technology with the effect that, as Donna Haraway explains, 'our machines are disturbingly lively, and we ourselves frighteningly inert' (Haraway 1991: 152). As Kellner and Best maintain: 'Marx's vision of commodity fetishism, where subjects and objects exchange characteristics, has become concretized is in a world of interactive technologies, "spiritual machines", artificial intelligence and life, natural and social engineering, and technobodies' (2001: 196). This leads to a number of positions taken up by a wide spectrum of cyberneticists, theorists or cyberpunks, extropians and transhumanists, as well as biocentrics and ecologists. Best and Kellner differentiate, accordingly, between: 'radical deconstructive posthumanists, who reject altogether the legacy of humanism, the Enlightenment, modern values and theory, the concept of progress, and a belief in some notion of agency', and 'moderate reconstructive posthumanists, who seek to rethink mind, body, and agency (and associated notions like reason and freedom) in improved forms, and do not completely sever themselves from the modern legacy' (Best and Kellner 2001: 196). Excesses can be found in the form of naïve scenarios of transcendence of the body and reality, or in the shape of radically anti-human activism, new age and gaia ideologies, such as, for example, 'Earth First!', whose motto in an Orwellian reversal is 'Four Legs Good, Two Legs Bad!', and which is prepared to demonize all things human. There is thus a rather crass opposition between technophile and hypermodern transhumanists and technosceptic, antimodern posthumanists with a great number of shadings inbetween. It is difficult, however, not to acknowledge the potential of the new and posthumanizing technologies in terms of the improvement of the quality and prolongation of human and other life. One cannot deny that the vision of the inventors of the 'new flesh' and technologies of 'enhancement' has certain attractions even while they picture future humans as 'cyborgs', 'whose consciousness and physical reality are dramatically expanded thanks to pharmaceutical and nutritional therapy, rigorous exercise programs, computer chips, memory implants, surgical alteration, and genetic modification' (Best and Kellner 2001: 197). In this context, human 'flesh' is consequently renamed as 'wetware' and is merely seen as the interface between technological hardware and infotechnological software. In order to escape its natural biological decay wetware itself needs to be transformed, through nanotechnology and genetics, and 'redesigned'. With such extended control over the human body more control over the natural environment and evolution itself can be achieved – which represents, in fact, a generalization and transposition of the power system described by Foucauldian biopolitics beyond human forms of self-discipline, technologies of the self and embodiment, onto the entire human and nonhuman environment. Apart from the utilitarian and scientistic incentive to reach perfection within the human there is of course also the age-old desire for a human resemblance to God and immortality, the desire for the 'forbidden fruit' and self-aggrandizement (from Adam, to Prometheus, to Frankenstein) which comes into play.

How then should one behave towards these different posthumanisms? Best and Kellner suggest:

> we should neither fear these changes and prohibit them on problematic philosophical grounds (appealing to the alleged norms of God or nature), nor uncritically embrace them in a technophilic ecstasy. Rather, society as a whole must carefully weigh and measure what our choices are, and what futures are available to us. This presupposes a number of conditions, including the imperative that citizens must be scientifically and technologically literate enough to grasp what is at stake.
>
> (198)

However, in the end, it becomes clear that Best and Kellner and their (post-)Marxist approach merely see posthumanism as another 'challenge' for modernity, which the rational subject with its autonomy to act and its social drive towards freedom and justice needs to confront. Whether posthumanism can be ring-fenced in this manner, however, seems questionable, because it is precisely the presupposed rational subject which has been exposed as fiction, or, at best, as an 'effect' of an entirely different system, which outside of human paranoia or anthropocentric narcissism might have developed an entirely other, 'inhuman', dynamic of its own. It could well be – if posthumanism was right – that the liberal humanist space for free choice, which in the '(little) theatre of the subject' (Althusser) and the Enlightenment stage of the human drama is always already presupposed, might be just an illusion, or, even worse, a form of self-deception. Instead, supposed free choice is always already a mere reaction, influenced by distorted perceptions and constructed truths. The technological aspect of posthumanization would thus be the logical outcome of an irreversible loss of control, which occurs within hominization. The initial human reaction to this loss of control was, precisely, that which started the process of technologization of the human species, and this process, now, according to its own dynamic, threatens to engulf its own 'creator'. It is therefore not surprising that a critical posthumanism under these circumstances has opted for a combination of deconstruction and psychoanalysis as its analytical approach. This deconstruction is of an (inhuman) system whose subject is ruled by a technological unconscious. It will therefore not be as easy to choose a pick'n'mix' approach and to avoid supposed 'extreme' positions, as Best and Kellner seem to suggest, who are here used as representatives of an 'enlightened' (but in our view not sufficiently critical) posthumanism. On the one hand, one needs to reject the metaphysical idea of a 'natural body' and human 'nature', which is still more or less compatible with transhumanist techno-prophecies even though or rather because they embrace the idea of augmentation in general to improve human (and nonhuman) life. On the other hand, one needs to critique posthumanism in cultural, materialist fashion, as part of an ideology of a technoscientific capitalist society. Economic neoliberalism, free market ideology and late capitalist individualism can no longer be separated from the various technological and cultural posthumanization processes. What remains in fact is merely a kind of 'flight forward'. As idealist and rational as Best and Kellner's programme might sound, one cannot help thinking that theirs is a late humanist rearguard battle, when they promise to link: 'a project of human transformation to a politics of radical democracy and social reconstruction' (199). The task would thus not merely be to articulate the complex connections between technology and society to avoid the fetishizing of technology as an autonomous dynamic beyond any social relationships. It might be even more important to welcome and embrace global network society, cultural change and human mutation, while, at the same time, remaining conscious of and continuing the critical Marxist and Enlightenment tradition of modernity.

The approach we have called critical posthumanism as explained above therefore occupies a somewhat oblique position with regard to this human-maybe-all-too-human perspective. It is an approach that attempts to think the crisis of humanism and its effect of posthumanization from the point of view of its excluded 'inhuman'. This inhuman is, according to Neal Curtis, paradoxically, a concept and a category, which, on the one hand, is opposed to the human at a moral level; on the other hand, it is actually the inhuman that creates the human in the first place through negative emphasis: 'it upholds the human in its certainty and rectitude, projecting all animality and barbarity outward' (Curtis 2006: 434). At the same time, however, this inhuman, especially in Lyotard's sense, and as already mentioned, is also a challenge to the category of the human as such:

> While the inhuman understood as evil reinforces our sense of self and secures our autonomy, this other inhuman, understood as that which escapes and yet animates us, is the moment of both radical disruption and radical dependence. In this regard the inhuman does not serve the human but is a challenge to it.
>
> (434)

In this sense, the inhuman or the nonhuman is a firm component of the humanist system of values itself. Its nonexistence would literally be unthinkable because it is essential to support the moral code of human society, its institutions and its world picture. If one now understands critical posthumanism as an ethical and political project, one has to start thinking this inhuman supplement or definitional remainder *within* the human itself *otherwise*, and one has to think of it in the sense of a 'politics of the inhuman', which:

> refuses the arrogance that celebrates the end of history and the victory of a single vindicated model of the good society; it demands probity when dealing with events in order that their singularity is not lost in the haste to comprehend them according to the well-known narratives of our habitual sense-making practices; it demands that we think in new ways, invent new concepts, new rules for understanding, new criteria for judgement and new modes of representation.
>
> (435)

The manner in which the figure of the posthuman is represented from various angles opens up political as well as ethical or moral questions that need to be put to the ideology and value system that is humanism. On the one hand, this concerns its 'politics of representation' with its associated question: How are concrete representations of the inhuman as the potentially 'posthuman' simply equated with the 'nonhuman'? This basically means that the inhuman is being integrated within an existing economy of representation. The question is whether the inhuman challenge to the existing humanist value system is being exoticized or demonized through the use of traditional symbolic means, or whether it is being reined in through some form of fetishization. It is exactly out of this selective and thus political and ideologically conservative practice that a moral and ethical responsibility arises, which every specific representational instance of the inhuman or posthuman provokes. Why is the nonhuman inhuman threatening? This recalls Jeffrey Jerome Cohen's formulation in his analysis of 'monster culture'. He invites us to finally take responsibility for 'our' monsters, who keep asking us provocatively, why we made them so monstrous, why we have represented them they way we did. More will have to be said about this in the following chapter, which deals with the multiplicity of posthuman representational 'forms'.

So even if there is uncertainty about the origin of posthumanism, conceptually it is inevitable that with the 'invention of the human' the posthuman as one of his or her 'others' also becomes thinkable, representable, possible, necessary, etc. As soon as some form of *humanitas* begins to characterize the species as a whole, nonhuman (un-, in-, pre- or posthuman) others start proliferating and the process of inclusion, exclusion and differentiation is set in motion. Literature – this humanist invention – might be seen as a privileged cultural practice that engages in this representational negotiation between the human and the inhuman. Where else therefore should one seek out the human/inhuman nexus than at the heart of the literary canon? Shakespeare, given his central position within early modern Western culture at the beginning of roughly 500 years of humanism, can thus be used as an important illustration in this context. Harold Bloom's monumental study *Shakespeare: The Invention of the Human* (1999) insists on the centrality of Shakespeare's position in the universal 'humanist' canon, which transcends individual national literatures through the creation of essentially 'human' characters like Rosalind,

Shylock, Iago, Lear, Macbeth, Cleopatra and, in particular, Falstaff and Hamlet, who represent the 'the invention of the human, the inauguration of personality as we have come to recognize it' (Bloom 1999: 4). 'The idea of Western character, of the self as a moral agent, has many sources: Homer and Plato, Aristotle and Sophocles, the Bible and Augustine, Dante and Kant, and all you might care to add. Personality, in our sense, is a Shakespearean invention, and is not only Shakespeare's greatest originality but also the authentic cause of his perpetual pervasiveness' (4). For Bloom, Shakespeare's importance does not so much lie in his central cultural aesthetic or social historical meaning but in his 'ingenious' creation of universal truths and profound spiritual and sublime, in short, in his authentic 'humanity': 'Our ideas as to what makes the self authentically human owe more to Shakespeare than ought to be possible (17). Bloom's insistent and almost 'dogged' liberal humanism represents, of course, the main target of the kind of constructivist or anti-essentialist 'antihumanism' that characterizes new historicism, cultural materialism and poststructuralism (especially, in the work of Stephen Greenblatt, Jonathan Dollimore, Terence Hawkes or Catherine Belsey). As a result of the politicization of Shakespeare studies in the last few decades Shakespeare is usually afforded an 'ambivalent attitude' towards rising and consolidating early modern humanist ideologies and modern anthropocentrism (cf. the discussion about 'subversion' and 'containment', which, from a cultural political point of view, are always 'present' as two characteristic moments in Shakespeare's plays; cf. Dollimore 1985: 10ff.). This ambivalence is then 'resolved' by both camps – the defenders of liberal humanism like Bloom or Brian Vickers, on the one hand, and champions of antihumanist materialism, on the other – and further used for their respective ideological purposes. On one side we thus have a Marxist-materialist critique of capitalist modernity, which targets alienation and individualism as the main evils of liberal humanism, whereas, on the other side, from a formal aestheticist point of view, Shakespeare is reclaimed as a monument of essential humanity and humanist cultural achievement.

Jonathan Dollimore in his more recent commentary places this caricature of an opposition into a longer historical and theoretical context. Neither Shakespeare's invoked universal humanity, nor his, or early modernity's, subversive radicality, neither the liberal humanist, individual genius, nor the proto-postmodern decentred subject of theory offer the entire truth, because:

> The crisis of subjectivity was there at the inception of individualism in early Christianity, and has been as enabling as it has been disturbing (enabling because disturbing). In other words, what we might now call the neurosis, anxiety and alienation of the subject-in-crisis are not so much the consequence of its recent breakdown, but the very stuff of its creation, and of the culture – Western European culture – from which it is inseparable, especially that culture in its most expansionist phases (of which the 'Renaissance' was undoubtedly one). The crisis of the self isn't so much the subjective counterpart of the demise, disintegration or undermining of Western European culture, as what has always energised both the self and that culture ... what we are living through now is not some (post-)modern collapse of Western subjectivity but another mutation in its enduring dynamic.
>
> (Dollimore 1998: 271)

This latest mutation could therefore without doubt be referred to as 'posthuman' or at least 'posthumanist subjectivity' – a new form of humanist identity in posthumanist clothes that calls forth our vigilance and scepticism. In the third and latest edition of Dollimore's *Radical Tragedy* (2004), he gives his preliminary verdict on the outcome of the so-called 'culture war' of the 1980s and 1990s that his book in many ways helped to spark: '*Radical Tragedy*, first published in 1984, attacked just these ideas: essentialism in relation to subjectivity, universalism in relation to the human, and the belief that there was an ethical/aesthetic realm transcending the political' (2004: xv). While the decentring of the subject and of universalism in late-capitalist society has become the everyday experience of our posthuman(ist) selves, 'aesthetic humanism', as Dollimore calls it, continues to survive in its commodified form as a kind of spiritualizing force. The conviction that art, literature and culture function as a humanizing force is (still) the foundation of the cultural industries as well as all educational institutions. Dollimore criticizes this attitude as rather complacent:

Far from being liberating, the humanist aesthetic has become a way of standing still amidst the obsolete, complacent and self-serving clichés of the heritage culture industry, the Arts establishment, and a market-driven humanities education system. The aesthetic has become an anaesthetic'.

(xxii)

The potential transformation of the traditional humanities into, for want of a better word, the 'posthumanities' of the future will be discussed in more detail in a later chapter. What Dollimore's analysis makes clear, however, is that in the age of the exposed crisis of humanist education there is no way back for theory and criticism, but also no clear-cut trajectory forward into some consensual posthuman(ist) utopia – a condition that Neil Badmington, with reference to Elaine Graham's work, calls 'oblique': 'a 'critical post/humanism' must actively oblique the order of things, Humanism must be obliqued, knocked sideways, pushed off course, declined' (Badmington 2004b: 63). The oblique or slash between 'post' and 'human' (post/human) proposed by Graham mainly serves to gain time and to create a critical space for a more thorough deconstruction of humanism, without which an uncritical reinscription of humanist ideology into posthuman(ist) forms would be inescapable. The liberal humanist and the cultural materialist 'antihumanist' positions described above can in fact be seen to compete for the same moral authority over so-called human 'nature'. Recent approaches within literary criticism are certainly not immune to this anthropocentric blindspot, even if or maybe because they pose as posthumanist engagements with the latest 'scientific' insights, for example by promoting a so-called 'cognitive turn'. One could take Robin Headlam Wells' *Shakespeare's Humanism* (2005) as an example, which takes a biological-*cum*-cognitive starting point in its attempt to 'transcend' the opposition between pro- and anti-humanists:

Where 'humanity' was once seen as a purely cultural construct, a consensus is now emerging among psychologists and neuroscientists that our minds are the product of a complex interaction between genetically determined predispositions and an environment that has itself been shaped by generations of human culture.

(Wells 2005: 2)

Wells uses the idea of the co-evolution of genes and culture to reposition the question about human nature as central within Shakespeare's work, in the hope that

> by listening to what other disciplines have to say about human nature, criticism can move on from an outdated anti-humanism that has its intellectual roots in the early decades of the last century to a more informed modern understanding of the human universals that literature has, in Ian McEwan's words, 'always, knowingly and helplessly, given voice to'.

(5)

The rhetoric of 'departure' and 'overcoming' makes clear that one cannot simply write off humanism that easily. On the contrary, humanism with all its essentialist values relating to some mystical form of human nature is currently being reinvented with the help of cognitive and neuroscientific concepts – supposedly ever-changing yet ever true to itself.

A critical posthumanism would thus need to overcome the ideological confrontation between liberal humanists and cultural materialists mindful of both the historical context and the current climate of cultural change. This also means situating Shakespeare's work formally and historically at a certain turning point within the process of 'posthumanization' – a process that already contains its own mechanisms of repression and exclusion and thus already inscribes its own demise and end. So, just as Shakespeare might be the possible starting point of a certain humanism he could also already anticipate its decline and ultimate ruin. A critical perlaboration of Shakespearean humanism should thus open up the possibility of a fundamentally different, more 'radical' understanding of 'in/humanity'. Recalling Donna Haraway's 'Cyborg Manifesto' (1991 [1985]) – in which Haraway hints at the permeability of the boundaries between human and animal and between humans and machines at the end of the twentieth century – Fudge, Gilbert and Wiseman (2002) explain that the early modern period provides other and much earlier problematizing accounts of humanness and humanism. The spreading of humanist and anthropocentric ideologies during the Renaissance and early modern period does not happen without tensions, contradictions and resistance. There is no immediate consensus about what constitutes some imaginary 'human nature'. This alone might be reason enough to abandon the simplistic idea of a monolithic (Western) humanism which might today be challenged by 'one' (global or globalized) form of posthumanism. Instead a critical posthumanism needs to link back to those critical discourses that run within and alongside the humanist tradition. The contributions in Fudge, Gilbert and Wiseman's *At the Borders of the Human: Beasts, Bodies and Natural Philosophy in the Early Modern Period* (2002) provide some clarification in this respect by pointing out moments of ambivalence in the early modern relationship to animals, machines, the rise of the natural sciences, cartography, sexuality, new concepts of the body and embodiment and modern medicine. Jonathan Sawday, for example, in his essay 'Renaissance Cyborg', emphasizes that body modification is not the privilege of our own, contemporary period:

> Enhancing or altering the body form artificially, whether through adornment – tattoos, cosmetics, padded shoulders, bustles, cod-pieces, wigs – or through more invasive procedures – silicone implants, surgical modification, scarification, the piercing of ears, lips, and other features – may be traced through a bewildering variety of cultural and historical moments.
>
> (Sawday, in Fudge, Gilbert and Wiseman 2002: 172)

Sawday illustrates this ambiguity by referring to a literary example, Shakespeare's Coriolanus and his progressing 'mechanization' during the course of the play, which corresponds to the more general mechanization of nature, especially after Descartes: 'When did we first begin to fear our machines?', Sawday asks.

> Certainly, by the end of the seventeenth century, the dominance of the mechanistic model within European modes of understanding

had become unassailable. The world, human society, the human and animal body, all could be analyzed in terms of the functioning of machinery.

(190)

Haraway's 'cyborgization' of the human can thus be seen to start at the same time as the historical rise of humanism and actually becomes an integral part of it. Without its ideological and philosophical anticipation the idea of cyborgization would have been literally unthinkable. As much as the metaphor of mechanization of nature and of the human and human behaviour allows for greater 'scientific' control over the environment by humans (and machines), it also provokes an 'unease' towards this new and self-produced and self-producing other which threatens to become an indispensible instrument of identification and delimitation and thus to erode the very core of this newly created humanity:

> The modern human relationship with machines, from its emergence in the earlier part of the sixteenth century down to the present, has always been tinged with a measure of unease. 'They' have always been nearer kin to 'us' than we have cared to admit; and in that lies their fascination, as well as their potential horror. It is an uncomfortable prospect that what it is to be human may be defined by 'forms such as never were in nature'.

(191)

In a similar move, Rhodes and Sawday, in *The Renaissance Computer: Knowledge Technology in the First Age of Print* (2000), argue for an anticipation of contemporary information and media society in the early modern period. Almost in analogy with the temporal mode we proposed for posthumanism and the 'invention of the inhuman', Rhodes and Sawday describe contemporary technological change in the form of 'remediation' by claiming that '[t]he experience of our own new technology has enabled us to re-imagine the impact of new technologies in the past' (Rhodes and Sawday 2000: 2).

But even the delimitation between the human and the inhuman as such, as for example in Lyotard's take on posthumanism, has its beginning in early modernity. Shakespeare's 'invention of the human' thus implies the invention of the inhuman. A case in point is Shylock, the Jew, in Shakespeare's *The Merchant of Venice* (1600). Bloom's classic interpretation of this profoundly ambivalent character of an all-too-human and at the same time constantly dehumanized villain can serve as emblematic of a humanist, as opposed to a critically posthumanist, understanding of the human. The central question in this context concerns the antisemitism of the play, as Bloom explains at the opening of his chapter on *The Merchant*: 'One would have to be blind, deaf, and dumb not to recognize that Shakespeare's grand, equivocal comedy *The Merchant of Venice* is nevertheless a profoundly anti-Semitic work' (Bloom 1999: 171). Humanists nevertheless venture either to defend Shakespeare against the accusation of antisemitism (e.g. in arguing that the text is not antisemitist but simply, at worst, ironically and critically reflects a rampant and popular Elizabethan antisemitism, which not only saves, but even ennobles Shakespeare as an author not of, but in his time), or they attempt to 'humanize' Shylock by characterizing him as a largely sympathetic figure and thus wilfully misunderstand the text. Bloom is aware of this contradiction and blames the ambivalence in Shakespeare's text on the rivalry between Shakespeare's 'arch Jew' and Marlowe's Barabas, in *The Jew of Malta* (1590). How else can one explain Shylock's bizarre cruelty and his thirst for Antonio's pound of flesh? 'Shylock simply does not fit his role; he is the wrong Jew in the right play' (Bloom 1999: 172). What Bloom seems to be missing in Shylock is the typical Shakespearean sceptical irony. Shylock impresses through his linguistic precision and expressivity, which constitutes another 'contradiction' at the heart of this social outcast – a contradiction which many modern and contemporary stagings have tried to 'even out' by giving Shylock a strong 'foreign' accent.

Bloom tries to make a Shakespearean virtue out of Shylock's 'vividness' and his extraordinary (human) realism in the face of the barbaric and comic evil he represents by interpreting Shylock as an example of the fascinating multidimensional character of human nature. Shylock is thus seen to shake 'our' fundamental and universal belief in human goodness and confronts this belief with 'our' racist, sexist and religious prejudice. Shylock simply is both a comic villain and the embodiment of tragic and embattled humanity. In this respect, his final conversion to Christianity must represent a sadistic act of revenge by Antonio. The other main characters of the play also do not remain without blame in this interpretation. Antonio, for example, is just as curious an outsider as is Shylock. In addition Antonio seems to entertain a homoerotical relationship with his friend and impoverished playboy', Bassanio. He suffers from the latter's betrayal, namely his decision to woo the rich heiress Portia, to pay off his debtors; however, first Bassanio needs another cash injection from Antonio which, leads to the whole credit and 'pound of flesh' episode. This part of the story is driven by Shylock's hatred of Antonio who has spat at him in public and dehumanized him by calling him a 'dog'. Portia, on the other hand, who is sometimes seen as the true main character of the play, displays some degree of frivolousness in her noble and rather romantic Belmont, while acting rather cunningly and implacably as a dressed-up judge in court. She tricks Shylock, who is rather obstinate in his literal interpretation of the bond, and has no hesitation in completely reversing the situation during the court scene by exposing him to ridicule, destitution, capital punishment and, ultimately, to public humiliation and violence in the form of an imposed conversion to Christianity. Thus it is not only Shylock who is characterized by his human, all-too-human, contradiction but the entire play plays with 'our' trust in the 'Christian' understanding of 'humanity'. Shakespeare's ambivalence, Bloom believes, 'diverts self-hatred into hatred of the other, and associates the other with lost possibilities of the self' (Bloom 1999: 190). And this is where ultimately Shakespeare's 'invention of the human' is located for Bloom, namely in the moral injunction that, in the name of universal humanity, we should not 'dehumanize' ourselves by giving in to our self-hatred or hatred of the other based on a projection of difference and alterity. It is probably also in this sense that Bloom's rather speculative concluding statement needs to be understood: 'I close by wondering if Shylock did not cause Shakespeare more discomfort than we now apprehend' (191), for 'the playwright, capacious soul, would be aware that the gratuitous outrage of a forced conversion to Venetian Christianity surpasses all boundaries of decency' (191). Mission accomplished, one could say: 'man', in standing up to his very own inhumanity, has been 'rehumanized' and, emblematically, in the figure of the Shakespearean genius, extracted, at least temporarily, from the evil mechanism of self-hatred and hatred of the other, and has thus been reinserted into the anthropophile sphere of humanistic self-elevation – court adjourned – at least until the next humanist or humanitarian crisis. As last reassurance, Bloom's final verdict is: 'Shakespeare was [merely] up to mischief' (191).

A completely different, namely posthumanist, way of reading the play is possible, however. In order to demonstrate this alternative, let us first look at Catherine Belsey's essay 'Cultural Difference as Conundrum in *The Merchant of Venice*' in her *Why Shakespeare?* (2007), as an example of poststructuralist 'antihumanism' with its undeniable merits but also its limitations. In a by now classic move, Belsey shifts the ambivalence of the play onto its linguistic plane and characterizes it as 'a play that depends so extensively on the instability of meaning and the duplicity of the signifier' (Belsey 2007: 160), which to a large extent is expressed in Shylock's stubborn 'literalness', as far as the bond is concerned. It is this literalness that will be 'outdone' by Portia, in the court scene, in order to 'undo' Shylock. Unlike Bloom and other humanist interpreters, who see this ambivalence as a pedagogical 'task', or as a moral 'admonition' to the reader or spectator, namely to acknowledge and understand their own human nature, Belsey reads it in a deconstructionist vein, namely as an impossible structural necessity of the play and its cultural context: 'A prejudice conventional in its own period goes into the composition of *Merchant of Venice*. At the same time, the play includes elements that radically unsettle the prejudice it produces. *It differs from itself*' (161). A central role is played by the contradiction between the untouchable and general nature of the law, on the one hand, and its necessarily linguistic interpretation, on the other – a point that Derrida (2001b) makes in a similar form, in his reading of the play. Belsey formulates the dilemma as follows:

> How, in other words, can the law be just to both Antonio and Shylock? And the answer, of course, is a quibble: flesh is not blood; a pound is not a jot more or less than a pound. Nowhere is the duplicity of the signifier thrown into clearer relief than in this exposure of the moneylender's worthless bond. Shylock's

ultimate antagonist is the language in which his contract with
Antonio is necessarily formulated — and he loses.

(Belsey 2007: 162)

The law is necessarily expressed in language ('inscribed in the signifier'); language, however has its own dynamic and is 'anarchic' (164). At this point, something very interesting happens in Belsey's reading, which, despite all its best intentions and absolutely consistent antihumanist conclusions, finds itself drawn back into the dialectic of de- and rehumanization as described by Bloom above. Belsey uses Derrida's notion of a 'monolingualism of the other' (Derrida, 1998), by which he describes his forced exile from his 'own' and his 'only' native language, French. The experience of being an Algerian Jew under the protectorate of the Vichy regime is represented by Derrida in the form of the following 'aporia': 'I have only one language; it is not mine' (Derrida 1998: 15). Belsey uses this to come to a general, almost existential, maybe even 'humanitarian' insight: 'we none of "us" own the language we speak, which was already there when we came into the world' (Belsey 2007: 163). 'In this sense, we are all aliens, all in exile from a state of perfect correspondence between what we want to say, or would want to say if only we knew what it was, and the signifying practices available to us' (163). However, what this disarming, almost humanist-*cum*-existentialist, 'universalism' necessarily downplays is that not all forms of linguistic exile are equivalent. Instead, and this is one of Derrida's main arguments in *Monolingualism*, every linguistic exile depends on a culturally specific power struggle between individuals and institutions, which attempt to control and establish a monopoly over the fixation of meaning by claiming 'ownership' of (a) language. Shylock becomes implicated in such a power struggle and as an outsider is duly stigmatized and excluded. He is stripped of 'his' language (which even more than in Derrida's sense is not his 'own') and is punished for his cultural difference to safeguard the imaginary homogeneity of Christian society and Venetian law.

The strategy that Belsey uses to 'save' Shakespeare from his 'own' contemporary culture seems ultimately, despite or maybe because of its diametrical opposition to Bloom's liberal humanism, as humanistically and universalistically motivated as in Bloom: 'How surprising, then that the play invests its fantasy-Jew with humanity. It is for this reason, however, that *The Merchant of Venice* does not just reaffirm prejudice, but draws attention to it' (167). If Shakespeare's text itself undermines or even 'deconstructs' the idea of a culturally homogeneous identity it can be used as an early modern testimony against any exclusivity in the process of identity construction at any time in history. Belsey's reading consequently does not fail to engage in a critique of contemporary multiculturalism, at the same time as it justifies the ongoing interest in Shakespeare as a thinker of great humanitarian and existential questions ('the reason why Shakespeare's play continues to haunt the imagination of the West'): 'can a society preserve cultural difference and at the same time do away with social antagonism?' (168). In relation to the contemporary, and especially the Anglo-American, cultural context, the question arises in the following *historically and culturally specific* form, despite its tacit universal assumptions: 'While enforced integration generates a justified resentment, our own well-meaning multiculturalism may inadvertently foster precisely the segregation, and thus the hostility, it was designed to prevent' (168). The similarity of the procedure with that of Bloom's 'liberal humanism' in this context is indeed striking. The play opens onto the 'abyss' of inhumanity, projected onto the outsider who, in turn, exposes the inhumanity of the entire society of humans. The same dialectic of self-hatred, hatred of the other and cultural improvement that constitutes Bloom's humanist ideology ironically appears to be at work in Belsey's reading as well. Our argument would be that as long as this dialectic is not questioned a critical posthumanist angle remains invisible.

Let us therefore briefly return to the 'essence' of humanity and look again at Shylock's famous speech in Act III.1 – a speech provoked by his previous personal and no doubt traumatic loss of his only daughter, Jessica, and Salarino's mocking reminder of her elopement. Shylock concludes his humanity speech with the words: 'The villainy you teach me I will execute, and it shall go hard but I will better the instruction' (III.1.56–7). Nothing, in fact, is more effective in unhinging humanism than this phrase, because the dialectic of similarity and difference is here seen at its turning point. The projected inhumanity, the repressed self-hatred returns, following the basic psychoanalytical logic of the repressed's return, and it begins to haunt the provisionally stabilized self, threatens it and causes it to repress afresh – which could be used to explain to what extent the escalation of inhumanity is an essential aspect of humanity itself, maybe even its very engine, drive or *telos*: the 'humanization' of history hides its own dehumanizing logic. Posthumanism can therefore not simply break with this logic because that would merely constitute a continuation of the escalating dialectic of humanization and dehumanization. Instead it is a question of a deconstructive 'working through' of humanism's represseds, of the inhuman and unhuman, in a radically different sense.

Scott Brewster summarizes this point in his introduction to *Inhuman Reflections: Thinking the Limits of the Human*:

> the inhuman is unsatisfactorily configured as somehow 'post' or as a mere *limen* or threshold, much less a crossing of the boundary. Rather it retains a sense of excess (plural potentiality) which continues to disseminate as it always has done and fulfilled an unfulfillable within the continuing 'technical mediation' of the human.
>
> (Brewster 2000: 9)

This techn(olog)ical mediation of the human, which has to be taken into account in any critical genealogy of the inhuman or the posthuman, testifies to the fact that any form of 'becoming-machine' (i.e. cyborgization as the one, predominantly contemporary, form of posthumanization) is always already a constitutive factor of being human and thus being necessarily connected with an 'originary technicity'.

Let us stress again that the prefix 'post-' in posthumanism can have a variety of meanings and that it allows for a number of discursive and argumentative strategies. Thus neither in terms of content nor as far as strategic usage is concerned do the terms 'posthuman', 'posthumanity' and 'posthumanization' presuppose any consensus. These terms are politically, radically open, which is the fact that gives rise to the demand for a critical posthumanism in the first place – a critical posthumanism that both takes the issue of the posthuman seriously and problematizes, contextualizes and historicizes it, at the same time.

In this respect this argument is in partial agreement with Halliwell and Mousley's approach in *Critical Humanisms: Humanist/Anti-Humanist Dialogues* (2003), which proposes to do justice to the complexity of humanism in its many disguises. Halliwell and Mousley distinguish between a romantic, existentialist, dialogic, civic, spiritual, secular, pragmatic and a technological humanism, on the one hand, and, on the other hand, they also subdivide antihumanism, as a reaction against each of these humanisms, into three phases. The first of these phases lasts from the mid nineteenth to the beginning of the twentieth century and contains important antihumanist precursors like Darwin, Freud, Marx, Nietzsche, Saussure and Weber, who all engage in a critique of anthropocentric metaphysics. The second phase of the 1960s and 1970s is that of the antihumanists proper (Barthes, Deleuze and Guattari, Derrida, Foucault, Baudrillard and Lacan), which leads, finally, within the postmodern context of the 1970s and 1980s, to the third generation of antihumanism in the form of a popularization. Among the proponents of the third phase Halliwell and Mousley include figures like Catherine Belsey, Geoffrey Bennington, Terence Hawkes, Christopher Norris, Peggy Kamuf, J. Hillis Miller and Paul Rabinow, who expose the 'cardinal sins' of 'Western metaphysics': logocentrism, phallocentrism and anthropocentrism. As antidotes they propose the decentring of language, the subject and the liberal humanist world picture in general. Despite the curious anglocentrism of Halliwell and Mousley's genealogy, their approach successfully problematizes a monolithic view of humanism by locating a radical self-criticism already within the humanist tradition and, on this basis, by arguing for a non-normative, 'post-foundational' humanism 'that refuses to define the human'(Halliwell and Mousley 2003: 9) and thus escapes the 'tyranny of naming and quantifying the human' (10). Against the 'reduction' of the human in the age of hypermodern, late capitalism, so-called 'high theory' and the endless 'plasticity of the human' Halliwell and Mousley propose a 'grounded humanism' which opposes the 'alienation, depersonalisation and degradation' (10) of the human and humanity. Despite Halliwell and Mousley's humanitarian reflex, however, it seems unlikely that the contemporary techno-savvy phase of posthumanization will have a lot of patience with such an attempt at rehumanizing. This is why our standpoint probably also implies a kind of 'alterhumanism', rather than a rehumanization, as an antidote for some of the undeniably dehumanizing tendencies within the prospect of posthumanization. However, projecting the inhumanity onto the 'system' in order to preserve the principle of human(ist) freedom seems an illusion, since 'human' and 'system' are thoroughly interrelated – humans create systems, which then 'reproduce' or shape humans as subjects or actors to guarantee the continuity of that system (an aspect which is further explored in the final chapter of this volume).

One has no choice but to face the prospect of posthumanism if one is serious about a critique of humanism and anthropocentrism without giving in to the rehumanization reflex, which does not really seem prepared to question humanist foundations. This might, for example, be particularly relevant for postcolonial theory and the discussion about how best to deal with ethnic difference and modern racism. The particular concern is that the dissolution of a universalist notion of humanity would foster a return of old racisms in a new form. As justified as this concern might be, it cannot lead to a renewal of a leftist radical humanism in the name of a Kantian cosmopolitan tradition as, for example, suggested by John Sanbonmatsu (2004), who argues for, what he calls 'metahumanism':

> With the arrival of post-humanism we may fast be approaching the zero hour of the critical tradition. With the subject as such now placed *sous rature* (under erasure), but this time not merely by clever critics but by scientists who *literally* manipulate the stuff our dreams of ourselves are made of, even the poststructuralist project self-destructs, as deconstruction is rendered irrelevant by the *fragmentation* of the ontological unity *Dasein*. This may seem a trivial point, but critical theory is already dangerously in collusion with the final obliteration of all things 'human' by capital ... Post-humanism will have to be met forthrightly – with a return to ontology and the grounding of thought in a meaningful account of human being.
>
> (Sanbonmatsu 2004: 207)

A lot could be said about the problematic reference to Prospero in defense of 'metahumanism'. Indeed, it would be quite wrong to idealize humanist universalism for the reasons outlined above.

The universalist ideal of a common and irreducible humanity that underlies, for example, the legitimation of any legislation against crimes against humanity has not succeeded in addressing the radical dehumanization underlying the entire history of colonialism and its current legacy of global migration and multiculturalism (this is also Belsey's motif above). Neither has an essentialist notion of humanity prevented the Holocaust or other genocides since. In our view, the 'perversion' of inhumanity is part of the logic of humanism itself. This is why a deconstruction of the humanist tradition has never been more important than today, i.e. in the face of a continued transformation of the human and of the humanistic question as such: What exactly constitutes the humanity of the human? It is precisely the connection between continuity, break and remembering that powers the dialectical drive, within humanism, between dehumanization and rehumanization. Only a deconstruction of humanism in its current globalized and technocultural posthumanist form and phase can unhinge this dialectic play and may eventually expose and disrupt it, provoking an opening towards a radically different, nonhumanist, post-anthropocentric view.

From its tender beginnings in Greek and Roman antiquity, to its neoplatonist and Christian Europeanization, Renaissance anthropocentrism, the Enlightenment and industrial and rational modernity, up to the antihumanist phase in the nineteenth and twentieth century and contemporary posthumanist age that includes the radically utopian stance represented by transhumanists – humanism has always displayed a remarkable resistance and adaptability. It has overcome its theological and religious beginnings in the face of modern developments and challenges (science, evolution, psychoanalysis, existentialism, globalization and technologization) and has secularized (French Revolution), politicized (liberalism) and economized (capitalism) itself and has perpetuated itself as 'common sense' on an international and, arguably, global level. In its name, wars have been and are being fought, as much as the world's poor are being helped. Its educational values underlie the modern institution of the university. Its aesthetic shores up globalized Western culture. Its moral values do not cease to inspire promethean historical accounts of human self-aggrandizement *and* humility, of the good and evil, of which the human in all his or her splendour *and* misery is capable and between which he or she constantly has to choose in order to overcome the suffering and the mortality the human shares with all the individuals of the species (and indeed with all known other species). Who could be so unfeeling and not be touched by this: humanism's 'heroic' self-account? Nevertheless, it is precisely this humanistic self-indulgence and uncritical complacency that might drive a critical posthumanist towards 'strategic misanthropy' – out of care for the human and a future of and for humans, including their natural and cultural environment, for 'who can fail to realize that the trope of misanthropy is the hope of society?' (Cottom 2006: 150).

3

Our posthuman humanity and the multiplicity of its forms

> *It has become a commonplace assumption that the present is a posthumanist era.*
> (GAGGI 1989: 157)

As Wolfgang Welsch explained in *Unsere postmoderne Moderne* (1991), with reference to the postmodern, the contemporary debate is not about an either-or between modern and postmodern but about a perlaboration and transformation of modernity. Some modern traits might disappear while others are kept and developed further (xiv). Something similar could be said about the present, posthumanist context: it is not so much a question of the detachment of some utopian or existing posthumanity from a more or less existing or idealized humanity or its opposition, but of the 'perlaboration', differentiation and pluralization of the latter. All the elements of the phrase 'our posthuman humanity' – 'our', 'posthuman', 'humanity' – have become problematic. 'Our' is problematic because of the crisis of universalism and universal values; 'posthuman', because of the ambiguity of its prefix and the resulting multiplicity of human and posthuman forms of representation; 'humanity', finally, because of the radical openness of and the lack of a consensus on the meaning of its concept. Nevertheless, the phrase, 'our posthuman humanity', in the multiplicity of its forms, seems well placed to characterize the current state of the discussion and also the extent of the crisis in which 'our' at least 500-year-old humanist tradition currently finds itself. Humanism's most fundamental question – What does it mean to be human? – is being asked with more urgency than ever before. Just as for Welsch's notion of the postmodern, plurality remains a key term in the context of the posthuman – a plurality which also works 'retroactively' so to speak, since the prefix 'post' tends to question the unity of its category and hence, the unity, uniformity and integrity of the human. The 'end of metanarratives, the dispersion of the subject, the decentring of meaning, the simultaneity of the asynchronic, the impossibility of synthesizing the multiplicity of life forms and patterns of rationality' (xv; my translation), which all describe postmodern plurality, also capture the crisis of the last remaining metanarrative, namely humanist anthropocentrism, and its origins. Posthumanization – to give this crisis a name – is the sign of a process in which accelerated technologization has led to a hastening of humanism's current crisis, but which nevertheless merely represents its latest phase within a long history of crises (starting with the 'invention of humanity' itself, as suggested in the previous chapter). It is also a sign that this process is not complete and that it is a process, similar to modernity that may be uncompletable by definition. Humanity cannot imagine anything except the worst to come after its projected end. And this is precisely what concerns us, namely the 'unimaginability' of the posthuman despite, or in the face of, the current proliferation of posthuman forms. This is not really a paradox since there is no alternative for 'us' humans, in the face of both the uncertainty and the inevitability of our own 'end', except to attempt to 'reinscribe' our anthropomorphism – our narcissistic projection onto the representation of 'others' – within our posthumanity, thus hoping at least to leave a human 'trace'. One cannot therefore take the expressions of posthumanism at face value; instead one has to read them as 'symptoms', as expressions of anxieties or desires, psychoses, phobias and hysterias produced by a still predominantly humanist culture, which is undergoing radical change – or, in short, as a kind of autoimmunitarian reaction. Through such a 'symptomatic' reading of posthumanist forms of expression an entirely different and much more positive meaning of posthumanization might become possible, namely an affirmative deconstruction of our humanist 'prison-house', not of language as such (cf. Jameson 1972), but of our obsessions; a reading which opens up the possibility to think of posthumanization as a much more radical and liberating form of 'humanization'. Maybe, to adapt Bruno Latour's argument on modernity, we have never been human (Latour 1993).

This chapter therefore engages in such a symptomatic reading of posthumanism through its expressive forms in order to make visible its underlying deconstructive process of posthumanization. Posthumanist forms of expression are not exclusively contemporary. However, it is certainly true that within current expressions technologically induced forms like cyborgs, artificial intelligence, robots and so on tend to dominate. We would thus propose to understand posthumanism as that crisis which has always been inhabiting humanism while posthumanization is the ongoing process of repression of 'our' in/humanity. The important transformations within modernity since WWII and its entering into a postmodern, postindustrial, late capitalist, globalized and infotechnological phase will serve as a sociological framework. While neoliberal globalization is ongoing, what is added at the beginning of the twenty first century is a new uncertainty, a military and political multipolarity and the beginning of a planetary ecological consciousness in the face of global warming, radical climate change and their social consequences. What is less clear is the extent to which the modern humanist notion of the human as the last remainder of Enlightenment grand narratives has already changed and will continue to change, as a result of the accelerated technocultural development that forms the problematic cultural inheritance of postmodernism.

There is little controversy about the fact that the postmodernization of modernity is either accompanied or largely determined by technological change. Lyotard's postmodern 'knowledge society' is based on the advent of new information technology, the access to which is (and still remains) in need of democratization on a global scale. This development, however, not only changes the mere quantity of information that is available or its distribution but also the quality of what actually constitutes information as such. Consequently, information becomes the most important resource, commodity but also the central 'ideologeme' within information society. Digitally based information technologies not only 'recognize' data exclusively as 'information' they actively transform everything into information as well. Information thus is the key metaphor and the driving force behind 'informat(ional)ization' on the trajectory towards a global networked information society. It thus makes sense to explain posthumanization as the disappearance of the modern metanarratives of the Enlightenment and human emancipation, of the idealist 'teleology of the spirit' and the historical 'hermeneutics of meaning', as Welsch calls them, following Lyotard (Welsch 1991: 32); or the loss of the totality and the liberation of its parts, in the context of technological change and the dissolution of the last (meta)metanarrative, arguably underestimated by postmodernism, namely anthropocentric humanism. Welsch, for example, argues for a co-operative model between postmodernity and technology, even if he sees a certain incompatibility between the thesis of a 'technological age' and a postmodern thinking of plurality (Welsch 1991: 215ff.). It is true that many theories of postmodernism or postmodernity are characterized by a sceptical attitude towards (techno) science. It is also true that the idea of progress based on technological development has taken serious blows, as early as WWI, but particularly since the Holocaust and WWII. Nevertheless, an entirely different form of technological determinism seems to have gathered momentum in the age of posthumanism, namely a dehumanized, subjectless, autotelic and system-oriented belief in technology, in particular in transhumanist quarters. This new belief in technology is disseminated to a wide audience via popular media and 'get-the-latest-gadget' consumption, a popularization which is an integral part of contemporary technoculture. The transhumanist movement and the posthumanizing effect of the media are subjects that are dealt with in subsequent chapters of this study. The present chapter is mainly concerned with establishing the link between postmodernity, the 'technological age' and technoculture as such.

In general it is probably safe to say that postmodern philosophy with its critique of rationality and reason is rather sceptical as far as technology and science are concerned. In terms of social theory this scepticism, which has had much influence within science itself, namely through figures like Thomas Kuhn, Vilém Flusser and Paul Feyerabend, and which has been further accentuated by the institutionalization of 'critical science studies', is related to the intensification of the alliance between late capitalism, technology and science – often referred to as 'technoscientific capitalism'. Communication, culture and media studies in particular, following Marshall McLuhan and Jean Baudrillard, are characterized by their ambiguous attitude towards technologization and mediatization of postmodern society. They either develop a fascination with the new 'tech(no)gnosis' (cf. Davis 1999, and Hassan 1987) or they succumb to some kind of phobia regarding the supposed technological suicide of the human in the age of networking, media convergence and the emergence of artificial intelligence (cf. Kroker and Kroker 1996, and Virilio 2005). Maybe postmodernism was too 'naïve' however as far as posthumanization is concerned, given its intensification in the age of 'technological hypertrophy' (Welsch 1991: 218). It seems that new technologies in combination with new media might have overpowered the pluralistic postmodern critique of rationality, or that they might even have benefited from it. Contemporary and ongoing globalization and informatization, on the one hand, might lead to a radicalization of plurality; on the other hand, however, these very processes also threaten to develop into a new global techno(mono) culture. In this sense, they lead to increased localization *as well as* to delocalizing virtuality (cf. 'glocalization'). A critical posthumanism thus needs to embrace technological challenge while at the same time it needs to think through a postmodern critique, both 'forwards' and 'backwards' so to speak, mapping change onto the long-term dimension of posthumanization, which in fact already begins with the very idea of hominization. It is no longer a question of a critique of technology as such, as Welsch argues (1991: 222), but of a deconstruction (and thus also not really of a 'third culture', as C. P. Snow suggested) of fundamental oppositions like human/machine, human/animal, nature/culture, mind/nature, etc. It is a question of thinking the implications of humanity and technics 'otherwise' than from a late capitalist and techno-logical point of view (for example, by following Lyotard's 'para-logy', or, Welsch's 'transversal reason'). In this sense, modern science can be said to be currently in its state of dissolution, while at the same time it might also be seen as omnipresent at a cultural and economic level. It thus faces its own 'postscientific' stage, as Crook, Pakulski and Waters already explained in 1992:

> A postscience would entail the final erosion of boundaries between the knowledges and practices of science and those of other domains. It remains unclear whether postscience will enjoy an open and pragmatic integration with public interests, or whether it will be subject to a commercially dominated hypercommodification.
>
> (Crook, Pakulski and Waters 1992: 223)

At the same time, it remains unclear whether contemporary technoculture constitutes a generalized form of surveillance or the liberation of the postmodern individual. In order to prevent the ambivalence of technological development from turning into a stalemate between freedom and survival, as Ulrich Beck formulated it (1998), and to save self-restriction from inviting new forms of authoritarianism, and also to avoid the acceptance of 'risk society' turning into a form of depoliticization, Beck, instead, calls for the 'invention of the political' within a second, radicalized and 'reflexive' modernization (Beck 1992). In analogy, a critical posthumanism might thus also be seen as a kind of 'reflexive humanization'. This would mean recognizing technology as the intrinsic risk, at the heart of human society, and using its inevitability 'reflexively' so to speak, namely as an integral part of the ongoing questioning of humanity, with the intention of seeing posthumanization, with its 'postanthropocentric' view of humans and their environment, as a 'second (radicalized) humanity'.

In summary, it thus seems convincing to describe the process of postmodernization throughout the second half of the twentieth century, which especially in the West coincides with the processes of globalization, postindustrialization and (technological) posthumanization, in terms of technoculture and technoscientific capitalism. As will be discussed in the next chapter, this combination of postmodern technoculture, which is characterized not only by the progressive miniaturization and computerization of production processes and the service industries, but also in everyday life practices and consumption, has reached a point at which 'our' contemporary lifeworld has *literally* turned into a 'techno-culture' and our social order *literally* corresponds to 'techno-scientific capitalism'. As a result, the traditional liberal humanist subject within this technoscientific, postindustrial, hypercapitalist information society is experiencing, under the economic, political and social conditions of technoculture, the most profound transformations. It is not only the transformation of the individual into the ever more present and cynical figure of the 'consumer' which represents a challenge and a threat to the liberal humanist principle of uniqueness as well as to the 'integrity' of the individual human being, but also the increasing dependence on technologization processes and their complete penetration of contemporary culture.

Below we will be analysing the plurality of posthumanist forms which appear under these conditions of posthumanization within contemporary technoculture. A fundamental aspect of a critical posthumanism beyond technophobia and techno-euphoria is to be found in the poststructuralist critique of a 'politics of representation' (as summarized in Stuart Hall (1997)), with a view to new posthumanist forms and constructions of 'posthumanity'. For the purpose of this kind of analysis it is worth remembering that the poststructuralist idea of a politics of representation, which has been dominating critical and cultural theory and cultural studies in the past decades, presupposes a number of points that are worth clarifying. First, one has to bear in mind theory's anti-realism, which has already been mentioned, and relies on a (moderate) constructivism. The main argument in this context is that the realist principle as one of the dominant ideologemes of capitalism and humanism has become suspect, because it builds on mystifying assumptions which have, on closer inspection, become untenable. In the main, this concerns the apparent 'transparency' of the medium and the 'elision' of the subject. A 'realist text', be it a fictional novel, a television documentary, a political or scientific statement, depends on the more or less hidden assumption that there is *one* reality which, in principle, is independent of its (human) communication and which, through appropriate (i.e. 'realist') means of representation, can be 'transferred' realistically, objectively and with universal validity. All humanist, liberal and capitalist institutions are in fact based on this assumption, whether they serve a political, religious, scientific, juridical or pedagogical end. A radical constructivism would go so far as to simply deny the existence of such an independent reality, and would instead see any reality merely as a social construct. It is thus based on a radical nihilism that can only speak of reality in the plural and that has to presuppose a competition between different constructions of reality. Poststructuralists usually are not radical or nihilist constructivists in this sense, but instead might rather be termed 'critical' realists. A certain measure of realism is probably inevitable for any 'critical' standpoint. However, one needs to be sceptical of any resulting 'truth claim' based on the specific realism of representation (including the realism at work in one's own position – which explains the extreme self-reflexivity that is usually at work in poststructralist thinking). One cannot trust language or any other medium as a means of expression for one's identity. Thought would be unthinkable without language, but language is naturally ambiguous and polysemic (two axioms of Saussurean linguistics, in particular, and of structuralism, in general – even though structuralism attempted, by systematic and quasi-scientific means, to reduce this plurality of meaning in 'modernist' fashion and force it into one single unified expression, while poststructuralism, in its 'postmodern' vein, turns the perceived problem of plurality into a virtue and embraces difference, including 'self-difference' or 'otherness' in order to celebrate it or at least to respond to it ethically). The result is a scepticism towards the apparent transparency of the medium and the associated claim of the 'naturalness' and 'obviousness' of its communicative and symbolic messages, as well as towards the idea that these messages might be in any way 'identical' to themselves, which means independent of context and perfectly reproducible. Instead, poststructuralism advocates radical contextuality and a highly critical view of any stable or 'circular' identity. Identity is never identical to itself, but necessarily differs from itself, it is a process, rather than a state – an insight gained in particular within post-Freudian, Lacanian psychoanalysis. The formula for this is the eruption of the other within the self-same – a process that is predominantly at work in systems which aim for coherence of meaning. A naïve realism pretends to its addressee that not only is the medium transparent but that its subject is a stable and passive entity – a point of critique that can, for example, be found in Foucault's well-known reading of Velazquez' *Las Meninas* in *The Order of Things* (1970).

The second principle of poststructuralist critique problematizes the notion of the addressee of any cultural symbolic form of representation. The addressee is a cultural subject who is 'interpellated' ideologically and who is only apparently a 'free', 'unique' and unified 'individual' – someone who takes predominantly rational decisions for which linguistic or symbolic expressions are purely secondary, or merely the expression of a pre-existing, mental or cognitive fact (cf. Althusser 1971). In contrast to this, a representational text 'creates' 'its own' subject, by positioning it. Cultural representation, for example of a cyborgized posthuman, is thus not 'neutral', but demands from its addressee either acceptance through 'embodiment' of the inscribed (or 'offered') position (which through its associated web of intertextual relations constitutes an entire world view), or active resistance, which nevertheless can only take place once interpellation has occurred and the subject position has been at least temporarily taken up. This resistance subsequently has to produce a revision and reinscription of the positioning, which means that a discursive 'negotiation' process of the presupposed, dominant (but not entirely determined) reading or meaning has to occur. To this end, new subjectivities are needed and have to be created, whose positions continue the 'game' by interpellating other subjects and so forth. It is important to stress, however, that not all subject positions are equivalent, because different subjectivities have different forms of power attached to them. When an influential and well-known institution like the MIT lab proposes new technological breakthroughs that will turn humans into subjects based on a fusion of organic and high-tech informatics, this has of course, thanks to popular dissemination through television, magazines, new media, etc., a much broader effect; and it is thus an effect in relation to which the individual 'consumer' of this message has to position him or herself. This usually functions somewhat like this: 'look at what "science" has come up with again! Now it will only be a few years until "I" will also become a cyborg'. The other possibility is, of course, doubt or disbelief given the perceived 'craziness' of the idea or the 'scientists' behind it: 'look at these "scientists", who, would you believe it, really think that through an alliance with high-tech-gear humanity might be "improved"!' However, even this more sceptical attitude still requires a negotiation of the (imaginary) cyborg scenario, which, with every repetition, gains credibility and power, probability and thus 'reality' – a self-enforcing discursive circle (cf. Chapter 1). There are, of course, also many intermediate positions and a whole spectrum of selecting reactions. Technological developments are never entirely 'realized' in exactly the way they were constructed and offered up by scientific, commercial, military or political discourses. Again, the classic case is the internet, whose intended original military use has by now transformed into an ideal environment for capitalist (cf. e-Bay, Google, etc.), political-ideological and social (cf. e-news, blogging) exploitation. It is also increasingly used for the creation of new forms of identity construction and 'identity work' (cf. MySpace, YouTube, Facebook, etc.).

The third presupposition for a poststructuralist understanding of a politics of representation, once the notion of representation and identity (both the identity of the representation and the identity of the subject of representation) have been problematized, is the 'politicization' of culture, on which the whole dynamic and project of 'cultural studies' is based. Culture, following Raymond Williams, is not (only) a civilizatory and humanist project, or human sublimation – to be understood as the best, most beautiful, most essential or truest and universal that humans have managed to produce. Not only is it the entire heritage of knowledge, human techniques, products or skills, but culture is above all 'a way of life' of any given 'symbolic community'. Culture is a lifeworld which, however, is not based on consensus but on the constant negotiation of conflicts and disagreement. Cultural conflict within one or between several cultures and their subcultures is the norm, and this is normally carried out at a symbolic level where meaning is contested, that is within discourses and texts, subjects and institutions, practices and experiences. The meaning of posthumanity and posthumanism, for example, becomes an issue for conflictual negotiation between individual, social, institutional and political actors with their concrete representations of the 'posthuman'. The present study is certainly part of this very process. It describes cultural practices (cyborgization, technoculture, virtualization, etc.) and their meaningful representation (in the media, scientific texts, manifestos, etc.). It thus intervenes within this cultural discursive conflict by promoting a very specific position and thus also a positioning of an 'ideal' subject, namely a critical posthumanist subject, who will neither withdraw from the discussion on posthumanization, nor give in to techno-euphorian utopias and who will instead continue deconstructing and contextualizing the phenomenon. In this sense, this intervention within and representation of posthumanist objects is culturally political, because despite all possible self-reflexivity it is based on some realist belief on the basis of which change is invoked. This would not be possible at all if culture was not indeed dynamic and conflictual, or a conjunction of social, and contextually historical and singular, subjective meanings. There is thus some good and some bad news in this: posthumanization, cyborgization, virtualization, etc. cannot be ignored, but nor are they fully determined or determining; however, on the basis of alternative forms of knowledge and cultural 'technologies of the self' (Foucault), these processes can also be reinterpreted as potentially 'empowering'. This summary of the politics of representation at work in culture should help to critically evaluate the diverse forms of representation within posthumanist discourse and those, in particular, which are concerned with the figure of the 'cyborg' and other posthuman 'monsters'.

An excellent approach which takes into account both the threatening as well as the positive potential of posthumanization by critically analysing the forms of expression within technoculture and technoscientific capitalism as symptoms can be found in Elaine Graham's *Representations of the Post/Human* (2002). Graham's project is to place the cultural representation of the posthuman between the extremes of enslavement and liberation of humans by the nonhuman other (machines, cyborgs, animals, gods and other 'monsters'), namely as cultural political process, and to show the 'ontological hygiene' that is at work in this process, which is supposed to 'purify' the category of the human. The monstrous or idealized posthuman is thus part of, or motivation for and a symptom of, a politics of representation within the contemporary social process of posthumanization. The interest in the terrifying, the monstrous, the uncanny, etc. has been at the centre of discussion within critical and cultural theory ever since the 1990s. This, again, has been happening under the influence of the 'philosophers of difference' (Ruby 1989): Foucault, Derrida, Deleuze, Lyotard, even though this list of names could easily be continued: Lacan, Levinas,

Said, Bhabha, Butler, Braidotti, Haraway, Žižek, etc. The 'philosophers of difference' and their critique of a dialectical relationship between 'the same and the other' (cf. Descombes 1980) tend to stress radical difference and alterity, a move which serves to escape the Hegelian dialectic of (self-)identity, in the form of attending to an indigestible remainder or as a necessary 'outside', which constantly returns to haunt self-identity as a threatening but at the same time fascinating 'monstrous' other. What is at stake, therefore, is the transgression of boundaries with its associated risks and pleasures and, hence, the nightmarish, the haunting, which nevertheless needs to be taken more seriously than some purely aesthetic, 'dark romanticism'. Instead, the monster poses an ontological challenge aimed at the foundations of 'Western metaphysics' and its value system. Monstrosity is, so to speak, a necessary 'supplement' (cf. Derrida 2002b) that was made 'acceptable' by Derrida and has been a topos in cultural criticism since the late 1990s. Let us take just one characteristic statement, which already applies this theme to a very specifically posthuman aspect of monstrosity:

> Monsters, denizens of the borderland, have always represented the extremities of transgression and the limits of the order of things. In the work of Jacques Derrida, the figure of the monster embodies a means of thinking otherwise – a means of passing 'beyond man and humanism' and reaching for other posthuman futures – that has travelled under the name deconstruction. The event of the Derridean text, signaling a 'rupture' with the discourses in which it gestated, terrifies with its unprecedented deformation of the normal and its threat to the boundaries of conventional thought.
>
> (Milburn 2003: 603)

What is at stake is the erosion of hierarchies with their boundaries and binary oppositions – Foucault, as a student of Canguilhem, as well as Derrida, deconstructs the opposition of the 'normal' and the 'pathological', not out of some perverse pleasure, but basically in the name of an ethics and politics of alterity. The humanist metaphysical dialectic of identity which uses radical alterity in order to reassure itself, or rather its self, by constructing cultural political forms of representation in the form of monstrosities of all kinds. In doing so it believes itself able to restrict and control this alterity. This dialectic engine is made to stall, however, by 'taking the monster seriously', and by reading it as a 'symptom' of a cultural politics of representation. This also opens up an entirely different attitude towards alterity and the injustice concrete others have experienced through their (mis)representation. This is not only important for reasons of justice but it also serves as a starting point for a radical political in(ter)vention of an absolutely new and unforeseeable future, as the prefix 'post' (for example in the 'posthuman') also implies. The posthuman can neither simply guarantee the human, nor can it differ in any epistemological sense from the human, because even opposition, variation, etc. would merely be repetitions of the same (cf. Deleuze 1994). The posthuman must, therefore, be entirely other and new in the sense of a 'monstrous monstrosity' (cf. Derrida 1989b), since behind the disgust of monstrosity is the fear of the uncontrollable and the unpredictable of a radical, or 'monstrous monstrosity', which erupts, beyond good and evil, in the form of an event or the unannounced advent of a Derridean, absolutely unforeseeable, *arrivant*. One could thus say, that the posthuman announces the inhuman in the Lyotardian sense outlined above. It is, in its very monstrosity *and* fascination, an apocalyptic statement of truth which remains incomprehensible to the humanist anthropocentric perspective. And yet, everything hinges on this incomprehension.

This monstrous dialectic of the self is arguably best articulated in a short and programmatic essay by Jeffrey Jerome Cohen called 'Monster Culture (Seven Theses)' (1996). Cohen here remarks on the proliferation of the monstrous in the age of techno- and mediaculture and of the ubiquity of the 'Frankenstein syndrome', as he calls it. This is regardless of whether one looks at science fiction or genetically modified foods. In the age of anxiety the monster becomes a fetish and the object of cultural-psychological 'foreclusion' [*Verwerfung*]. Thus, it is the task of cultural criticism to investigate the temporal geographical and technological boundaries that constitute culture and through which culture is implicated within the construction of monstrosity (Cohen 1996: ix). The monster as a symptom of culture's 'unease' (Freud) is an embodiment of projected difference and at the same time it poses a danger for any form of categorization. In the shape of its otherness, it is the embodied resistance to an absolute dialectical sublation [*Aufhebung*]. The monstrous posthuman embodies our historical, identitarian and technological anxieties. Cohen proposes a new *modus legendi* which reads culture through its (culturally specific) monsters – a kind of teratological cultural criticism (Cohen 1996: 4). In this sense, the body of each monster is seen as a 'displaced' projection of fears, desires and phantasms and can thus be understood as 'pure' culture in its utter 'legibility'. The way specific posthumans are represented is a sign of the human fears and human phantasms which have to be read 'against the grain', so to speak (an approach we propose to call a critical 'posthumanist reading', cf. Herbrechter and Callus 2008). For the monster has the structure of the Freudian uncanny – in its ghostly haunting it is both present and absent. It does not stay on the operation table but constantly 'escapes' in the sense of a Derridean 'hauntology' (Derrida 1994b). A critical posthumanism will therefore have to be adept at reading traces, since the posthuman monster is (also always) a sign and a symptom of an entirely other cultural unease. Because of its ambiguity and hybridity the monster represents a category crisis: what is there *between* the human and the nonhuman, for example? The chimera, the beast, but also zombies, vampires and other ghosts, the ghost in the machine included of course. 'Ontological liminality' is Cohen's term for this (1996: 6) as the result of which, according to Elaine Graham, an 'ontological surveillance of boundaries' is taking place. The monster is a symptom of an epistemological and ontological situation of crisis within culture that can be seen in the vibration of its boundaries and taboos, in the darkening of its hermeneutic horizons, as a sign of struggle over meaning within culture or between cultures. The monster functions as a dialectical other, it is 'difference turned flesh' (Cohen 1996: 7), and thus asks for cultural 'consumption' as 'taming'. Its difference is articulated at a cultural, political, racial, economic, sexual, etc. level and, in the case of the posthuman, also at a technological level. The monstrous exaggeration of its attributes within a politics of representation is referred to as 'monsterization' and 'teratogenesis' by Cohen (9). Such monsterizations of the posthuman are symptoms of human fears and desires. Why, after all, are monsters so fascinating? They represent an epistemological danger which, similar to René Girard's idea of the scapegoat, contains both a promise and a consolation:

> The political-cultural monster, the embodiment of radical difference, paradoxically threatens to *erase* difference in the world of its creators to demonstrate: 'the potential for the system to differ from its own difference, in other words not to be different at all, to cease to exist as a system ... Difference that exists outside the system is terrifying because it reveals the truth of the system, its relativity, its fragility, its mortality ... Despite what is said around us persecutors are never obsessed with difference but rather by its unutterable contrary, the lack of difference'.
>
> (Girard, quoted in Cohen 1996: 11–12)

In its ontological liminality the monster 'polices' the boundaries between the possible and its realization, especially in a technocultural society, and it functions as a warning: if 'you', if 'we' transgress this boundary, we ourselves are in danger of becoming monsters! But in fact this warning should read: then we no longer know 'who' or 'what' we are. Monsters thus have cultural geographic and controlling functions and are positioned between known and unknown territory, while they themselves dwell in no-man's land or in limbo. They are a projection of the anxiety but also of the (often sexual) desire of contamination, the breaking of taboos and fetishization, because the fear of the monster in truth is a kind of desire to live out forbidden practices in a 'secure' fashion, for example, without loss of identity, in the form of exotic, escapist and exorcising phantasms.

The posthuman monster *à la* Frankenstein thus poses the question to 'us', as representatives of an imaginary humanity: Why have you created me like this? And in doing so it vents its scorn: 'So you think *you* are human?' The future of human evolution will be accompanied by such popular scientific or fictive Frankenstein scenarios. Donna Haraway, for example, dedicated one of her books (Haraway 1997) to the genetically modified 'OncoMouse™', which, on the one hand, was seen as an almost Christ-like figure of salvation, and, on the other, as a Frankensteinian monster. Similar phenomena regularly occur in the context of genetically modified foods, which in the press are often referred to as 'Franken(stein)-food'. The 'almost human', or the 'monstrous inhuman' – aliens, cyborgs, chimeras and so forth – contribute to the gradual normative reformulation of exemplary humanity. They can thus be said to constitute a form of continuation of Foucault's idea of 'technologies of self', or as posthumanist forms of biopower. While modern technologies of the self arise out of institutions and practices like the confessional, the clinic, the asylum or the prison, posthumanist technologies of the self are articulated in such new locations as cyberspace, laboratories or in the neuroclinic or the sperm bank (cf. Graham 2004: 21). Genetic manipulation and transgenic practices presuppose a porosity of the boundaries between species, while the resulting potential of anxiety and risk needs to be managed and reduced discursively, normally by attempts by 'experts' to reassure humans that they are still in control of scientific and technological development. In this way, scientific practices are legitimated (together with their associated economic and political interests) and, at the same time, the history of human dominance or dominion over 'his' nature continues to be inscribed, which thus confirms the radical boundary between human and nonhuman (maybe with 'slight' adjustments, but without questioning its absolute and universal validity). The impression is thus created that under posthumanist conditions culture and science more or less completely interpenetrate each other, and, consequently, that under these conditions, it is necessary to further promote the dissolution of the mechanisms of 'ontological hygiene' that have been responsible throughout the 'last three hundred years' for policing the boundaries drawn within Western culture, between human, nature and machine (Graham 2002: 11). One strategy in this context is to emphasize the 'symbiotic' relationship between humans and their techniques and artefacts, in the form of a co-evolution between humans and technology, which also erases the boundaries between an 'active subject' and 'passive object', exterior and interior, organic and artificial (33). It is not so much a 'reontologization' or a transfer of one ontological state (i.e. human) into another (posthuman), but a deconstructive problematization of human 'nature' as a historical construct (and a construct which is in the process of changing), which is at stake. Accepting this view is the first step towards the 'demystification' of humanity and technology and the beginning of a critical posthumanist discussion about the future of the human.

Graham is characterizing the main aspects of our contemporary posthuman state thus: we experience the mechanization of the human and the technologization of nature (for example in the form of implants of self-regulating cybernetic mechanisms, or in vitro fertilization and the Human Genome Project; these coincide with a 'medicalization' of birth and human reproduction in general, which may also represent the end point of this process); further, there is an erosion of species boundaries (thanks to transgenic processes such as, for example, the production of human-animal chimeras used in medical research); there is also the abolishment of clear boundaries of the body (the increasingly internalized process of 'prosthesization', from tool use of external objects such as, for example, a hammer, towards the integration and ergonomic or bionic fusion with technologies through implants, synthetic drugs, the digitalization of sensory perception and experience in virtual realities or Bluetooth technologies); and finally, one needs to mention the creation of new personal and social worlds (digital environments, virtual reality in games, forums, chatrooms, MySpace, YouTube, Facebook and so on, with the possibility of creating and living out more or less fictive identities in the form of 'avatars'). It is important to neither demonize nor idealize these developments but to show how specific posthuman 'figures', 'scenarios' and metaphors are being represented ideologically. Let us take the decoding of the human genome as an example:

Within the discourse of the Human Genome Project and throughout contemporary molecular biology the gene occupies a number of discursive spaces simultaneously. It is a thing of nature and the very essence of life. For a biochemist it is the catalyst for the formation of essential proteins. In the bio-informatics systems that record the genes' sequences, it is a string of binary data that encodes its own peculiar molecular 'signature' ... In sociobiological discourse, it is an icon of destiny; and for the biotechnological corporations that stand to profit from the patenting and marketing of genetic information for medical research purposes, it is a highly lucrative commodity.

(Graham 2002: 24)

It is the connection between nature, technology and economy on which the discussion about posthumanity needs to focus. The slippage of the signifiers between 'gene' or 'nature', and between 'information' or 'commodity', underscores the role of linguistic discursivity in all the areas involved: science and technology, economics, politics and religion, and it also shows the central importance of close textual analysis of the actual forms in which the posthuman and the process of posthumanization is represented.

The central role of the information metaphor is also the starting point for N. Katherine Hayles' groundbreaking study *How We Became Posthuman* (1999). An emblematic role for the informatization of human knowledge and the knowledge of humans, according to Hayles, was played by the Turing Test, which represents the birth of artificial intelligence. This test, proposed by Alan Turing in 1950, was supposed to show that under specific circumstances it would be impossible to distinguish between computer and human intelligence. As soon as there is uncertainty, however, the idea of human uniqueness is threatened and there is no further obstacle to the advent of information society. What is lost, however, in the 'transubstantiation' of the human 'embodied' mind into machine intelligence is embodiment as such. In fact, Hayles' original motivation, as she explains, was to denounce the widespread delusion that human consciousness might be downloadable, under ideal infotechnological conditions, into a computer without any loss: 'how could anyone think that consciousness in an entirely different medium would remain unchanged, as if it had no connection with embodiment?' (Hayles 1999: 1). In accordance with the Turing Test, Hayles calls this mind-downloading scenario the 'Moravec Test', after Hans Moravec, who first propagated this idea in *Mind Children* (1988). Machines would thus become the depositories of human consciousness, while machines, at least according to the conclusions drawn by many of Moravec's transhumanist colleagues, would thus themselves become 'human', or even better, the 'new human' – *homo sapiens cyberneticus*, or simply *robo sapiens*. Hayles summarizes this circular argument thus: 'you are the cyborg, and the cyborg is you' (Hayles 1999: xii). There is something else happening in the course of the Turing Test, however, as Hayles points out. In fact, prior to the actual Turing Test, which was designed to test whether humans and machines can be differentiated, another, seemingly negligible, test had to be carried out. Before any difference between 'embodied reality' and pure verbal production (or 'code') could be abolished Turing, in fact, had to ask himself whether under similar conditions it would be equally impossible to distinguish between a man and a woman. Hayles thus rightly asks:

> If your failure to distinguish correctly between human and machine proves that machines can think, what does it prove if you fail to distinguish woman from man? Why does gender appear in this primal scene of humans meeting their evolutionary successors, intelligent machines? What do gendered bodies have to do with the erasure of embodiment and the subsequent merging of machine and human intelligence in the figure of the cyborg?
>
> (Hayles 1999: xii)

By (re)introducing the question of gender difference into the context of artificial intelligence Turing unwillingly and unwittingly points to the fact that in the process of shifting the boundaries between human and machine more might be at stake than the mere transformation of: 'Who can think?' into: 'What can think?' In fact, Turing ends up emphasizing precisely what was supposed to remain unproblematic, namely the idea that in transferring human into machine intelligence the liberal humanist subject will not escape unscathed, because its reality is an 'embodied' and hence necessarily 'gendered' one. Even worse, on the one hand, informatization stresses the specific bodily and material existence of the humanist subject, on the other, however, it exposes the problematic self-denial within Cartesian humanism of the duality between 'enacted' embodiment and 'projected' or represented, visible body image:

> Thus the test functions to create the possibility of a disjunction between the enacted and the represented bodies, regardless which choice you make. What the Turing test 'proves' is that the overlay between the enacted and the represented bodies is no longer a natural inevitability but a contingent production, mediated by a technology that has become so entwined with the production

of identity that it can no longer meaningfully be separated from the human subject.

(Hayles 1999: xiii)

At the point at which gender threatens to reappear as part of the posthuman potential within informatization – and thus might spell out a return of the liberal humanist subject within the machinic sphere, but now merely in idealized cyborgian form – an entirely other possibility arises for a critical posthumanist thinking, namely the problematic of the liberal humanist idea of embodiment as such:

> What embodiment secures is not the distinction between male and female or between humans who can think and machines which cannot. Rather, embodiment makes clear that thought is a much broader cognitive function depending for its specificities on the embodied form enacting it. This realization, with all its exfoliating implications, is so broad in its effects and so deep in its consequences that it is transforming the liberal subject regarded as the model of the human since the Enlightenment, into the posthuman.

(Hayles 1999: xiii)

What turns us into posthuman subjects is thus the ideology of information (the cybernetic transposition of 'embodied thought' into 'disembodied information'), which, of course, has to be met with extreme scepticism. On the other hand, playing with exactly this idea makes it possible to overcome the traditional Christian and Cartesian mind-body dualism, which has sought its ultimate retreat within the liberal humanist subject, possible. As a result, Hayles argues, in her critical analysis of cybernetics and its social aspects of informatization, in favour of an 'embodied virtuality' in the age of global information society, whose credo must be the free and unchanging circulation between 'information and material substrates' (1). A central aspect of a critical posthumanism is therefore to remind information of its forgotten or repressed materiality (cf. also Kittler 1999; Poster 2001a, 2006). Hayles investigates how the ideology of information was able to establish its current dominance, and in the process she discovers three 'narratives' that underlie cybernetics, the information sciences, autopoietic systems theory, computer simulation technologies and the cognitive sciences: namely, 'how information lost its body' (until WWII); 'how the cyborg was created as a technological artifact and cultural icon' (after WWII); and 'how a historically specific construction called the human is giving way to a different construction called the posthuman' (Hayles 1999: 2). The ambivalence of opportunity and danger that inhabits this development has to be *critically* pursued, contextualized and historicized and ultimately deconstructed. One should neither ignore the potential of posthuman technologies of the self and new forms of posthuman subjectivity, nor should one give in to the temptation of radical dematerialization, disembodiment and dehumanization. The yardstick to be used, according to Hayles, is the resistance to the 'erasure of embodiment', which can be seen at work both in the universalist tendencies of liberal humanism and in the transhumanist techno-utopian scenarios. With this proviso in place, posthuman subjectivity may also be understood as an opportunity, namely as the possibility to stop 'disembodiment' from being constantly reinscribed within the dominant notion of subjectivity (5).

No 'postbiological' future, then, but a posthumanist humanness that is sceptical of both, the supposed becoming human of the machine and the mechanization of the human, and which, instead, investigates the process of cyborgization, following Haraway, as a process of embodied 'sedimentation' (284) of human history – understood not as the 'end of man' but rather as the end of a very specific notion of 'humanity', or being-human. The traditional concept of humanity: 'that may have applied, at best, to that fraction of humanity who had the wealth, power, and leisure to conceptualize themselves as autonomous beings exercising their will through individual agency and choice' (286). On the one hand, this means a relativization regarding the illusion of sovereignty and autonomy, on the other hand, it also promotes a new understanding of the interactions between humans, their environments and technics, as 'emergence' of human subjectivity in co-operation with nonhuman actors, and thus not as humanist 'teleology' (288).

What is of central importance for a discussion about posthumanism and any politics of representation is thus the question of embodiment. It is a case of defending a material anchoring of humanity in embodiment against techno-idealists and transhumanists; however, it is also important to 'dynamize' the humanist idea of a duality of mind and body, mental consciousness and physical reality and so on. This is also the argument the French sociologist David Le Breton is making in *L'Adieu au corps* [A Farewell to the Body], against the Gnostic and Cartesian 'hatred of the body' (1999: 7ff.), as well as against the modern scientific notion of the body as pure 'matter' and as the biological 'support' of personality. Moreover, Le Breton also criticizes the posthumanist and postbiological 'disappearance of the body' (he refers in the main to Moravec and the Australian performance artist Stelarc). Contemporary technoscience and the phenomenon of virtuality in particular propagate a 'sketchy' image of the body and thus invite technological enhancement. Embodiment becomes a 'task' (as in Benjamin's '*Aufgabe* of the translator', with its double meaning of 'task' and 'abandonment' or 'surrender'), and thus a challenge. The body itself turns into the hyperreal (cf. Baudrillard 1994: 23) ultimate signifier:

> In our societies the importance of symbolic bricolage is growing and the choice of knowledge forms and services at the disposal of the individual has grown disproportionately. The malleability of the ego and the plasticity of the body have become commonplace. Anatomy is no longer destiny but a provisional feature, a basic material that remains to be transformed, redefined and adapted to contemporary *design*. For a number of our contemporaries the body has become a provisional form of representation, a *gadget* and an ideal stage for the performance of 'special effects' ... The body in our contemporary societies is no longer the allocation of a tangible identity, the irrevocable incarnation of a subject, or its being-in-the-world, but a construct, an interface, a terminal, a volatile object which can be decorated with diverse accessories.
>
> (Le Breton 1999: 23–4; my translation)

In this way, the body becomes our double, our *alter ego* and ultimate prosthesis; the human self is constantly looking for new forms of expression and confirmation of its identity. The current posthumanizing technologies of this self are thus no longer so much designed towards the control function and the exercising of power by modern institutions (cf. Foucault's notions of 'biopower' and 'governmentality'), but they are completely internalized by the posthumanist or posthuman individual, who is striving for the control and transformation of his or her own body (Le Breton refers in particular to practices of body building, sex change, 'body marking' and 'body art', as examples of current practices in this respect). The new spectrum of available relationships to one's own body also provides new forms of reconciliation with and overcoming of the Gnostic and Cartesian antimaterialism, for example in the notion of the body as one's 'privileged partner', in the process of self-realization (Le Breton 1999: 49). On the other hand, Le Breton also sees the danger of a technologically radicalized form of body hatred, which is expressed, for example, in many contemporary science fiction films and in 'neognostic' technosects like the Extropians and other transhumanists. These see their task as 'fighting the body, separating the subject from its decaying flesh and privileging the mind as the sole interest for immortality' (210). While Le Breton seems to draw exclusively apocalyptic conclusions, however, and dismisses the postbiological age as inhuman cynicism and the 'overcoming of the body' as absurd (219–23), the kind of critical posthumanism that is proposed in the present study situates itself strategically between materialist and antimaterialist notions of the body. This more complex approach will be needed to understand the increasing extension of the body into virtual spaces and also in relation to new forms of 'mutation' and bodily techniques. This kind of strategy can be found, for example, in Alain Milon's *La Réalité virtuelle: avec ou sans le corps?* (2005), which, on the one hand, just like Le Breton, criticizes antimaterialist (or neognostic) forms of disembodiment in virtual reality, especially within the genre of cyberpunk (including its most recent filmic expressions, for example, in the *Matrix* trilogy); on the other hand, Milon emphasizes an evaluation of living in virtual reality as a bodily 'limit experience'. It is not a question of disembodiment, either of virtual bodies as 'artificial' entities or of displacements of boundaries within human body experience and body image. It is thus not obsolescence or replacement but displacement and expansion. This virtualizing aspect – which constitutes another form of cyborgization – will be dealt with in more detail in a subsequent chapter. However, let us dwell a little on the first form of cyborgization, namely the biological-technological-physical mutation of the human body and its consequences and its opportunities for a 'post-gender' society (cf. Haraway 1991).

There is indeed a close kinship between Haraway's early technofeminism and Judith Butler's idea of sex and gender as 'performance', or, as one could say, acquired forms of 'embodiment' and social 'scripts'. Sex and gender thus represent one of the most fundamental 'technologies of self', in the context of the so-called 'heteronormative matrix' (i.e. the tacitly presupposed heterosexual social norm), which underpins the 'naturalness' of sexual reproduction (cf. Butler 1993). Embodiment itself can thus be seen as a form of prosthesization, and 'posthuman bodies', according to Judith Halberstam and Ira Livingston (1995), make visible the connections between power and desire, virtuality and reality, sexualitiy and its consequences: 'The posthuman body is a technology, a screen, a projected image; it is a body under the sign of AIDS, a contaminated body, a deadly body; it is ... a queer body' (Halberstam and Livingston 1995: 3) In this 'posthuman zoo' of (techno-)subcultures, embodiment, sexuality and gender grow radically fluid without losing any of their materiality or physicality, however. On the contrary, anamorphism is one of the key terms of this new, radicalized, materialism: 'technology makes the body queer, fragments it, frames it, cuts it, transforms desire' (16). And therefore a distinction between posthuman bodies and their material extensions has to be rejected (17). In accordance with a general critical posthumanist framework, this is a materialistically inspired deconstructive critique of the existing humanist grand narrative against which new, 'smaller' narratives are set, as far as the relationship to embodiment is concerned:

> Bodily masternarratives authorize a very narrow range of responses: that it is maturing or evolving or deteriorating or remaining the same, becoming dependent or independent; that it is threatened by, succumbing to or recovering from illness; that it is gaining or losing, for good or ill, various features or functions (weight, hair, muscles, mobility, etc.); that it is growing, reproducing or dying.
>
> (18)

In contrast to this, posthuman bodies with their multiple possibilities precisely accentuate the precariousness of traditional characteristics of body-related identities like gender, sexuality but also ethnicity or race. Instead, the body, according to Ollivier Dyens, in *Metal and Flesh* (2001), is becoming the 'interface between being and living; on its surface, being and living mesh' (55). This does not constitute a disappearance of the body but, on the contrary, makes the body omnipresent but in increasingly hybridized, mediatized and consumptional form, which corresponds to a fragmentation and dynamization of the body after the end of the myth of unity and identity between body and body image, or of the body as a given, presupposed as either abject or sacred, untouchable physical-biological entity. In this sense, Mark Hansen, in *Embodying Technesis* (2000), argues that the new technoculture requires a new recognition of the 'affective' and experiential, practical understanding of embodiment. The clearest formulation of this question can be found in Teresa de Lauretis's work, who, already in *Technologies of Gender* (1987), proposed that – following Foucault's notion of sexuality – gender also has to be thought of as a 'technology of sex', both as representation and as self-representation: '[gender] is the product of various social technologies, such as cinema, and of institutionalized discourses, epistemologies, and critical practices, as well as practices of daily life' (de Lauretis 1987: 2). And, as with gender, one can argue that the question of ethnicity or race may also be understood in terms of such a social 'production' process. And thus one should also, in this context, enquire about the future of such productions under technocultural conditions (cf., for example, Nakamura 2002 and Terranova 2004).

As a preliminary conclusion one could say that the positive aspect of posthumanism lies in the propagation of a new form of human self-understanding, namely as an 'embodied self' based on an interpenetration of mental and physical processes, which may lead to a bodily identity in the first place, but which also constitutes an identity that is not fixed but dynamic. This is the central meaning of the cyborg figure and its strategic use by Donna Haraway. She sees the dissolution of the boundaries between human and machine as an opportunity to weaken other humanist boundaries, namely the ones between genders and species. On the one hand, she attempts to wrest away the cyborg figure from its popular apocalyptic, hyper-masculinist and militarist image and thus to 'reontologize' it; on the other hand, she wants to move it out of its cybernetic-informational-technological corner and make it usable for cultural criticism. Ultimately, Haraway's project is a transformation of a cultural into a technocultural imaginary, which accepts the coimplication of humans and technology and uses this as a resource for posthumanist creativity in relation to all life forms and new social, technological, economic, etc. challenges. New figures and new characters are needed for new forms of narratives, which can answer the question: 'How can humanity have a figure outside the narratives of humanism; what language would such a figure speak?' (Haraway 2004: 49). The cyborg – originally a contraction of 'cybernetic organism' – in contemporary culture, is as much a social reality (cf. the ongoing medical and informational cyborgization process) as it is of course 'merely' a figure of science fiction; it thus constitutes both a number of social relations between bodies and machines as well as a metaphor and a figure for new forms of stories and narratives. It is therefore important in terms of the creation of new subject positions and their cultural meanings. According to Haraway, the distinction between social reality and science fiction is to a large extent an 'optical illusion'. In her 'Cyborg Manifesto' (1991), Haraway wishes to create an 'ironic political myth'. 'Ironic' and 'blasphemous' are the words she uses to describe the radicalization of cyborg intervention within late capitalist biopolitics (for which the cyborg has long since become a usable reality and a new 'market'), but also in the film industry, medicine, technologies of reproduction, the defence budget and military operations. The cyborg is the real subject of technoculture, but, as with all subject positions, there is also some space for negotiation as to how cyborg embodiment can be understood, and this is the space which needs to be discussed and actively used. In particular, according to Haraway, this relates to spaces and technologies of gendered identity. Her cyborg- or technofeminisim aims to break the traditional patriarchal predominance of the domains of science, technology and politics and instead use the cyborg as material for alternative fictions and imaginations, in order to produce new cultural forms and to imagine a world without gender. This might thus be a world without 'genesis', but also a world without *telos*. As part of this announcement, the cyborg is a 'creature of a post-gender world' and the 'illegitimate offspring' of militarism and patriarchal capitalism as well as 'state socialism', without a clear origin or father figures (Haraway 1991: 150–1). As a kind of 'trickster' or liminal figure, the cyborg accompanies the dissolution of diverse boundaries within contemporary Western cultures of science: the boundary between human and animal, between human-animal and machine and the one between physical and nonphysical processes. In the face of global technological dominance and its dangers, the question of the cyborg, for Haraway, becomes a question of life and death:

> From one perspective, a cyborg world is about the final imposition of a grid of control on the planet, about the final abstraction embodied in a Star Wars apocalypse waged in the name of defence, about the final appropriation of women's bodies in a masculinist orgy of war ... From another perspective, a cyborg world might be about lived social and bodily realities in which people are not afraid of their joint kinship with animals and machines, not afraid of permanently partial identities and contradictory standpoints.
>
> (Haraway 1991: 154)

It is, therefore, clear that the cyborg remains a 'contested techno-cultural space' which, on the one hand, is seen within the milieu of informational sciences as the next logical stage of bio-info-cultural evolution for humanity; on the other, it is seen by transhumanists as a necessary but only intermediate stage, not the endpoint of evolution, which, instead, must lie in complete dematerialization and disembodiment. A key figure in relation to the former aspect of this process is, for example, the already mentioned Kevin Warwick, who in several books and television documentaries and on his own website publicly presents himself as his own cyborg guinea pig by reporting on his adventures and emotional experiences of having a microchip implanted into his body. In *I, Cyborg* (2002), with reference to Isaac Asimov's *I, Robot* (1950), Warwick begins by saying:

I was born human. This was merely due to the hand of fate acting at a particular place and time. But while fate made me human, it also gave me the power to do something about it. The ability to change myself, to upgrade my human form with the aid of technology. To link my body directly with silicon. To become a cyborg – part human, part machine. This is the extraordinary story of my adventure as the first human entering into a Cyber World; a world which will, most likely, become the next evolutionary step for humankind.

(Warwick 2002: 1)

What follows is part autobiography, part *Bildungsroman*, and another part science fiction 'without' the fiction, almost like a television 'docudrama' (with its underlying claim of 'this is what it realistically might look like if', or 'this is with all probability what it is going to be like'). Reality is 'extended' on the basis of current indicators and is thus extrapolated into the future, in this case obviously with the institutional cachet and infoscientific legitimacy of the self-experimenting scientist. This is, of course, not to doubt Kevin Warwick's expertise in any way but it is part of an analysis of the 'discourse' and the politics of representation that are at work here. These are, despite the fact that they are speaking of a posthuman future, surprisingly and reassuringly human, if not humanist, for Warwick's self is in fact being projected into this posthuman future without major problems it seems. Like most pioneer subjects he interpellates his readers in missionary form: look! I have already undergone this transformation and I welcome it! I survived! So follow me without fear into the future 'cyber-world'! We can do something about the baseness of our human condition by upgrading ourselves and thus escape our biological 'destiny', we can even accelerate evolution. We thus have a perfect illustration of the typical combination of a free humanist subject, that in order to achieve its own potential for freedom and happiness has to make a decision – a 'free choice' between good and evil – a teleology, which is, on the one hand, inevitable, and which, on the other, paradoxically, is represented as remaining to be realized, and all this in view of a better, truer and (even more) universally valid future. Warwick's *March of the Machines* (1997) is merely the utopian side of the usually more dystopian and 'apocalyptic' representation to be found in the *Terminator* science fiction scenario, according to which humanity lost its control over the machines a long time ago, or in the *Matrix* saga, in which the last battle over world dominance between humans and machines is still undecided.

This techno-idealism and determinism is even more obvious within the circles of self-professed transhumanists. This second group of radical techno-idealists is the main target of Oliver Krüger's study, *Virtualität und Unsterblichkeit* [Virtuality and Immortality] (2004). The idea of overcoming the biological human body within a transhumant(ist) environment is coupled with the notion of immortality within the medium of virtuality. Krüger also mainly focuses on central figures like Max More, Frank Tipler, Marvin Minsky, Hans Moravec and Raymond Kurzweil, as well as the World Transhumanist Association and the Extropian Society and places them within the context of a history of ideas based on the notion of the man-machine, from La Mettrie's *homme-machine* (1747) to Norbert Wiener's cybernetics, to cryonics, the futurology of the early space age programmes, and further to contemporary art in the wake of Marinetti's futurism (in particular, in the form of self-proclaimed posthumanist performance artists like Stelarc, Orlan or Natasha Vita-More). Instead of seeing the transhumanists as representatives of a technological gnosticism, as, for example, in Erik Davis's *Techgnosis* (1998), which refers to the 'spirituality' of the cyborg, Krüger describes posthumanism – which he fails to clearly distinguish from transhumanism – as a kind of 'utilitarian' philosophy. Posthumanism is concerned with human 'improvement'. In this sense, posthumanist virtualization would be merely a means to an end, namely reaching a higher state of humanity.

Just like Krüger, Graham is also establishing a connection between posthumanism and religion. Graham points towards the presence of religious and theological issues in many posthuman visions, and shows that the fascination with technology is an expression of spirituality. It therefore also requires a critical analysis from a theological perspective, whose task it would be to investigate the pseudo-religious discourse of figures like Moravec (cf. the analogy between downloading human consciousness and the idea of the transmigration of souls), Eric Davis (who calls virtual communities 'technopagans'), or David Noble (who characterizes technology as an instrument of 'salvation') (Graham 2004: 23ff.). Ideas of techno-transcendence and digital cities of god in cyberspace, of the overcoming of the flesh (cf. William Gibson's notion of the 'meat world'), the 'technological sublime' and the technological (re)enchantment of the world (Graham 2002: 230ff.) abound within the transhumanist scene, which consists of a mixture of self-proclaimed experts, spiritually inclined scientists and technoprophets. What these have in common is a technological determinism, which, on the one hand, engages with apocalyptism and, on the other, announces human apotheosis in the form of evolution. Be it the idea of figures like the 'metaman' in Gregory Stock's work (1993) or the idea of human transcendence into a 'global superorganism' (cf. Vernor Vinge's notion of the 'singularity'), which has its predecessor in Teilhard de Chardin's world-spanning noosphere (1955); or major figures of the history of artificial intelligence like Marvin Minsky, who sees human replacement by robots as inevitable – a tendency which by the way can already be found in the 'father of cybernetics', Norbert Wiener (cf. Wiener 1954 and 1964); or technosocial utopian prophets like Max More and his neofuturist 'Extropian Society' (cf. Moore 2003). Programmatically, the new techno-ideology is expressed in Robert Pepperell's 'The Posthuman Manifesto' in *The Posthuman Condition* (2003), which begins with the general statements:

1. It is now clear that humans are no longer the most important things in the universe. This is something the humanists have yet to accept.

2. All technological progress of human society is geared towards the transformation of the human species as we currently know it.

(Pepperell 2003: 177)

It is probably wise to be open-minded towards the potential of dissolution that the process of posthumanization contains, especially as far as the breaking up of traditional humanist ways of thinking is concerned. However, one should remind the sympathizers of a new techno-idealism of the fact that it has a somewhat dubious and questionable history and that its analysis of the present is based on greatly simplified forms of abstraction, which in the main rely on the propagated ability to separate what indeed are interpenetrating life spheres, like consciousness and embodiment, individual and society, and technology and culture.

Opposed to this is the kind of neovitalist understanding of the human and technics that can be found in the works by Gilles Deleuze and Félix Guattari, which constitutes another way of conceptualizing human cyborgization. Deleuze and Guattari's notion of *devenir machine* [becoming machine] is one of several strategies proposed in *A Thousand Plateaus: Capitalism and Schizophrenia* (1987) designed to critically undermine the fluid system of late capitalism. Other possible forms are 'becoming animal', 'becoming woman' and, in general, 'becoming minoritarian' or 'becoming other'. Their project is designed to dissolve identity and to construct a new materialist body politics. According to Rosi Braidotti, the Deleuzian body is nothing but 'embodied memory' (2000: 159). A Deleuzian body is an 'assemblage' of forces and emotions that congeal within time and space to a singular configuration, and which, in general, is referred to as 'individual'. Braidotti characterizes the current state of posthumanization as 'techno-teratological' and thus as a cultural imaginary which, as already seen, is fascinated with and terrorized by monstrosities that are made imaginable and realizable by new technologies. Similar to Haraway, Braidotti sees in this state of radical fluidity, dynamics and ambiguity a chance, namely the opportunity for the repressed cultural unconscious to be worked through, expressed and thus made conscious.

The task that arises for the posthuman individual is to find a politics of representation that would be able to resist 'techno-hysteria', on the one hand, and which, at the same time, would produce positive and agreeable forms of expression, and which would thus use the process of becoming-other to overcome the modern humanist deep-seated fear of the bodily roots of subjectivity (Braidotti 2000: 162). The return of the repressed body under techno-teratological, posthumanist conditions has to be a time of vigilance as well as of new possibilities. The challenge of posthuman monstrosity in the plurality of its forms requires a critical teratology in view of what Braidotti calls the latest episode within the process of 'decentring' Western thinking. Being human is now inevitably shot through with posthuman variables, Braidotti claims, to the extent that it makes our collective sense of superiority, acquired over centuries of humanism, more or less irrelevant (172).

At a more concrete level, however, the 'becoming machine' of human society, with its human individual, whose definition becomes more and more problematic, does not merely represent an individual-ontological embodiment, but also, of course, a political, ethical and legal challenge. Chris Hables Gray, in particular, has been focusing on the conflictual aspect and socio-political implications of cyborgization in his work. In his *Cyborg Citizen* (2001) he developed a 'Cyborg Bill of Rights', following Haraway's 'cyborg politics', which he calls the 'Turing Test for citizenship' (31). Gray favours a participatory repoliticization of the public under posthuman conditions. While cyborgization contains new militaristic threats of course. it also allows for new forms of political action (e.g. new forms of political participation through new, virtual media). The posthumanist subject has to reinvent itself within these new technologies.

To summarize thus far, it is worth stressing once again that a critical posthumanism stands for a postanthropocentric (post)anthropology with its promise of a non-normative description of the human and its others. Whether this can still be thought of as an anthropology at all is, of course, a legitimate question. Philosophically, however, a critical posthumanism opens up the possibility of a return to some fundamental aspects of humanism and philosophical anthropology. Apart from the question concerning the essence of technology (Heidegger), there is also the aspect of the ontological status of the machine, the mechanical 'object' and the subject, and thus also the renewed urgency of the question concerning the nonhuman in its plurality of forms.

4

Posthumanism and science fiction

Yet there is a utopia to be found in the science fiction film, a utopia that lies in being human, and if utopia is always defined in relation to an other, a nonutopia, then the numberless aliens, androids, and evil computers of the SF film are the barbarians storming the gates of humanity.

(BUKATMAN 1993: 16)

Contemporary technoscientific and media-fictional futurology is almost indistinguishable from coinciding parallel trends in popular culture (cf. the already mentioned ongoing prosthesization, digitalization, cyborgization and virtualization of a growing number of humans in the Western techno-consumer societies). In a time of change and accelerated posthumanization the danger arises that the age-old question of philosophical anthropology ('What is man?') will become the exclusive domain of a combination of the philosophy of technology, economics and systems theory. At the same time, however, the contemporary crisis of humanism also opens up possibilities for new and promising approaches within critical and cultural theory. After all, as already mentioned, the crisis of humanism is nothing new. 'Antihumanism' has not only attacked the foundations of humanism but it has also problematized humanism's understanding of technology. Within the current spectrum of feelings between euphoria and apocalyptism, provoked by technology, the genre of science fiction seems more or less resigned to chase the latest technological developments and reproduce new modes of technoreality. In this context, the critical deconstructive potential of posthumanism is often overlooked. The present chapter will therefore not only investigate the notions of 'technoculture' and 'technoscience' at work in science fiction, but it will also, in the form of critical posthumanist readings of some examples of science fiction, analyse the general relationship between humanism and technology. Let it be said from the start, however, that these readings will restrict themselves to well-known science fiction films, and Hollywood productions in particular, and will leave aside literary examples, many of which are much more critical and nuanced. This is not the place for an aesthetic analysis of the genre but of the cultural political influence of science fiction on the current process of posthumanization.

Within twenty-first century, everyday-life popular culture, one is constantly confronted with posthuman visions of technology. A short survey of a variety of press examples within the past few years shows the ubiquity of new technologies, which question humanist notions of human 'integrity'. Articles like 'First brain repair cells cultivated' (*Sunday Times* 16 November 2005: 10) refer to the use of stem cells in the reconstruction of brain damage and the rebuilding of neurons. 'The face of the future' (*Times Higher Education* 21 July 2006: 16) reports on the psychological and physical implications of a full face transplant which has recently become technologically feasible. 'Bionic eyes give sight to the blind' (*The Times* 17 February 2007: 1) describes the first attempt in the USA to cure congenital blindness by implanting an artificial retina made of light sensitive electrodes. 'Tender touch with bionic hand' (*Daily Express* 19 July 2007: 36) introduces a new 'bionic' prosthetic hand designed specifically for Iraq War veterans. In 'My life as a cyborg' (*Guardian* 3 December 2002, G2: 15) a man suffering from Parkinson's disease reports on his experience with a microchip implant. 'Computerisation of the body: Microsoft wins patent to exploit network potential of skin' (*Guardian* 6 July 2004: 3) describes the plans of the computer industry to use the human body as interface for information technologies (for example in the form of bionic keyboards, sensors, receptors, electrodes and the like). The subtitle of the article is also quite representative: 'Fact or fiction – carrying a keyboard on your arm'. The South African athlete Oscar Pistorius started making headlines in 2008 when he declared that he wanted to compete in the 400m race at the 'regular' Olympics in Beijing. Pistorius is known under the name 'Bladerunner' because he had both his legs amputated as a child and now runs with the aid of two specially designed hyperelastic blades. The international Olympic committee declined his request arguing that his blades would give him an unfair advantage! (Cf. *Guardian* 10 July 2007: 9 and 10 January 2008: 33.) Pistorius went on to dominate the races in the Paralympics. In the 2012 Olympics in London, however, Pistorius *was* finally allowed to compete in the 400m race and – came 23rd, while at the 2012 Paralympics he again won but faced serious competition from other 'Bladerunners'.

The *Times Higher Education* (22 June 2007: 4) warns in 'Man and machine joined in deadly harmony' of the military interest in creating neuronal signal links between soldiers and their uniforms. 'Put your finger in your ear and take that call' (*Daily Telegraph* 6 November 2003) shows a possible development of portable mobile telephone technology, which uses the human body as its conductor. Even if some of these technologies have not had their breakthrough (yet) it doesn't seem so far-fetched anymore that in future we might just press our thumb and index together to have a telephone conversation. The already mentioned rubric 'Futures' in the French daily *Le Monde* for a while brought regular news about current science and research with an openly posthumanist agenda. 'Will robots get rights?' and 'A cell turned computer analyses its own state of health' (9–10 September 2007: 17) discuss the nanotechnological compression of cells and the question of whether in the age of artificial intelligence robots may have to become legal persons. 'An adhesive strip like a frog's leg' and 'Cyborgs already exist' (21–22 October 2007) explain bionic copying of animal techniques by humans and provide a review of Ollivier Dyens' book *La Condition inhumaine* (2008), respectively. There is also an explanation of the 'Lifelog' principle – an initiative pursued by the Pentagon since 2003 – which is aimed at recording the entirety of a person's data and thus creating cognitive systems which may become a human's constant 'companion' similar to a 'guardian angel'. The question concerning the future genetic modification of athletes and the interactivity between humans and their electronic environment via quasi 'telepathic' means is the focus of another *Le Monde* issue (4–5 December 2007: 17). The question of the future of aging in a robotized, self-administrating, remote-assistance environment – 'Growing old in the year 2030' (*Le Monde* 9–10 March 2008: 17), as well as the future of love in the year 2050 on the basis of new 'haptic' technologies, or robots with 'emotions', are also discussed (*Le Monde* 23–24 March 2008). Examples like these have been proliferating ever since.

In the face of the omnipresent popularization of the cyborg scenario it becomes clear that old as well as new media play a key role in the transformation of a humanist cultural imaginary into a posthumanist twenty-first century technocultural imaginary. Two more detailed press examples follow to conclude this little survey: the *Newsweek* issue of 25 August 2003 was entitled: 'Bionic kids: how technology is changing the next generation of humans'. It describes the influence of new technocultural practices and their changes to childhood and to growing up. Computer games, mobile phones, text messaging, chatrooms, Facebook, all these new forms of experience and communicational spaces not only change personalities but also human abilities and thus affect the cognitive patterns of the 'next generation'. One article, for example, claims that children are becoming more and more astute at processing a multiplicity of visual impulses, which raises the question to what extent pedagogical models will have to adapt to the changes of their subjects, or to what extent 'interhuman' relationships are being affected by the omnipresence of mediating technologies and, also, to what extent the technologization of childhood (and the reduced importance of traditional humanist media, and books and print media in particular) will affect or might already have changed the humanist ideal of childhood as an 'oasis' of time, space and 'free imagination', or 'free (role) play'. Are we indeed facing, after Neil Postman's announcement of the 'end of childhood' (1983), the complete disenchantment of children's environments due to technological virtualization? Are our children becoming 'strangers' to us through cyborgizing technologies, especially since younger subjects usually seem to demonstrate greater preparedness towards experimenting with new media and usually display a far more positive attitude towards these technologies than their parents and educators? As Jennifer L. Croissant explained in her article 'Growing Up Cyborg':

> Children are growing up cyborgs between the extremes of disembodiment presented by the possibilities of life in cyberspace and the complete reduction to embodiment posited for production workers subject to the machinisations of hypermobile global capital in export zones.
>
> (Croissant 1998: 285)

In pedagogical circles this leads to the application of new educational models to learning and teaching processes, which are using metaphors that are largely taken from cybernetics (for example the idea of 'informatization' of learning processes or analogies like hard and software with brain and consciousness). It is, however, her humanist-pedagogical instincts which cause Croissant to fear for the survival of 'common sense':

> With evolutionary narratives naturalizing the emergence of cyborgs as anthropomorphized robotic systems, and cybernetic metaphors playing an increasingly important role in describing and normalizing development, flexible bodies and unhappy decentered subjectivities are part of the erosion of collectivities for refashioning politics and the public sphere.
>
> (Croissant 1998: 296)

As justified as Croissant's scepticism seems, it would be dangerous to blindly trust the underlying humanist reflexes in her argument. The bemoaned 'decentred subjects' are not only the product of posthumanizing technologies alone, but are an integral part of modernity as such – this is precisely what the so-called poststructuralist 'antihumanist' reaction focused on. Following poststructuralism's footsteps might therefore lead to a new critical position that helps to avoid the current extremes of techno-utopian and techno-dystopian visions.

Bionic kids, however, are only emblems of the tip of the (global and melting) iceberg of what is happening to 'us'. The popular science weekly magazine *New Scientist* in May 2006 (13 May

2006) published an issue entitled: 'Better than human: Why settle for what you were born with?' It expresses the new symptomatic plasticity of the human in the age of technological posthumanization. Interestingly, the introductory commentary by Graham Lawton bears the caption 'The Incredibles', after the eponymous Disney/Pixar animation movie, which appeared in 2004, and which represents an entirely 'average' family of super(human) heroes. This is noteworthy because it hints at a general trend in which movie culture, popular culture, the popularization of science and technological development – and hence 'science fiction' in the literal sense, of the fictionalization of science and technology – is being made accessible on a large scale and offered as *the* new 'life style'. Lawton expresses this in the following enthusiastic terms:

> They're here and walking among us: people with technologically enhanced senses, superhuman bodies and artificially sharpened minds. The first humans to reach a happy 150th birthday may already have been born. And that's just the start of it. Are you ready for your upgrade ...?
>
> (Lawton 2006: 32)

The significant turn in this context is the 'embodiment' of technological modification. Until now humans have 'applied' technology to their environment so to speak and now, in the age of informatics, genetics, neurology and cognitive science (usually referred to under the formula 'nano-bio-info-cogno'), they tackle their own modification through technologies which are designed to change human consciousness, metabolism and the personality of future generations. Gene repair, the convergence of diverse technologies like informational technology, robotics, bio- and neurosciences, for example, are aiming for the event that Vernor Vinge described as the 'singularity', which, through accelerated change, will radically and irrevocably change the life form called 'human'. Telepathic communication between humans and machines, designer kids, spare body parts, mental and physical forms of augmentation through 'smart drugs' and prostheses are becoming part of posthuman everyday life.

What most of these examples have in common, however, is the apparently 'natural' amalgamation of fiction and reality, future and present tense, all based on an underlying principle of extrapolation – one of the fundamental principles of technological determinism. It is this circumstance which justifies seeing science fiction as the posthumanist genre *par excellence*, not just on the basis of content, however, but also because of the role it plays within the formation of a techno-posthumanist and technocultural imaginary, for which the naturalization of the cyborg myth, as Croissant explained above, is merely one aspect, but a central one. Science fiction thus needs to be understood as a 'symptom' of change which should be investigated through a critical reading that reveals the hidden causes and the inscribed but repressed desires at work in it. Most visible is the importance of science fiction in its Hollywood blockbuster incarnation. But also, at a micro-cultural level so to speak, at the level of everyday cultural practice, in advertising, in the vocabulary of personal media usage, everywhere where the combination of science and fiction plays a key role. Since science fiction is such an integral part of the contemporary human imagination, technological and scientific developments are increasingly being 'explained' to, or are being made explicit for, the public through analogies with well-known science fiction scenarios or topoi. Hence, quite legitimately, the question arises: is fiction still following any reality here? Is science fiction inspired by the possibilities of scientific research, which are then exploited and 'extended' so to speak? Or has reality, following Baudrillard's well-known claim, long disappeared within this nexus of fictionalization and de-realization and turned into something like 'hyperreality'? First, a few examples to demonstrate the erasure of the boundary between science and fiction: expressions like 'beam me up, Scotty' from the *Star Trek* series have become synonymous with any kind of technological developments that in any way resemble 'teleportation'. Titles like 'Hollywood got it wrong, this is how you stop an apocalyptic asteroid' (*Sunday Telegraph* 25 February 2007: 13) refers to the film *Armageddon* (1998) in which Bruce Willis sacrifices himself to save humanity by deflecting an asteroid on a collision course with Earth. What is interesting is not so much the factual correction of a science fiction film but rather the fact that the knowledge of the film and the topical scenario is presupposed (within the cultural imaginary) and is strategically used to hand the reader a more 'scientific' explanation without, however, in any way dispelling the apocalyptism of the film. It is as if science was buying into the 'cultural capital' (cf. Bourdieu) of the media in general, and powerful genres like science fiction in particular, and turning this mediacultural capital into 'profit' in terms of an increase in science's own legitimation and 'presence'. Slightly earlier, the *Guardian* had already asked this question of 'inspiration' (17 November 2006: 3): 'Wanted: man to land on a killer asteroid and gently nudge it from path to Earth':

> It is the stuff of nightmares and, until now, Hollywood thrillers. A huge asteroid is on a catastrophic collision course with Earth and mankind is poised to go the way of the dinosaurs. To save the day, Nasa now plans to go where only Bruce Willis has gone before. The US space agency is drawing up plans to land an astronaut on an asteroid hurtling through space at more than 30,000 mph.

Examples of this form of 'reporting' have been on the increase ever since. The article in the *Guardian* (9 February 2007), 'The brain scan that can read people's intentions' refers to the film *Minority Report* (2003 [2002]) to explain to its readers the problem of 'free will' and the implications of new neuroscientific scanning technology that can make 'intentions' visible through neurological changes in the brain even before a specific subject has actually become 'conscious' of them. To this end, the reduction of the quite complicated plot of the film, not to mention the fact that its literary model (Philip K. Dick's short story) is dealing with the underlying philosophical problem of free will in much greater detail and nuances, seems irrelevant. The media and popular culture by far prefer working with clichés of mad scientists like 'Doctor Frankenstein'. In any case, science fiction has increasingly been exercising the role of a cultural trendsetter. One could even see this as the beginning of a new hybrid media genre, namely 'science faction' (cf. also Colin Milburn's phrase 'nanowriting' (Milburn 2002) in this context), which consciously mixes the fictionality and facticity of scientific culture. 'We have the technology' *the Guardian* (25 March 2007: 10) promises its readers: 'Bionic eyes, robot soldiers and kryptonite were just film fantasy. But now science fiction is fast becoming fact. So how will it change our lives?' Another article runs 'Forget robot rights, expert says, use them for public safety – Scientists call for public debate on possible roles: work in military, as carers or as sex toys mooted' (*Guardian* 24 April 2007). The article poses the question of whether future forms of artificial intelligence and robots should be granted 'human rights' and explicitly refers to the film *Bicentennial Man* (1999) and *I, Robot* (2004). 'It's magic: science gets closer to creating the Invisible Man' (*Sunday Times* 28 May 2006) draws explicit parallels between Harry Potter's invisibility cloak, the film *Hollow Man* (2000) and new technologies that 'make invisible', which are of special interest to the military. Cryonics – freezing the human body for preservation and subsequent 'reawakening', practised by Walt Disney himself – would be unthinkable without regular representation in science fiction of freezing people in 'pods' for all forms of space travel. At regular intervals there is also Arnold Schwarzenegger's image – whenever there is talk of prostheses – who, in *Terminator* in 1984, first revealed his steel entrails and his metallic arm to a film audience. Compare, for example, the article 'Artificial limbs used by mind power' (*Guardian* 14 October 2003: 3), where you can read below Arnold's photo: 'From fiction to fact ... Terminator star Arnold Schwarzenegger flexes muscle power, shown to work in tests on monkeys'. Also the already mentioned 'Man and machine joined in deadly harmony' (*THES* 22 June 2007: 4–5) uses quite 'naturally' a film still with Dolf Lundgren from *Universal Soldier* (1992). Brake and Hook (2008) call this phenomenon, which can be traced back as far as to the speculative texts at the beginnings of modern science in the Renaissance – Kepler, Copernicus, and later Cyrano de Bergerac and Jonathan Swift – a 'symbiosis of science and science fiction', which influences what we see, do and dream.

It is thus no coincidence that the genre of science fiction has gained so much importance within the cultural representations of technoscientific capitalism. The interpenetration of film, media and culture has gone so far that it makes sense to speak of contemporary posthumanist culture as 'mediaculture' and 'filmculture'. Technologization and mediatization go hand in hand in the process of social posthumanization – this circumstance has provoked a number of prominent apocalyptic formulations, not least in the work of Jean Baudrillard. For Baudrillard, the genre of science fiction is not just any genre; it is the one that is closest to 'theory' and thus to his own way of thinking and writing. Science fiction is indeed 'simulation' *par excellence*, because it represents a form of consciousness that aims to depict scientific and technological transformation 'realistically' and thus discusses the questions of probability and 'realizability' with their associated problems of teleology, or inevitability, ontology and ethics. As a mediating (and popularizing) force between science and everyday life practice, science fiction floats in a simulative space, in between realism and fictionality – a space, as we suggested earlier, one might call 'science faction'. This may be a space of futures as yet unknown, as well as fictional pasts or *verfremdet* (defamiliarized) presents. Science fiction is thus the most posthumanist of all genres because it usually deals with a definition of the human through science and technology and thus serves to explain 'our technocultural condition'. As Istvan Csicsery-Ronay explains:

> SF, then, is not a genre of literary entertainment only, but a mode of awareness, a complex hesitation about the relationship between imaginary conceptions and historical reality unfolding into the future. SF orients itself within a conception of history that holds that science and technology actively participate in the creation of reality, and thus "implant" human uncertainty into the nonhuman world.
>
> (Csicsery-Ronay 1991: 388)

In the age of Baudrillardian 'hyperreality' and the interpenetration of culture and simulation technologies, science fiction becomes the typical form of expression of a 'technological imaginary', a fiction, which has lost its dialectical other and for which 'reality' has become the highest and most unattainable form of utopia. As a consequence, the boundary between social reality and science fiction has become an 'optical illusion', as Haraway already mentioned in her 'Cyborg Manifesto' (1991 [1985]). For Scott Bukatman, the resulting (posthuman or at least posthumanist) subject position that is made available by the genre of science fiction might be referred to as 'terminal identity':

There is simply no overstating the importance of science fiction to the present cultural moment, a moment that sees itself *as* science fiction ... science fiction has, in many ways, prefigured the dominant issues of postmodern culture ... it is the purpose of much recent science fiction to construct a new subject position to interface with the global realms of data circulation, a subject than can occupy or intersect the cyberspaces of contemporary existence.

(Bukatman 1993: 6, 8–9)

The main challenge within science fiction is thus the interface between humans and technology so that Bukatman's 'terminal identity' may be understood as that form of identity that is compatible with the computer terminal and, at the same time, as the 'terminal phase' of humanist identitarian culture as such (9). Science fiction visualizes the dissolution of ontological foundations like the distinction between organic and inorganic, masculine and feminine, original and copy, natural and artificial, human and nonhuman, etc., and thus serves as a reflection of our science fictional everyday life. Through the extensive use of visual special effects, science fiction tries to achieve a 'defamiliarization' of an already posthumanized environment. It thus shakes the humanist value system to an extent where the ontology of the human becomes precarious and the subject of utopia as such. Contemporary science fiction films in particular therefore portray the 'loss of control over the human form' (Bukatman 1993: 17), referred to by Bukatman as 'terminal identity', which constitutes a 'transitional state produced at the intersection of technology and narrative' (22).

Contemporary cultural criticism is therefore well advised to take science fiction seriously, not in the sense of its factual 'realizability' but rather on the basis of its cultural influence. In other words, a critical reading of a society which is in the process of becoming posthumanist if not posthuman uses science fiction as one of its most important sources for analysing the symptoms that are at work within the contemporary cultural imaginary. This imaginary includes the futurologically oriented sciences with their bio-, nano-, cogno-, info-, etc. technologies within science fiction. A clear separation between 'science' and 'fiction', between scientific fact and futurological fiction is neither possible nor desirable in the age of radical miniaturization, digitalization, cyborgization, virtualization and mediatization. The transmission of scientific research is being effectuated (as shown in the various press cuttings above) by means of science fiction within popular and everyday culture, in order to gain political and economic support for research ventures and the development of new technologies. In this sense long-standing dreams of humanity like space travel, intergalactic peace-keeping missions and technological progress are literally *made* true and, what is more, represented as the aim of becoming (more than) human. It thus becomes clear that the diverse utopian and dystopian science fiction scenarios are serving to police the boundaries within the negotiation of morality, values and taboos, and that they foster the acceptance of cultural change that is caused by eventual displacement of these boundaries. They are thus visualizations of symptoms of repressed desires and anxieties as a reaction to diverse posthumanizing tendencies. A critical posthumanist reading of science fiction films is thus a working through and a deconstruction of certain humanist values at work almost 'despite' the posthumanizing potential portrayed.

For such a reading, however, we still need a few clarifications concerning reading technique. It is by now fairly well established to speak of films as 'texts' and that within the structures of these texts there is a catalogue of values inscribed. These values comprise amongst other things humanist foundational beliefs about what it means to be 'human'. Even if maybe not all texts lend themselves to the same extent to such a reading it is legitimate to start from a hypothetical posthumanist position from which these values can be interrogated, and thus to act *as if* it was possible to read from an 'inhuman', or at least no longer quite so human standpoint. This is an 'artificial' position it is true, however, it stands against an equally constructed 'humanity', which does not stop it from observing precisely the constructedness of such a no longer entirely embodied, anthropomorphized and anthropocentric perspective. The basic humanist presuppositions of a text thus have to be read 'against the grain'. To read from a posthumanist perspective means to put in question one's own (human) self at least temporarily and to suspend one's fundamental self-understanding as a member of a certain 'species'. One therefore projects an otherness onto the always presupposed human and sympathizes with a view that undermines the human identity principle but which, at the same time, may also find new foundations for that which defines the human and what is familiar to it. This means positioning oneself between identity and alterity while reading or deconstructiong the organic foundations for this very opposition. Up to a certain point this way of reading is consciously counter-intuitive for it wishes to transcend a participation in a universal humanity which, strictly speaking, is defined as unsurpassable. How can one as a human read differently, or as 'nonhuman', since neither machines nor animals can be said to be able to 'read', at least not in the human sense. Is this position not entirely absurd, then? This absurditiy is dissolved, however, the moment that the connection between speculation and reality, fiction and truth, possibility and actuality, as, for example, in science fiction, is at least momentarily suspended. This displacement of the boundary between the human and its other renders the deconstruction of the humanist value system feasible. Deconstruction is here not meant negatively but instead is based on profound 'empathy'. Almost 'inhuman' does not mean 'dehumanized' but instead calls for a strategic 'misanthropy' (cf. Cottom 2006). In what follows, it is not a question of analysing films in their entirety but of focusing on some central scenes in which this posthumanist misanthropy comes to the fore. In most cases, these are films that are so well known that their general content can be safely presupposed.

Arguably, what characterizes many contemporary science fiction films is a kind of 'subversion' and 'containment' dialectic that cultural materialists like Jonathan Dollimore discovered to be at work in early modern literature a few decades ago. There are what might be called 'posthuman moments' in science fiction. They more or less deliberately threaten the integrity of a given 'human essence' and are fetishistically indulged in, but all too often they are in the end closed off by the reaffirmation and reconfirmation of the human on a different plane. The closing off mentioned above was maybe first discerned by Tom Cohen in a little 'coda' to his book on *Anti-Mimesis* (1994). The coda's title – 'Post-humanist reading' – announces its particular relevance to what we are discussing here.

The focus of Cohen's posthumanist reading is *Terminator 2:*

Judgment Day (1991). Cohen focuses on one aspect of that film in particular – the T2000's 'anamorphism'. As opposed to the old Terminator model (which was more or less happy to retain 'Arnoldoid' form), the latest cyborg killing machine sent back in time to destroy the future hero of human resistance against the machines is strictly speaking no longer a 'machine' in the 'mechanical' sense of the term. 'He' is a nightmare for human representation because 'he' can take on any animate or inanimate shape. He is literally anamorphic by substance, his 'nature' as liquid metal allowing him to metamorphose into humans of any gender and objects of any shape. In that regard, and emphasizing a different connection to that between posthumanism and meta(l)morphosis studied by critics like Rosi Braidotti, Cohen's question goes right to the heart of humanist assumptions behind this obvious 'crisis of representation' caused by 'anamorphosis': '

> he [T2] is able to assume myriad anamorphic shapes as liquid metal, a virtual melt-down through all representation ... – is cast as the to-be-evaded-assassin this time. Yet assassin of what? And why is that which burns through all representations, including the commodity form of the human, *evil*?
>
> (Cohen 1994: 260; *Cohen's emphasis*)

Why indeed? The humanity that had accommodated itself to the earlier cyborgian threat of new robotics (the android as 'Arnoldoid', as T1, is John Connor's armoured protection machine – a kind of virtual 'pet' and 'replacement father' at once) now regroups in the face of an even bigger threat that goes to the core of the human. This core appears coextensive with the survival of human shape and with recognition of it. It implies trust in human representability and in the representedness as human of even that which is scarcely human. We remain humans – even cyborgs are 'humans' of sorts – because we recognize human form and humanist content, this content being that which explains Cohen's focus on 'mimesis'. Hence the T2 is 'the invasion, from a fantasized "future", of an *anti*-representational and post-humanist logic' (260; Cohen's emphasis). Hollywood, as a representative of defending the status quo, namely late capitalist liberal humanism and its cultural logic, could be said to be the last bulwark of *representationalism* (and the image-commodity) against 'an anamorphic logic, humanism's low-tech mimesis against the implementation of the supplement' (261). Basically, Hollywood desperately positions itself as the legitimate source of representation in the face of 'anamorphic' (i.e. unrepresentable) threats to its bread-and-butter business of filmic representation of possible, maybe even likely (fictional) scenarios. Consequently, exploring the future of what it means to be human involves encountering the very logic of the inhuman while of course creating the parameters through which this human, extended into the inhumanity of the future, may still be 'captured' on film and consumed by actual contemporary human subjects. This is not too far from Jameson's point that in science fiction 'the alien, fully assimilated, its Difference transmuted into identity, will simply become a capitalist like the rest of us' (Jameson 2005: 141). On his part, Cohen reads this defensive 'pseudo-humanism', which is only really interested in protecting some human essence as long as it can be sold (down the river), as a 'reply' by popular culture to the impacts of anti-representational 'theory', in the following way:

> The film, subtitled 'Judgment Day', strives to put an apocalyptic slant on what is a recurrent aesthetic evasion on which the future may indeed be said to rest. Humanity as a now empty trope opposes, here, the post-humanism that grows out of its own logic, and it opposes that with star power. Here the pseudo-humanism of Hollywood representationalism (parodically symbolized in the real machine-man, the Kennedy-Republican Arnold) beats off the invasion of French post-structuralism and non-representational logic, cast as a threat to the human, as materiality as such.
>
> (Cohen 1994: 261)

Here Cohen strategically uses the so-called 'theory wars' to illustrate how SF cinema opens up post-humanist possibilities only to foreclose them and restore the more or less repressive status quo. The 'anti-mimetic Other' is literally undone in the end. The T2000 is in fact 'amalgamated' into the 'melting pot'. His radical difference is thereby blended away. In a strange reverse anamorphism, all the human forms the T2000 had taken on (and, by taking on, killed off) reappear and are almost exorcized until the final image, the shape of a human skull, remains as the ultimate de- and re-humanized form. Representation seems reinstalled, anamorphosis appropriated, but the unleashing of an 'Other' (fictional or not) is never entirely recuperable. The 'irruption' of such an ambiguity, the haunting of a terrifying 'real', a what if-scenario (what if we take the anamorphic threat seriously and even start seeing it outside the logic of 'threat', i.e. anxiety-desire), leaves a trace in the form of radical posthumanist moments in which the vulnerability of the humanist model is exposed or at least remains exposable.

The question of why an anamorphic other is to 'die' (with death here understood as the ultimate loss of 'form', the 'unrepresentable') as a result of the 'expulsion' of all forms and of melting away into 'formlessness' (and perhaps complete anonymity) is only one such posthumanist moment out of which a challenge to representationalist or 'mimetic' humanism arises. Another is also pointed out by Cohen. It is the last scene where the 'good' Terminator must also 'disappear' to guarantee that the techno-logic that will lead to the disappearance of the human in the future can be destroyed here and now. But since the representationalist machine has now become an ally, indeed in many respects 'more-human-than-the-human-itself', he-it is granted a humane and dignified, even heroic opportunity for self-effacement – suicide. Tellingly, and in sharp contrast to the T2000's meltdown, the last scene the spectator visualizes is the machine's 'own' perspective. The spectator 'becomes' or 'inhabits' Arnold's vision one last time before the mechanical eye-I 'shuts down'. One could argue that this is the ultimate 'imagination' (representation) of the essential humanist 'self' that 'envisages' its own death as the 'end of seeing' and the descent into absolute 'darkness'. It ties in with Jameson's discussion in *Archaeologies of the Future* (2005) of the 'android cogito' and of the difficulty that what is alien to the human 'can never be "empathized from within"' (140–1). Under technocultural conditions this envisaging and this attempt at impossible empathy has, ironically, been computerized and digitalized – and internalized. Our death is now imaginable only as a 'switching-off' process. In a literal, maybe even 'digital' sense, we have become (posthuman) machines in the process of warding off the inhuman other. This seems quite a high price to pay, as Cohen explains:

Of course, in this scene, the machine-as-human, Arnold, must go through the misleading gesture of (human) self-sacrifice at the end, virtually erasing not a terrifying future but the opportunity of the 'human' present to read itself. The (inhuman) 'human' wins out over the real – suppression is restituted.

(Cohen 1994: 262)

Cohen's wider claim, namely that 'commodified forms of humanism prevail through mimetic ideology that suppresses figural logic' (262), means that for a 'posthumanist reading' these moments in which humanism is threatened and the posthumanist other is unleashed need to be taken seriously (maybe even 'literally') and forced back onto the texts. In fact, it is a kind of ethical demand that confronts texts with their own liberal humanist conservatism. The aim is not in any way to 'overcome' the human but to challenge its fundamental humanism, including its theoretical and philosophical underpinnings and allies (e.g. anthropocentrism, speciesism, universalism, etc.).

Another ally in this attempt to characterize a specifically 'posthumanist' critical practice is the work of Neil Badmington. In *Alien Chic: Posthumanism and the Other Within* (2004a), Badmington investigates the inevitable 'contamination' of the human by its inhuman others, and in particular in the representation of aliens in science fiction. Humanism – the hegemonic belief system that ultimately relies on 'an absolute difference between the human and the inhuman' (Badmington 2004a: 124), and which manifests and reproduces itself through cultural texts – reveals itself, if read against the grain (or *in a certain way*, as Badmington says; 134), 'to have been always already housing the alien of posthumanism' (124). There is thus a deep affinity between the Barthesian idea of 'demythologization' understood as 'denaturalization' (i.e. there is nothing 'obvious' about the human as such, instead there is only a 'discourse' – humanism – that is trying, through the construction of 'myths', or through 'mystification/mythification', to legitimate a hierarchical system in which the human manages to retain its absolute supremacy by expelling differences outside its 'own' category and projecting them onto constructed 'others', i.e. nonhumans). And culture, ironically, is precisely that which is designed to guarantee human 'nature'. Humanism's 'work', however, is never done because the otherness constructed and projected into the world (which might be the equivalent of a 'posthumanist' definition of culture: the sum of the otherness projected by humans into their world) comes back to haunt and threaten the borderlines of difference drawn around the human as its protection. It is a dialectic of 'probing' and 'haunting' that keeps the play of humanist hegemony alive. But the threat is already the beginning of a contamination. The purification process is never complete and grows more desperate and tragic as more borderlines are crossed and eroded.

It therefore becomes equally clear that there is also a close affinity between deconstruction and psychoanalysis in any 'critical posthumanist reading'. For example, what Badmington calls 'humanism's faith in identity' (2004a: 129) is undermined through the very process of differentiation and 'othering'. In setting up a binary or absolute opposition between humans and aliens, for example, it becomes clear that the alienness used to distinguish between the two has a side effect. It is the invasion of the selfsameness (or, the identity of the human) by 'its' other. As Badmington shows, '[a]liens differ from humans, but humans differ from themselves' (130). The other ends up being 'in the same' – a process that might be referred to as the 'deconstruction of the human' – so that 'the human is never quite at home with itself, and never without the alien' (134). Though it may be glib to say this, there is therefore a sense that the kind of critical posthumanism we are advocating is far from a threat to the human(ist). Rather, it may be viewed as a strategy in meeting the fear that governs humanism's logic of contamination/purification. By problematizing humanness or the human' we are not in the least advocating a 'dehumanizing' process. On the contrary, and as will be argued later, dehumanization and annihilation are precisely the 'terror' humanism itself helps to construct or at least to maintain, which means that humans might have to become critical posthumanists out of humanitarian interest.

Before we explore that, let us dwell a little on another science fiction film. The invasion of the human by its other(s) could not be more drastically and intriguingly represented than in *Invasion of the Body Snatchers* (1956). The idea here is that humans are surreptitiously 'supplanted' by the inhuman other – in this case alien 'plants', seeds falling out of the sky producing pods that gradually generate a perfect copy of a human body and then eliminate the real human body to replace it. The strange familiarity and uncanny resemblance – the 'legumes'/aliens *look* human – requires the generation of difference. How can you 'tell' the difference? Humans, apparently, have feelings and these aliens do not. As Badmington explains,

> [t]his binary opposition supports the film's humanism in four principle ways. First, there is a belief in an absolute difference between the human and the inhuman. Second, this difference is hierarchical. Third, there is an appeal to a uniquely human essence that cannot be replicated. Fourth, there are clearly identifiable rules according to which a simple versus – humans versus aliens – may be maintained.
>
> (2004a: 137)

This 'versus', however, is what is 'in crisis'. The other, by definition, brings not only control but uncertainty. It is an uncertainty, at the very centre of humanism, about the meaning of the 'human'. In *Invasion of the Body Snatchers* it is the very ambiguity of human emotion, used as an absolute marker of distinction between humans and nonhumans, which threatens to break down the barriers set up to protect the integrity of the human. As Badmington says, 'love is the problem' (138). Love, figured ultimately as an essentially human characteristic, remains 'alien', mysterious and inexplicable. It is ungovernable, inextricable from desire. Can one 'love' the alien, the inhuman, the nonhuman? Desire, as psychoanalysis tells us, is at once blind and uncontrollable. It is an essential aspect of the human but at the same time it is a threat because it does not distinguish in its object choice between human and inhuman. 'To be human is to desire', Badmington claims, 'but to desire is to trouble the sacred distinction between the human and the inhuman' (2004a: 139). Desire makes humanism 'tremble'. The most essential means by which the human is defined must remain mysterious and somehow exterior to it. It is predicated on a necessary ambiguity, on a certain *'je ne sais quoi'*. Love, basically, is no guarantee. It will uphold neither the essence of the human nor the institutions cherished by humanism.

Interestingly, a simple reversal of humanism is often played with in certain instances of contemporary apocalyptic science fiction where the human is explicitly under threat of becoming extinct or in a curious way has already lost the final war – for example, the one against the machines (cf. the *Terminator* scenario) – and is merely 'surviving'. We agree with Badmington, of course, when he claims that posthumanism is not to be understood as a simple 'after-humanism', but rather that posthumanism 'inhabits' humanism: that is, it is always a repressed possibility *of* and *inside* humanism. Hence, the necessarily psychoanalytic-*cum*-deconstructive approach favoured by a critical posthumanist reading of texts and their humanist tradition. In this sense, anti-humanism is not enough because anti-humanism is still humanist. In other words, anti-humanism may not take the dialectic between human and nonhuman seriously or 'literally' enough. While Badmington's focus is the subgenre of science fiction he calls 'Alien Chic', it might also be possible to extend this 'deconstruction of the binary opposition between the human and the inhuman that is forever happening *within* humanism itself' (Badmington 2004a: 151) to other subgenres of science fiction, and ultimately to all cultural texts, past and present.

Within the parameters of this chapter, meanwhile, a good third example may be the way in which the film *Minority Report* (2003 [2002]) goes about policing another boundary around a fundamentally humanist concept: free will. John Anderton (Tom Cruise) undergoes a transformation from a firm believer in the idea and execution of crime prevention through the use of 'precogs' (specially gifted humans whose nightmarish preconscience predicts murders that are about to happen) to a sceptic and victim of the system. The particular 'posthumanist' moment or angle of this film lies in the question of whether the absolutely essential humanist value of free will should be overruled in the case of the imminent murder of a human being. As countless critics of detective fiction have argued, there is something 'special' about murder as opposed to other crimes, so that it is significant that the film portrays society as having moved 'beyond' trusting the human to be 'perfectible' and capable of that judgement which, in the moment of an absolute decision, makes the morally right choice in a 'better' world. This world seems in many ways *post*-humanist in the sense that it has moved beyond human decision taking towards dehumanized automated bureaucratic systems driven by efficiency and pre-emption or, to use another current buzzword, 'pro-activeness'. These systems are supposedly 'infallible'. The age-old problem the systems encounter, however, is the uncertainty around human 'intentionality' – probably the most crucial aspect of human law. An 'intention to kill' is precisely the proof that needs to be 'established' for there to be a murder case. The sceptic investigator into the precrime unit's practices voices this concern: 'It's not the future if you stop it!' The context for this is that the 'precrime unit' evades the problem of judging intention by absolute 'trust' in the accuracy of the precogs' visions: 'Precogs don't see what you intend to do, only what you will do'. Intention is in fact no longer needed, because the vision of a murder that is about to occur is taken literally as a murder that has already been committed and is punished accordingly. Yet the matter is not so simple, as it is in the suppressed complexity of that outlook that the film's drama positions itself. For predetermination is everywhere, as John explains: 'The fact that you prevent something from happening doesn't change the fact that it was going to happen'. In simply presupposing intention, the idea of precrime abolishes the doubt over what constitutes human intentionality and drastically circumscribes the space for conscious choice, or free will. This implies that the desire to protect humans (from each other) leads to a denial of what, for humanism, ultimately constitutes the human as such: the uncertainty necessary for a possible choice between right and wrong to exist. Not surprisingly, this dystopian vision is put forward by the filmic narrative as an illustration of the fact that free will needs to be defended in the face of an inhuman(e) system that is less perfect than it makes itself out to be. The 'posthuman scenario' the film paints therefore needs to be rejected and humanism reconstituted and reconfirmed.

This is seemingly achieved through two ideas that are connected with human free will: fallibility and vulnerability, or the possibility of suffering. Fallibility turns out to be the 'repressed' of the system. The precogs do not always agree in their vision. There are so-called 'minority reports' where there is one alternative scenario in which the predicted murder does not in fact occur. The system needs human interpretation and decision if it wants to do 'justice' to the complexity of life and human unpredictability. Fallibility is therefore put forward as a necessary component of human(ist) constitutivity. Vulnerability is the other narrative lever against the film's posthumanist vision. Who, in fact, are the 'precogs', and what links them with the embattled hero, John Anderton? Initially John is offhand about them. 'Don't think of them as human', he tells his rival, the policeman who will go on to investigate the murder John is predicted to commit himself. However his rival, as the representative of a 'religious' form of humanism, explains that 'they are much more than [human], namely our connection to the divine'. In this sense, the precogs are both less and more human than human, and thereby also the 'most' human: representatives of the human as such. They have attained their 'gift' of prescience through suffering caused by humans (the mother of Agatha, 'author' of the minority report that drives the film's plot, was both a drug addict and a murder victim herself). John shares this background of suffering. He has lost his son and endures mental instability as a result of his drug use. He is the typical Hollywood hero in the sense that his suffering leads him to doubt the human and trust the inhuman system until he becomes a victim of the system himself, so that in fighting his own demons he reconfirms his human essence through a decisive moment of 'free choice' (he resists his urge to kill the presumed murderer of his son and instead entrusts him to the 'law').

The most curious association and the one which is just as necessary as it is unintended by the deeply humanist desire that drives *Minority Report*'s narrative is the very 'metaphysics of murder' which acts as the unacknowledged force behind the affirmation of the human in the face of posthuman adversity. The 'metaphysics of murder' is briefly explained early on in the film. The inventor of the precrime programme, Iris Hineman, is quoted as saying: 'There is nothing more destructive to the metaphysical fabric that binds us than the untimely murder of one human being by another'. But what is one to conclude from this rather strange logic in which the most human act, the act of human self-legitimation, is also the desire for the elimination of the human? What makes 'us' human is the capacity for murder. Murder is more than a crime, it is a sacrilege for humanism. What is terrifying is that it is a *necessary* sacrilege (like, ultimately, all sacrileges). One is most human in the moment of annihilating another human. Animals kill, humans murder each other. The affirmation of the human, according to humanism's 'metaphysics of murder', passes at once through the committing and the suffering of murder. Murder as the most in/human(e) act affirms the fallibility *and* vulnerability of the human *at the same time*. Strange logic indeed, but, at least, in articulating the logic, a critical post-*humanism*, i.e. a humanism intent on working through its own repressed, may be the starting point for a more open and less metaphysical definition of humans and their laws.

What, then, binds these films together? It is the instinct to affirm the human in the face of posthumanist scenarios, to discover in subjectivity and fallibility and vulnerability themselves the resources through which to allay the unease envisioned by the very thought of the enhancements promised by 'our posthumanist future'. Human lack and weakness, therefore, are figured as strengths in those moments where the human is most at crisis and most precarious, particularly when they are mobilized in the name of values like love, loyalty, free will and self-sacrifice. They are what secure the integrity of the human and justify the desire for non-contamination, for non-assimilation within the posthuman other. Human(ist) integrity is thereby preserved in the face of posthuman(ist) othering. Set in posthumanist settings, these stories are therefore impeccably humanist parables. And yet the unease persists.

In the face of that unease, we would like to point towards some other erosions of the human/nonhuman opposition that have been under way for some time in science fiction. Take the figure of the 'cyborg', for example – not, of course, an innocent example, but rather striking in its specificity, as Donna Haraway has shown. More recent films, like *Artificial Intelligence: AI* (2002 [2002]) and *I, Robot* (2004 [1995]), all testify to the working through of the boundary between human and nonhuman. The desire for and anxiety of 'becoming-machine', or 'cyborgization', is irrepressible. What happens to the human once it is invaded by its machinic other? And what happens to the machine? Is there such a 'thing'? A rather more quiet and low-tech representation of this anxiety is of course already present in, for example, *Stepford Wives* (2004 [1975]) and then again in classics like *Blade Runner* (1992 [1982]). In each case there is a necessary contamination of the categories 'human' and 'machinic human other' – a temporary blurring of boundaries which justifies a subsequent purification process. The machinic other is allowed to temporarily threaten, invade and hybridize the selfsameness of the human in order to indulge both: the desire of the 'what if?' (for example, what if there was no real boundary between human and machines?) and the anxiety of maintaining the status quo (that is, to reconfirm the humanist essentials in the face of posthuman threats). Usually, doubting heroes overcome their obsessions at the price of first 'becoming other' (e.g. like the machine) and then regaining their true self and redrawing the blurred lines (e.g. the machine 'becomes' human, indeed more human than human, to affirm human control over it). Alternatively, in somewhat 'darker' scenarios like *Blade Runner* and the early version of *Stepford Wives*, but also in *Artificial Intelligence: AI*, doubt is sustained as an additional 'thrill' (in other contexts it also helps set up subsequent sequels, of course). What makes science fiction such a powerful genre and, ironically and unintentionally, such a strong ally for critical posthumanism, is the fictional indulgence in the desires and anxieties of 'becoming posthuman' while remaining in the ultimate safety of a fictional framework. A posthumanist reading thus merely needs to 'force' the narrative a little to arrive at a 'meta-fictional' level. What if the 'what if' was not just fiction? Not in the sense of 'not-yet-reality' (which would just be a more radical notion of science fiction itself) but rather in a deconstructive sense of 'what is a fiction of fiction?', comparable to what if 'difference' differs from itself (*différance*) – in which case the opposition between identity and difference begins to break down.

There is thus at once a desire to take the constructed posthuman scenarios 'seriously' while critically working through the narcissistic humanist baggage that even the most radical and transhumanist vision of the human future or non-future carries around. All this for the sake of the human probably, since 'care' for the human paradoxically departs from posthumanist horizons. The cue for understanding this comes from a rephrasing of Bruno Latour. If it is true that we have never been modern, it would equally be possible to say that science fiction and critical posthumanist readings of them make clear that 'we have never been human'. This fearful doubt is expressed throughout the genre of science fiction, from the fear in *I, Robot* of 'becoming machine' to *Blade Runner*'s fear of 'unauthenticity'. It is 'as if' the unimaginable (the 'end of the human', of human 'after-life') has at once already happened and in having done so actually never manages to arrive. The posthuman future of *Artificial Intelligence: AI*, for example, is and remains remarkably human in the sense that the robot-boy, like some hi-tech Pinocchio, is captured in his desire for a human mother and for becoming human. It seems there is no choice for humanism but to humanize the machinic other, the animal, the object, God, etc. Whereas, if one took the idea of 'artificial intelligence' seriously, this would of course not leave the human, never mind humanism, unchanged. Indeed, the insistence on projecting human(ist) values and assumptions as essentially unchanged within posthumanist scenarios is one of the most intriguing instincts in this form of science fiction.

Nor is otherness exclusively para-organic in those scenarios. As Donna Haraway pointed out in her 'Cyborg Manifesto', the erosion of one human/nonhuman boundary inevitably leads to breakdowns in other boundaries. The whole humanist edifice is under threat. While the cyborg threatens from one end of the technological spectrum, the animal threatens from the other. Animalization, cyborgization, biotechnology, robotics and cybernetics bring about an accentuated 'hauntology' of the spectralized human. The animal-threat, already apparent in *Planet of the Apes* (1968), is even more apparent in *Gattaca* (2004 [1997]). In *Gattaca* the narrative desire is to overcome genetic determinism through affirmation of human mortality and imperfection. Jerome, the hero, cheats by putting his imperfections against those of the system. He demonstrates that human freedom lies in overcoming one's material, biological and other limitations by sheer will power and determination and belief (in oneself, his ideals, etc.). He is helped at critical moments by the most human of sentiments: love and compassion. When the fulfilment of Jerome's dream to travel into space is confronted with one last hurdle, one final urine check, the 'scientist' overrules the system because his son is in a similar (genetically imperfect) position to Jerome. In denouncing 'genoism', the 'future' form of discrimination that is based on perceptions of genetic 'deficiency', as it is called in *Gattaca* (the title is an allusion to the chromosome sequencing in human DNA, *Gattaca* being composed of the initial letters of the four DNA nucleotides:

adenine, cytosine, guanine and thymine), the film affirms free will and idealism as the core of what it means to be human. In this respect the film's tagline is an emblematic posthumanist moment in itself: 'There's no gene for the human spirit'. It is tempting to compare the stirring assurance of that line with the doubt, which is much more deconstructive and critically posthumanist, that drives Jacques Derrida's essay on the topic, 'The Aforementioned So-Called Human Genome'. 'What might the so-called *genome* of the said *man* be?' Derrida asks in an essay which 'call[s] for a deconstruction and reconstruction of the legal and of the legal concept of the "human"' (Derrida 2002a: 202–3). Here, however, commentary on the film must take priority, and it is interesting to note that ironically but rather representatively, the most human (i.e. deficient) hero must first expel all humanity (must become like the genetically perfect, automated, uniform, 'machinic' other – the 'inhuman' *par excellence*) to fulfil his dream of 'humanity' – his very own conquering of space. The reversal follows the (self)deconstructive logic already described. The 'longing for the human' as the driving force behind humanism's constant self-replication expresses itself through the variation produced by constant self-transformation. It recalls Nietzsche's most humanist expression in anti-humanist disguise: become who you (already) are!

Similarly, in *Planet of the Apes* (1968) the distinction between human and animal is explored, challenged and reconfirmed under different conditions. Humans first have to experience 'animality' – being treated like animals by a superior species – to be able to overcome their own animality and live in peace with and respect for animals (at least with simians, of course). The film never breaks out of its anthropocentrism, however, in first projecting human 'evil' onto the animal other and in the end presupposing the need for atonement and humility within 'the animal'. First, humans have to become more animal than (the 'worst) animal, and animals more human than (the 'best') human, before 'animality' (and not humanity – which means that the hierarchy and absolute distinction between the two is never fundamentally challenged) can be safely contained. The end, as usual, proposes a re-establishment of 'happy family' as the cornerstone of humanist society, while humanity is almost extended (at least partially) to the apes (the ultimate taboo, namely 'miscegenation' – evoked throughout the film in the female ape's sexual 'desire' for the male human hero – is quickly discarded). It seems that similarities between 'speciesism', racism and sexism are not only intended but absolutely necessary to safeguard the humanist system of values.

Ultimately, however, neither biotechnology nor robotics, neither animalization nor cyborgization constitute the 'real' threat to the survival of the human under current technological and cultural conditions. Rather, 'digitalization' and 'virtualization' promise to question humanism and human essence much more radically than humanism – including its most 'advanced' genre, science fiction – might be able to imagine. It is no coincidence that many recent science fiction films start not only from the hypothesis that the human might not be what 'he' used to be or what 'he' seems, but that 'culture', humanity's web of signification and purveyor of (social) reality, might not be so human, after all. The *Matrix* trilogy (1999–2003) might be seen as representative of this 'subgenre'. At stake is not only the 'integrity' of the human form – questions of embodiment are fundamental to the *Matrix* scenario (i.e. Am I where my body is?) – but whether the human as human can survive its translation into (digital) information. In this sense, it is not so much a case of whether 'Thought can go on without a body', as Jean-François Lyotard has it (1991: 8–23), or whether the mind is downloadable into a computer, as Moravec speculates (1988: 109–10), as much as a question of what constitutes 'digital embodiment'. The reason why the first part of the *Matrix* trilogy gives the general impression of being so much 'deeper' and 'interesting' than the sequels is that it probes this possibility of a digital body. To follow the narrative's Christian undertone (one among others), what happens in the analogue telephone lines through which the cyber rebels can access virtual reality and interfere in 'real life' is the absolute mystery of transubstantiation. How, indeed does one become 'code'? Is the genetically coded information inscribed in humans compatible with or translatable into the digital? Neo's final mastery over the matrix and its digital environment and laws could make him the first 'posthuman' completely immersed into a new, digital culture. His two bodies – the physical and the virtual, so to speak – become one. The curious thing is, of course, that Neo has to become 'real' first before he can master the 'virtual' (in which, however, he has grown up and already been the 'hacker' he is supposed to become).

This ultimate confirmation and reinscription of humanism into the film happens at the end of the first part and in the playing out of the story in the sequels. First of all, what is necessary for Neo's posthumanization is again a very human ingredient: Trinity's unconditional love and self-effacing femininity. It seems that the posthuman digital future will not have to worry about the continuation of sexual difference, gender and race (compare the mapping of race onto space in the sequels). Second, in filling in the void left at the end of the first part, and inevitably providing explanations for philosophical 'problems' put forward, the sequels are much more 'conservative' in giving shape to a possible posthuman scenario. Neo, it turns out, is not and never has been human, after all. He is that third, largely metaphysically blank element between fiction and reality called 'software'. Neither hardware nor wetware, Neo is in fact a 'medium', or 'translation itself'. Neither human nor inhuman, he is technoculture's (posthuman) 'angel', ministering to both human and inhuman at once. In this sense he is the very incarnation of *programmed* 'care'. It is the gradual and simultaneous 'divinization' of 'Neo' as code which makes watching the trilogy 'progress' so painful to witness – an expulsion of the sacred within the human into the realm of spirituality, and into the 'city of the machines' which is also the city of God. With that kind of contaminative logic, it is no wonder that these posthumanist parables are troubling. Their 'posthuman moments' are unnerving and thus have to be deconstructed by a critical posthumanism which tries to do justice to both the human and the posthuman.

5

Interdisciplinarity and the posthumanities

> *If we are willing to reflect seriously and critically, we will readily be able to demonstrate that fields like cultural anthropology, structural linguistics, women's studies, cybertheory, and posthumanism are indeed addressing the Big Questions: the Who Am I questions, the What Am I Doing questions, the What Lies in the Future questions that all attach themselves to the heritage of 'human nature'. These questions have never been more pressing – nor more 'human' – than they are today. And you can quote me on that.*
>
> (GARBER 2003: 267)

Under the conditions of social and cultural posthumanization through bio-, nano-, cogno- and infotechnologies not only humanist tradition and education has come under siege but also the future of the humanities. As an example, we can take the seemingly unstoppable rise of cultural studies and 'theory' (in the UK since the 1970s, in the USA since the 1980s and in Europe and elsewhere since the 1990s). This is, of course, not the place to analyse the history of this phenomenon in detail, which would have to look at the specific socio-political context in which this process of institutionalization has taken place, and what strategies of (cultural) translation, and applications of critical and cultural theory have been employed in the respective national and globalized contexts. Also the connection with the discussion about postmodernism outlined above would have to be taken into account. As far as the perspective taken up in the present study is concerned, we will point towards those aspects that will be relevant within cultural theory and cultural studies for a critical evaluation of the contemporary technoscientific posthumanization process. In the main, this will be a focus on the analysis of the so-called 'science wars', the problem of interdisciplinarity and the question of the future of the humanities and cultural studies in the age of technoculture and technoscientific capitalism.

A good starting point is Lyotard's *The Postmodern Condition: A Report on Knowledge* (1984 [1979]), whose basic assumption is the transformation of knowledge within postindustrial society and its postmodern culture. This transformation into a knowledge society is characterized by the 'hegemony of computers' (4), which is not only concerned with the transmission of knowledge but also promotes the transformation of knowledge into 'information' (or 'data'). In this process the Humboldtian notion of an inseparability of knowledge acquisition from *Bildung* [learning, education] has come under immense pressure. Instead, knowledge under neoliberal, capitalist, market-economy conditions is turned into a commodity for consumption: 'Knowledge in the form of an informational commodity indispensable to productive power is already, and will continue to be, a major – perhaps the major – stake in the worldwide competition for power' (Lyotard 1991: 5). This 'mercantilization of knowledge' is coupled with an ideology that propagates 'communicational "transparency"' (5), which, in turn, has consequences for the political exercise of power of the state, the structure of the public sphere and the influence of economic actors at a global level. The result is the general crisis of traditional processes of legitimation which Lyotard refers to as 'incredulity toward metanarratives' (xxiv). While the 'narrative knowledge' in Western societies and their dominant ideologies (Enlightenment, liberalism, Marxism and, as we would argue, humanism) are in an ongoing crisis of legitimation, scientific and technical knowledge have been growing exponentially and have become more or less 'autonomous'. Science is that discourse which is recognized by the scientific community and its subjects as 'scientific'. In the context of informatization it increasingly decides what may be recognized as 'legitimate knowledge' – one might call this, following Foucault, a 'scientific regime of truth', which, through digitalization, informatization and neoliberalization is expanding globally. However, it does so no longer in the enlightened liberal fashion – scientific legitimation based on the idea of 'progress for humanity' and 'expansion of human freedom' – since the consensus model on which these ideas were based has disappeared, under the conditions of postmodernity:

> In contemporary society and culture – postindustrial society, postmodern culture – the question of the legitimation of knowledge is formulated in different terms. The grand narrative has lost its credibility, regardless of what mode of unification it uses, regardless of whether it is a speculative narrative or a narrative of emancipation. The decline of narrative can be seen as an effect of the blossoming of techniques and technologies since the Second World War, which has shifted emphasis from the ends of action to the means; it can also be seen as an effect of the redeployment of advanced liberal capitalism after its retreat under the protection of Keynesianism during the period 1930–60, a renewal that has eliminated the communist alternative and valorized the individual enjoyment of goods and services.
>
> (Lyotard 1991: 37–8)

The legitimation of science after the end of the grand emancipatory and humanist narrative no longer occurs on the basis of an interaction between a social and a scientific discourse but only depends on the latter with its utilitarian and administrative principle of 'performativity'. Science thus becomes pure 'knowledge production', and technology becomes the performative means of dissemination of science and also the legitimation of scientific practice. Science positions a 'reality' which at the same time guarantees 'performatively', so to speak, its legitimation with all its juridical, ethic and political implications. By defining reality through 'exact' description, science 'creates' its reality, so that it then can, in turn, 'master' it through technological intervention. This circular process – 'legitimation by power' (47) – is supported by the 'informatization' of communication with its principle of performativity borrowed from cybernetics and systems theory. This has obvious consequences for the humanist notion of education, since education becomes the mere pragmatic and utilitarian transmission of knowledge assisted by the mercantilization of information.

This is what Bill Readings' work takes as its starting point. In his The *University in Ruins* (1996) he describes the neoliberalization of the institution of the university and how its change towards the location of 'knowledge production' has caused a crisis, especially in the social sciences and the humanities whose traditional model of a 'liberal education' no longer fits with the 'posthumanist' principle of performativity. It might be argued that this change merely occurs within a very specific, namely Western, late humanist idea of the university, but it is an idea that, in the context of cultural imperialism and its current continuation in the form of a media- and economy-driven globalization process, is being exported across the world. The neoliberal, global 'internationalization' of the university with its new 'corporate' structure spells out the dissolution of the national-humanist state or public university. The consequences are that:

> The current crisis of the University in the West proceeds from a fundamental shift in its social role and internal systems, one which means that the centrality of the traditional humanistic disciplines to the life of the University is no longer assured.
>
> (Readings 1996: 3)

Special leverage lies in the 'deligitimation of (national) culture' for which the traditional humanities (like philosophy, literature, history) have always played the role of guardian. The democratization, 'anthropologization', neoliberalization and commercialization of culture which happened within the postmodern context of a levelling of 'high' and 'low' (or elite and popular) culture can be measured, on the one hand, in the progressive institutionalization of cultural studies, and, on the other hand, in the rise of the new formula of 'excellence' as the quality measurement for scientific production. Readings calls this contemporary form of the university 'posthistorical' in the sense that as an institution it has survived its own original 'project of the *historical* development, affirmation and inculcation of national culture' (6). As the site of excellent knowledge production the university selects a scheme of quality assurance mechanisms which professionalizes and 'ecomonizes' the administration of the institution. The former central position of the professor as the teaching scientist is more and more pushed towards the side of administration – a process which further boosts the autonomy of university administration and which imposes onto the by now 'corporate' university, with the help of the latest neoliberal instruments, a permanent verification process of its 'excellence'. Readings thus asks what remains to be done for a university which can no longer assume that its teaching and learning subjects continue to understand themselves as embodiments of the liberal humanist ideal of education, while at the same time the consensus on the central aspect of a liberal humanist idea of education, namely a traditional (national) culture as the object of teaching and learning, can no longer be presupposed. We are left with a university whose character has become purely functional and corporate and no longer educational and cultural:

> Since the nation-state is no longer the primary instance of the reproduction of global capitals, 'culture' – as the symbolic and political counterpart to the project of integration pursued by the nation-state – has lost its purchase. The nation-state and the modern notion of culture arose together, and they are, I argue, ceasing to be essential to an increasingly transnational global economy. This shift has major implications for the University, which has historically been the primary institution of national culture in the modern nation-state ... this new interest in the pursuit of excellence indicates a change in the University's function. The University no longer has to safeguard and propagate national culture, because the nation-state is no longer the major site at which capital reproduces itself. Hence, the idea of national culture no longer functions as an external referent toward which all of the efforts of research and teaching are directed. The idea of national culture no longer provides an overarching ideological meaning for what goes on in the University, and as a result, what exactly gets taught or produced as knowledge matters less and less.
>
> (Readings 1996: 12–13)

The rise of cultural studies in this context is not a paradox but the direct consequence of a 'dereferentializing' of culture as such. Only when culture as the model of national consensus has disappeared does it make sense to speak of culture, as in cultural studies, in a 'non-normative' sense. Cultural studies' non-normative notion of culture, however, is also perfectly suited to the idea of excellence. As a result of the implementation of excellence as the main institutional legitimation of the university, not only 'excellence' but also 'culture' becomes a mere placeholder sign without true referent. Culture indeed becomes one 'object' among many – just as natural science can explain 'natural' phenomena, cultural studies analyses 'cultural' phenomena.

It is important to note that Readings' analysis is neither nostalgic nor enthusiastic of this development but aims to reinscribe certain ideas under these new conditions, in particular the idea of a scientific community, of interdisciplinary practice and an awareness of their renewed centrality for a discussion about posthumanist values. As far as the new dynamics with regard to interdisciplinarity is concerned, questions about the 'distribution of knowledge' arise (one could, for example, ask how to prevent the fact that the new 'life sciences' will develop a monopoly, as far as defining and legitimating 'life' and any related knowledge production are concerned). Readings was hoping for a 'community of dissensus' which would abandon the idea of transparent communication and instead would point out the problematic aspect of translation processes between scientific discourses in the sense of (Wittgensteinian) 'language games'. As far as the discussion about values is concerned, Readings preferred a 'pragmatism' which was conscious of the fact that the university might survive in its own 'ruins' – a process which requires heightened self-reflexivity, however, based on the strict separation between 'accountability' (the responsibility of the individual for the system and vice versa) and 'accounting' (the neoliberal orientation towards market economy and excellence). The question of what should be researched and taught at a university and why should indeed be asked, as long as this question is not based on the idea of cost efficiency and administrative institutional politics. One could argue that a university thus understood would constitute what might be called a 'critical posthumanist university' – a university which is conscious of the dissolution of its own humanist tradition, but which taps into the constructive and critical potential of this new condition, and which might thus again do justice to its social and global mission but in new forms. The humanist model of an ideal universal human community of knowledge in which each national education model merely strives towards the best form of embodiment of this 'universal' model (based on the humanist dialectic of particularity and universality explained above), according to Readings, has to give way to a (posthumanist) community based on dissensus. This community would not always already presuppose a common model of communication based on transparency and the subordination of discursivity to 'higher ideals and goals': 'We need to think about a community in which communication is not transparent, a community in which the possibility of communication is not grounded upon and reinforced by a common cultural identity' (Readings 1996: 185).

A posthumanist ethics of knowledge would thus have to follow Levinas's notion of the always already existing incalculable responsibility towards a preceding other, on the basis of a primacy of dissensus. Because, if we knew exactly what responsibilities we had towards others, we would probably be able simply to fulfill our obligations and pay our debts. In reality, however, 'we do not know in advance the nature of our obligations to others, obligations that have no origin except in the sheer fact of the existence of Otherness – people, animals, things other to ourselves – that comports an incalculable obligation' (Readings 1996: 188–9). The posthumanist university – or, as one might preferably call it, the university of the 'posthumanities' – might thus become a forum for the interdisciplinary and dissensual knowledge community to face these responsibilities. These responsibilities are posthumanist precisely because they are owed to the 'inhuman' or 'prehuman' and thus exist 'before' (however not in a simply chronological or teleological sense) the distinction between human and animal, human and environment, etc.:

> Our responsibility to others is thus inhuman in the sense that the presumption of a shared or common humanity is an irresponsible desire to know what it is that we encounter in the other, what it is that binds us. To believe that we know in advance what it means

to be human, that humanity can be an object of cognition, is the first step to terror, since it renders it possible to know what is non-human, to know what it is to which we have no responsibility, what we can freely exploit. Put simply, the obligation to others cannot be made an object of knowledge under the rubric of a common humanity.

(189–90)

Paradoxically, the informatization of a global knowledge society and its associated accelerated knowledge production, described by Lyotard, do not create greater communicative transparency but rather place an excessive demand on the posthumanist subject – they threaten with 'information overload'. In the same sense, globalization does not produce either dreaded or desired cultural homogeneity, because the community of human subjects whose consensus would be necessary to actually be able to experience a 'global consensus' is destroyed by the very process of globalization and informatization. Globalization, one could argue, is inherently posthumanist because at the very moment something like 'humanity' seems geographically and representationally realizable, the 'referent' of this humanity disappears and dissolves into its constituents and its others.

As a result of this analysis a clear distinction between 'technical' and 'cultural' posthumanization is no longer feasible. This is also reflected in the development of cultural studies itself. One way of making sense of the development of cultural studies, which also takes into account the idea of it being an inherently political project, is by looking at the succession of its institutional and interdisciplinary conceptual 'wars': the canon wars, theory wars, culture wars and, finally, the 'science wars' (in each case, these 'wars' were, respectively, fought over the meaning of literary, cultural, etc. canons of knowledge and values, or over the notions of theory, culture and science). Originally, cultural studies was designed as a cultural political counter attack on educational politics that were too exclusive and class-specific, and migrated from adult working-class education initiatives in the UK towards departments of English, where its main effect was the 'explosion' of the literary canon by the use of a generalized notion of 'text' or 'textuality'. This helped to transpose literary reading techniques developed in hermeneutics and phenomenology onto all culturally produced, signifying practices and objects. During the generalized 'theory wars' English (and, in the USA, comparative literature) departments transformed themselves into strongholds of poststructuralism and theory (a mixture of Lacanian psychoanalysis, Althusserian Marxism, Barthesian semiotics of everyday life, Foucauldian analyses of power and Derridean deconstruction). In the 'culture wars' an anthropological and descriptive or non-normative notion of culture (culture as 'a way of life' among many others) imposed itself, and, in combination with poststructuralist theory, the task of English or literature departments developed from the study of literature and language to text-based cultural criticism. This critical and cultural theory or cultural studies approach takes advantage of the newly 'discovered' readability of the entire world, which is seen as proof of its 'constructedness' and 'arbitrariness'. On the other hand, the democratization of culture and cultural change become cultural studies' main objective. To this effect, cultural studies not only embraces a linguistic-textual approach, but it also employs speculative-philosophical and social theory and media analysis and practice, as well as a more sociological, social empirical aspect. In this interdisciplinary constellation the idea of cultural studies has entered universities in the English-speaking world in many guises and within many disciplines (or, rather, non- or post-disciplines) by multiplying the forms of 'studies', from 'legal studies' to 'science studies', or from 'women studies' to 'religious studies', 'film' and 'media studies', etc. The paradoxical outcome of the culture wars is, according to Readings, the 'disciplining' and institutionalization of cultural studies as such, on the basis of the dereferentialization of culture already pointed out:

> Cultural Studies arises as a quasi-discipline once culture ceases to be the animating principle of the University and becomes instead one object of study among others. The problem of participation becomes most acutely the object of reflection when we no longer know what it would mean to participate, when there is no longer any obvious citadel to be captured.
>
> (Readings 1996: 118)

In opposition to this, the task for 'posthumanist' cultural studies would be a coming to terms with the loss of meaning and loss of reference in culture, which could be taken as an alternative starting point for developing a key role for the 'posthumanities' in the posthumanist university of tomorrow.

However, the ascendancy of cultural studies was halted quite abruptly by the 'science wars' in the 1990s and in particular by a return of a debate originally launched by C. P. Snow about the 'two cultures' – or, the idea of an unbridgeable gap between the humanities and the sciences. From the point of view of cultural studies, the science wars are the logical continuation of the democratization of culture, which should include all social 'discourses'. Science from a culturalist point of view is first and foremost a cultural practice, which tries to gain legitimation through a specialized discourse, and which uses the knowledge it produces to gain social power. Science is helped in this by political, economic and military forms of agency and institutions. What is questioned is therefore not so much scientific knowledge as such but, for example, the role of the scientist as a cultural subject and his or her relationship with the scientific institution. Other aspects under scrutiny would be the role of the scientific institution in relation to other social institutions, and the selection process at work in the production of knowledge as such. Questions therefore arise concerning the role of scientific 'narratives', ideologies and 'constructions' of truth and reality; the role of sociopolitical structures within science – questions of gender, institutional racism at work in science as practice and science as institution, or the speciesist legitimation of animal testing, and economic and military interests in the development of new technologies, the importance of science fiction in the production of knowledge and so on. All these aspects might be grouped under Bruno Latour's phrase 'politics of the lab'. In addition, an important aspect for cultural criticism of scientific practice lies in the public self-presentation of science and scientists, the history of science and the analysis of popularizations of scientific knowledge (for example, in popular science magazines or television programmes, as discussed above) – all this might be implied in the phrase: 'the cultural construction of knowledge and science'.

From the point of view of the sciences this might merely be seen as the latest 'provocation' in a long list of 'arrogant' and snobbish attempts to critique science from a humanities and popular culture position. Two culprits easily identified and targeted are 'postmodernism' and 'radical constructivism', which 'illegitimately' subject scientific processes of knowledge production to hermeneutic analysis. The battle lines are thus quickly drawn between truth and reality as social or cultural constructs and a more or less uncritical realism which remains convinced of the notion of empirical objectivity and the existence of a naturally 'given' reality, independent of human perception.

This contest, which is not purely philosophical but has concrete social and economic implications in the form of funding decisions and popular as well as political support, has been aggravated by the so-called 'Sokal Hoax'. In 1996, Alan Sokal, a New York University professor of physics, managed to place an article in the influential cultural theory journal *Social Text*, entitled 'Transgressing the Boundaries: Toward a Transformative Hermeneutics of Quantum Gravity'. This article, at least from the point of view of physics, was a 'parody', full of postmodernist jargon as well as 'physicist nonsense'. The editors printed the article because of their lack of knowledge of science (so, in effect, out of (misplaced) 'respect' for physicist expert knowledge) and because of their enthusiasm for a perceived congeniality (thus in hope of an interdisciplinary encounter). The article was subsequently 'exposed' as a hoax by Sokal in *Lingua Franca* and the editors of *Social Text* were stigmatized as representatives of a 'scientistic', misguided, 'leftist' social science clique which has been 'deradicalized' by postmodernist constructivism. A highly polemical and largely destructive debate about the importance of expert knowledge ensued in the international press (cf. *Lingua Franca* 2000). Sokal teamed up with a Belgian scientist, Jean Bricmont, to publish in France – presumably to take the polemic back to its perceived 'origin' – a generalized attack on the main figures within Anglo-American 'French Theory' and its misuse of scientific metaphors: *Impostures intellectuelles* [Intellectual Impostures]. Apart from venting their anger at cultural theorists who adorn themselves wrongly with scientific credit without having any detailed knowledge of the scientific context, Sokal and Bricmont criticized the rampant 'epistemological relativism, as well as the idea that modern science is merely a "myth", a "narrative" or a social "construction" among many others' (Sokal and Bricmont 1999: 10).

However, even if the intention behind the parody might have been motivated by serious political ideas, like the liberation of the humanities and social sciences from immobilism and the excesses of postmodernism, its relativism of values in particular and its radical anti-enlightenment stance, it was interesting to see that it also demonstrated the level of internationalization at work in movements like theory or postmodernism (the attacked French intellectuals, for example, did not recognize themselves in what was in fact an Anglo-American translation, appropriation, homogenization and institutionalization of their work). On the other hand, it turned out to be quite counter-productive from the point of view of scientific practice (if the Sokal Hoax had aimed for greater 'interdisciplinary' knowledge and understanding between humanities and the sciences, the effect has arguably been the exact opposite). In the end, Sokal's and Bricmont's absolutely legitimate question – What is specific about scientific discourse? – was perceived as 'status anxiety' and as an attempt to police 'scientific correctness'. This was, of course, also due to the fact that Sokal and Bricmont were very eager to show the metaphorical 'misuse' of scientific concepts by humanities scholars without being prepared to engage with the equivalent specificity of cultural theory's concepts, as, for example, in Derrida's *différance* or Lacan's use of *jouissance*. In the end, the discussion just petered out in the form of a quasi-agreement about the untranslatability of 'language use' and thus practically led to a reinscription and confirmation of the traditional gap between two mutually exclusive 'language games' or social discourses. While scientists tend to question the epistemological status of hermeneutics as such, language-oriented critical and cultural theorists, as a result of the 'linguistic turn', tend to exaggerate the blindness of science to its own metaphoricity and its dependence on language, the role of symbolism in the production of knowledge and in the description of scientific 'reality'. The result of the science wars was probably a paralyzing stalemate.

However, it is quite clear that within the context of progressive posthumanization referred to above an understanding between the 'new' sciences, and the life sciences in particular, and the 'new' humanities, social sciences and cultural studies (located in the emerging 'posthumanities' or, also, 'digital humanities') will be becoming ever more important. And so will interdisciplinary practice. Vincent B. Leitch expresses the need for a 'postmodern' (or maybe 'posthumanist') interdisciplinarity as follows:

> From a postmodern perspective, 'interdisciplinarity' has two very different forms. In its most ambitious modern version, it dreams of the end of the disciplines of knowledge with their hideous jargons and false divisions of knowledge; it wants to unify the disciplines, rendering them transparent. But insofar as postmodern thinking seeks to multiply the differences and respect heterogeneities, the recent proliferation of (inter)disciplines is an encouraging turn. The postmodern version of interdisciplinarity seeks, therefore, not to unify or totalize, but to respect the differences.
>
> (Leitch 2003: 170)

It is thus rather a 'contamination' of disciplines, a hybridity and translation, than some fictive 'purity' of disciplinary reduction of knowledge, and not a transdiciplinary dissolution or transgression or even less a dialectical transcendence of disciplines that is at stake. If, for example, science is analysed as a cultural practice, new and hybrid forms of knowledge arise, which, on the one hand, question traditional disciplinary forms of knowledge, but at the same time complement them. Because of its hybridity or contamination, this new knowledge sometimes also manages to create 'third spaces' between disciplines (from an institutional point of view these are mostly located in 'centres', 'clusters', graduate schools or the so-called Institutes of Advanced Study at research intensive universities), which represent contact zones in which the temporary transgression of disciplinary boundaries is being strategically encouraged. Even in 1979 Lyotard saw interdisciplinarity as a central element of the 'deligitimation' of the humanist grand narrative he was describing. However, he did so with a certain level of scepticism:

> The idea of an interdisciplinary approach is specific to the age of deligitimation and its hurried empiricism. The relation to knowledge is not articulated in terms of the realization of the life of the spirit or the emancipation of humanity, but in terms of the users of a complex conceptual and material machinery and those

who benefit from its performance capabilities. They have at their disposal no metalanguage or metanarrative in which to formulate the final goal and correct use of that machinery. But they do have brainstorming to improve its performance. The emphasis placed on teamwork is related to the predominance of the performativity criterion in knowledge.

(Lyotard 1991: 52)

A central aspect in this is the absence of a transcendental metadisciplinarity which inevitably would lead to the legitimation of a new grand narrative. In the age of advanced posthumanization a critical posthumanism has to make sure that the dissemination of new forms of interdisciplinarity, for example in the new life sciences, does not lead to new forms of knowledge exclusion. Without doubt humanities and cultural studies scholars have valuable aspects to add to the question of 'life'. Similarly, on the other hand, cultural studies and cultural theory do not own the monopoly on the phenomenon of 'culture'. They will have to seek a dialogue with neuro- and cognitive scientists and evolutionary psychologists whose explanations, as far as the meaning and evolution of culture is concerned, provide an important corrective from 'outside' – a perspective which alone can prevent everything from becoming 'culture' or a 'cultural construct' and thus, ultimately, being devoid of any meaning. There is thus at the very heart of interdisciplinarity a danger of totalizing knowledge as soon as it becomes institutionalized or '(re)disciplined'. Therefore, a critical posthumanism, as far as interdisciplinarity is concerned, does not focus on the desire for disciplinary establishment but merely on the investigation of objects constructed by a variety of discourses – or so-called 'interdisciplinary objects', like, for example, 'culture', 'human', 'technology', 'identity', 'science', 'life', etc. – from as many angles as possible. In this sense, Readings also calls for the dissolution of all disciplinary boundaries but he adds that 'the loosening of disciplinary structures has to be made the opportunity for the installation of disciplinarity as a *permanent question*' (Readings 1996: 177). For, the return of the knowledge gained through interdisciplinarity is always also a challenge to disciplinary tradition and thus constitutes an intradisciplinary, political issue. It is also, however, the trigger of necessary renewal, expansion, flexibility and restructuring.

Interdisciplinarity is always a very specific, historically and socially contextualized, transgression of particular disciplinary boundaries and in this sense the current situation, in which the question of the human is increasingly formulated in the language of 'technologization', interdisciplinarity represents a concrete challenge to the humanities, inviting them to turn into 'posthumanities' in order to create the necessary foundations for an interdisciplinary dialogue with the posthumanizing new (life) sciences. This is crucial to avoid the emergence of a new monopoly in relation to the question 'What does it mean to be human?' On the other hand, this also means that the humanities and cultural studies must be able to critically engage with scientific practice, as, for example, in the so-called 'critical science studies' ('technocultural studies' or 'cultural studies of science').

Seen from an interdisciplinary point of view, the culturalist observation of science starts from the assumption that technics, technology and science are interdisciplinary objects whose knowledge production is governed by a competition of explanation. In the age of accelerated technologization, technoculture and technoscientific capitalism (i.e. the nexus of science, technology, politics and economy), the interdisciplinary object called 'technology' generates exactly the kind of critical discourse we have called 'critical posthumanism', namely a critical return to the role of technics in the process of becoming human (or hominization). It is thus a question of finding out how the technology changes and subverts the epistemological foundations of disciplinary practice and cultural analysis. The complexity of the relations between technology, science and culture thus form the starting point for critical science studies:

> Technology shapes culture; science epistemologically grounds technology; science as an epistemology presupposes the technological; (techno)culture produces (techno)science; culture is always technological but not always scientific, and so on. Furthermore, science often legitimates one cultural practice over another as in the normative approach to physiology in which science distinguishes/legitimates what is 'natural' and prescribes corrective therapy for what it deems 'unnatural'.
>
> (Aronowitz and Menser 1996: 7)

Some of the most prominent aspects of these forms of investigation therefore concern the analysis of technics and technology as a connection between science and culture.

Technology is generally seen as a phenomenon of modernity in the sense that modern science develops technologies which it uses for its own further knowledge production, which, in turn, is seen as social progress. Modernity is thus, for example, unthinkable without the Industrial Revolution, and the Industrial Revolution cannot be explained without technological innovation, like the steam engine, the mechanical weaving loom, etc. These technologies in turn depend on scientific discoveries (for example, electricity). Modern technology is thus more or less the practical use or application of scientific knowledge. In this sense, technology as a 'human invention' or as 'artificial' is diametrically opposed to 'nature', which it controls and transforms. Originally, however, the word 'technology' is derived from the Greek *technē*, which means art or craft, and *logos*, meaning knowledge or reason. Some contemporary philosophers of technics are trying to reconnect to this early understanding of technology. Philosophy of technics, however, is not merely thinking about technology. Technics is a much broader term which includes all human techniques, swimming techniques for example, or the ability to express oneself with style (rhetoric is amongst other things a 'technique'). In order to apply a specific technology, a number of techniques are presupposed in the (human, or indeed nonhuman) 'operator'. What happens in late modernity, at the advanced stage of rationalization and automation, so to speak, is that, on the one hand, the human operator because of his or her technical abilities merges ever more closely with certain technologies (i.e. cyborgization, which, however, occurs not just at a strictly physical level but also, maybe even primarily, at a mental and psychological level); on the other hand, with the increase of automation the degree of technological autonomy also rises. When computers are networked with each other, they 'communicate' and take 'decisions' without human subjects getting involved in the process (which constitutes the 'virtualization' process that accompanies (digital) cyborgization). As this development continues, the object-world becomes 'smart' and thus humans, willingly, for reasons of convenience or time saving, might make themselves dependent on these technologies, which, in turn, increasingly leave humans out of their information loops. This can happen to an extent where one could say, with N. Katherine Hayles in *My Mother Was a Computer* (2005), that the translation of the environment by intelligent machines into (digital) 'code' that is understood by fewer and fewer people, is creating a gigantic 'technological unconscious' which might one day come back to haunt 'humanity'.

This form of technoapocalypse is also the standard scenario for an understanding of posthumanity which has been popularized by science fiction films like *Terminator (1984)*, where, similar to the effects of trauma, the humanity of the 'future' in which machines and humans are fighting a deadly war of survival, travels back into the past to reverse the original handing over of power from humans to artificial intelligence or to rewrite history after the fact. Ironically, this can only be achieved with *more* technology, which leads to the necessary differentiation between 'good' and 'evil' technologies, or at least 'good' or 'evil' use of technology by the 'liberal humanist subject', whose task it is to choose between these two forms. The contradiction is obvious: on the one hand, technology is what 'spoils' the human, on the other hand, it is also that which leads the 'good' human to greater insight and freedom. In this sense the history of the relationship between 'humans' and 'technology' becomes a history of 'taming', which, in turn, emphasizes the analogy between the animal and the machine established by Descartes (cf. Sloterdijk 2001). The fear by humans of being replaced by their quasi 'natural' evolutionary successor, the machine, or artificial intelligence, is a symptom of 'technoculture', which, however, merely constitutes its logical conclusion (cf. for example Truong 2001; Dyens 2008). The fact that this mainly informational vision is occurring at the same time as the rise of biotechnology is no coincidence. Human environment is undergoing a technological alienation process and this includes what is most 'proper', the innermost *bios* of humans, which is being contested by genetics with its desire to 'map' and thus control the human genome. This is an alienation from a recoded environment in parallel with a decoding of the last human mystery, the secret of human identity to be found in the human genome, which, in a literal and economic-technological sense, is to be 'externalized' – all this makes the diverse horror stories, but also the positive utopias of 'our' imminent posthumanity, more than understandable.

In order to, on the one hand, relativize these horror visions and, on the other hand, to remind the neognostic techno-utopians of their responsibilities, a critical posthumanism has to produce a reevalutaion of technics and thus to appeal to a new ethics and politics 'after' humanism and 'outside' of modern technological determinism. Let us thus start with technics. As already mentioned, modern technologies should not be seen in opposition to but rather as extensions of techniques in the sense of abilities. Human culture is unthinkable without technics – without the technique of making fire, hunting, tool making and the developing of symbolic code systems for communication and the transmission of knowledge something like 'humanity' would not have been able to emerge (cf. for example Stiegler 1998). This does not necessarily or 'automatically' lead to an anthropocentric view, because animal communities without doubt have their complex techniques, arguably with the exception of complex techniques of symbolic coding, which enable humans to use abstraction and 'dematerialized' information technologies, which, in turn, allow for extension across time and space. Culture in a sense is therefore always 'technoculture', namely achieved and transmitted by technics. One could argue that as a result of the verbalization of cultural techniques the kind of potential is released that is necessary to objectify and externalize these techniques. As soon as one is able to think about a specific technique at an abstract level, it becomes possible to instrumentalize and refine it and to transfer it, for example, onto objects, which will lead in turn to a 'tooling' and rationalizing process. It is, therefore, not surprising that Martin Heidegger's notion of technology has become highly influential again. Let us recall here that Heidegger's main claim is that 'the essence of technology is by no means anything technological', but metaphysical or even 'poetic' (cf. Heidegger 1978: 311). Dominique Lecourt interprets this in the following words: 'Technics corresponds to a certain attitude of reason towards the world, in which reason feels compelled to place the resources the world offers at the disposal of human being' (2003: 40–1). The human species, therefore, does not need to adapt to its environment but instead transforms its environment according to its needs:

> The essence of technics if one wishes to use this term is this: thanks to technics the human who separates itself from its

animality but also retains it, can see itself no longer as a pure being of necessity, nor as a being of rationality but as a being of desire, who within the contest with its 'milieu', which turns into its 'environment' (i.e. the milieu of all milieus), uses cunning and calculation to elude its inherent powerlessness and thus to correspond to the insatiable aspirations which its imagination constantly evokes.

(Lecourt 2003: 42; *my translation*)

What the notion of technics also makes clear is the inseparability of technology and culture, and of the individual and technology, or what Gilbert Simondon (1964) called 'individuation', which later is taken up by Michel Foucault and reinscribed in the notion of 'technologies of the self' in the context of modern society. Humans 'individuate' themselves by means of technical interaction and adaptation to their respective object and social environment. New technologies like, for example, the mobile phone cause new relations to emerge with the environment and within human sociality, which every single user through acquiring certain techniques uses for his or her own individuation, or for the manifestation of his or her own individuality:

The human type who develops with the mobile phone has not really exhausted its full potential. However, it already differs from its predecessor for whom this object was unknown. This is not because it was missing a capacity which it today has but because its being as such – namely its becoming – has been profoundly changed, whether this may be its 'objective' relation to time or the entirety of its affective relationships to others – absence, waiting, impatience, jealousy, love – have found in this technical object a possibility to refine and to extend the spectrum and the logic of emotions, whose expressions they are ... No, technics is not outside human life. It emerges from life and finds a place in it, constructs its norms within it and inserts them into it. This positioning means that technics is the instigator of individuation, which concerns both the object and the subject.

(Lecourt 2003: 87–8; *my translation*)

To understand the essence of technology it is important to see the continuity and the interconnectedness of humans, culture and technology. What constitutes the specificity of that relation between humans and technology within the history of technics in the late twentieth and early twenty-first centuries is not so much a radical break but an intensification and, above all, an 'economization' of this relationship. The principles of rationality and progress inherent to modernity, on the one hand, and the commodification of technical objects, on the other hand, are changing and intensifying the original and foundational 'cyborgization' into the modern form of 'individuation' as such. What should be referred to under the term of technoscience or technoscientific capitalism rather than technoculture is a complex of political, military, economic and scientific interests which constitutes the modern state, and which intervenes through its institutions between the individual and technology. What happens under the conditions of globalization, however – with its related changes in the role of the nation-state – is a partial regaining of people's own individuation through new technologies like the internet and new and social media. However, this also leads to intensified mediation between humans and their individuation (cf. the virtualization process already mentioned) via information technologies, which are in the process of transforming the historically specific form of individuation predominant within modernity, namely the so-called 'liberal humanist subject', into a new, namely 'posthumanist' understanding of individuation (or 'posthumanization').

This happens in conjunction with the already mentioned biotechnological 'externalization' of posthumanization: 'the way in which one becomes a singular human being is changing as soon as there are technologies which control the birth (or non-birth) of a future being' (Lecourt 2003: 94). In this sense, the cloning of humans threatens to radicalize a development that has been in process ever since, in the 1960s, modern contraception and thus birth control became widely available, namely the 'decoupling' of sexuality, love and intimacy from reproduction. While this differentiation has certainly created new forms of individuation, new biotechnologies also harbour the danger of a 'mediacalization' of human procreation, whose potential risk is at least as big as the informatization of the human environment outlined above. The role of biotechnology in the process of posthumanization will be dealt with in a later chapter. At this point, however, we are still concerned with the clarification of the terms 'technoculture' and 'technoscience' and the ethical and political task these pose for a critical posthumanism. Together with Lecourt, we would maintain that this task first and foremost lies in resisting any form of determinism, be it biologically, technologically or politically and ideologically motivated. Neither stories of human enslavement nor of liberation by technology but rather stories of hybridization and co-implication will be able to do justice to the necessarily 'reflexive' relationship between humans and technology.

Reflexivity and co-implication between humans and technology (what might be termed the *longue durée* view of human cyborgization) can safely be assumed to have become the dominant view in critical and cultural theory. We are thus positioned between two forms of technological determinism, the one that is dominant in modern science, and the other, the cultural pessimist one, based on the autonomy of technology and technics, which can be found in the work of techno-sceptics like Jacques Ellul or Martin Heidegger. Ellul begins his main analysis of technology, *Le Système technicien* (originally in 1977) by saying: 'Technics is not content with merely *existing*, not even with being the *principal factor* or destiny of our world. It has itself become a system' (Ellul 2004: 13; my translation). The implied system analysis announced in this statement will be the focus of the final chapter of our study. At this point we will merely investigate the deterministic view of technology in relation to the notion of 'technoculture'. Ellul, the sociologist, perceives an entirely different attitude towards processes in modern technocultural societies, which leads to the rationalization processes that affect all aspects of humans living together. Under these circumstances, the technical is about much more than just mere 'skill' or 'craft', but instead it has become the true subject of history. It is technology that drives scientific, economic and social development: the technical, for Ellul, is pure functionality. What he has in common with Heidegger is that the proper or essential of technology is nothing technological as such but merely a kind of *telos* or ontological mode of 'unconcealment of being'. What is characteristic for technology, however, according to Ellul, is the elimination of choice – and hence also the autonomy of technology, which takes its own decisions. The moralizing conclusions that Heidegger as well as Ellul draw from this, ironically, are almost 'automatic' with their typical apocalyptism, which dominated the 'nuclear age' of the Cold War.

In his 'Letter on Humanism' Heidegger explains that technology is an integral part of the age of metaphysics:

> Technology is in its essence a destiny within the history of Being and of the truth of Being, a truth that lies in oblivion. For technology does not go back to the *technē* of the Greeks in name only but derives historically and essentially from *technē* as a mode of *alētheuein*, a mode, that is, of rendering beings manifest [*Offenbarmachen*]. As a form of truth technology is grounded in the history of metaphysics, which is itself a distinctive and up to now the only perceptible phase of the history of Being.
>
> (Heidegger 1978 [1947]: 244)

For Heidegger, one might think, the hope for a posthumanism would lie outside technology (cf. also our demand elsewhere for a 'posthumanism without technology' – Herbrechter and Callus 2007) or at least in an ethics that would be prepared to think through the technological 'captivity' of humans. This thinking would have to start from the premise already mentioned, namely that the essence of technology is nothing technological. As opposed to the widespread 'instrumental' definition of technology, Heidegger develops a cultural anthropological or 'poetic' understanding. To generate, to discover and to challenge these are the modes of technology, which 'enframes' the human within its *Ge-stell* [enframing], over which humans do not have ultimate control:

> I see the essence of technology in what I call the frame [*das Ge-stell*], an expression which has often been laughed at and is perhaps somewhat clumsy. The frame holding sway means: the essence of man is framed, claimed, and challenged by a power which manifests itself in the essence of technology, a power which man himself does not control. To help with this realization is all that one can expect of thought. Philosophy is at an end.
>
> (Heidegger 1993 [1966]: 107)

Cybernetics, or 'the other thinking', thus takes the place of philosophy whereas the essence of technology threatens to become 'unthinkable' as such.

Heidegger sees the 'task of thinking' in obtaining an 'adequate relationship with the essence of technology' – a task that has become more and more urgent given the 'planetary' extension of technology. It is worth stressing, however, that Heidegger does not see technology as a 'destiny that cannot be disentangled or escaped', but it is also not something that 'man can master by himself' (Heidegger 1993 [1966]: 105). It is precisely in this context that Heidegger claims that we have not yet really begun thinking (Heidegger 1978 [1947]: 341–68). What is called thinking, or what calls for thinking, thus relates closely to the question of posthumanism and the 'future of thinking' – human and nonhuman – it could be argued. In fact, Heidegger's question, in the age of cognitive science and biotechnology, has taken on a new 'edge'. The question of What is called thinking/What calls for thinking? [*Was heißt Denken?*] therefore returns with some urgency onto the scene of thinking. The ambiguity of the questions – What does it mean to think? and What is the origin of or what 'provokes' thinking? – might have become even more relevant than it was some 60 years ago. Who or what calls for thinking, or calls whom or what to 'think'? If posthumanism is a rethinking of the human – as we have been arguing, with special emphasis on 'critical posthumanism' and 'posthumanism without technology' – thinking (the posthuman) remains an *Aufgabe* – a task and a surrender (in analogy with Walter Benjamin's task [*Aufgabe*] of the translator, who, necessarily has to surrender or abandon 'himself' to complete 'his' task). Does thinking thus necessarily have to betray itself? This is what Heidegger seems to imply in confronting the classical humanist definition of 'man' as the *animal rationale*, as that being which has the possibility to think. But thinking is to remain a possibility, and hence a task, a call, but also, possibly, a self-abandonment. Just like the radical openness of the human, his or her innermost and essential characteristics are, at the same time, always already implied while they also remain unattained and unattainable. For Heidegger, the task of thinking is thus a 'recollection' of thinking that focuses on the *zu-Bedenkende* [that which remains to be thought *and* that which is the most alarming]. The radical relevance of (future) thought which is posed in the question 'What calls for thinking?' aims at that which is most alarming, which remains to be thought and which is the real motivation behind the call for thinking. What remains most unthought and most alarming in this question thus remains to be thought. For Heidegger, this task was located in the 'forgetting of Being in metaphysics', the 'end of humanism' and 'the question concerning technology'. In this sense, posthumanist and maybe even more so 'posthuman' thought – thinking 'after' the human and 'outside' the human – remains the most unthought and alarming task and surrender.

In the light of this, a critical posthumanism would have to take up the Heideggerian challenge to think the essence of technology as something non-technical (which 'calls for thinking'), as well as to engage with cybernetics and its 'machine thinking' in order to establish what would for Heidegger be an 'adequate' relationship to the essence of *technē*. Some starting points can be found, on the one hand, in Bernard Stiegler's work on the philosophy of technics, which is influenced both by Simondon and Derrida, and, on the other hand, in the sociology of technology and critical science studies, and especially, in the work of Bruno Latour. Simondon's influential concepts regarding the first of these two approaches are individuation and 'transduction'. While transduction designates the multiplicity of (psycho- or neurobiological) amalgamations between humans, tools and technics, which problematizes any simple subject-object relation (especially as far as the boundaries between human body and the 'externality' of tools, machines and so on is concerned – cf. also Marcel Mauss 1934; Leroi-Gourhan 1945, 1964–5), technology forms the very condition of hominization within the process of individuation. The individual is the sum of its (social, cultural and individual-psychic) 'technical' abilities, which make it into the individual that it is in the first place. It does so, however, in the form of an ongoing process and not in opposition to a society or community, but in constant negotiation with these. In a similar way, *technē* is always already inscribed as a 'trace' or Derridean *différance* within the human and its difference (to other humans and nonhumans, the world, objects, etc.). The history of the relationship between human and *technē* is thus a history of the continuing deconstruction of the opposition between human and (nonhuman) technologies, always already in relation to a repressed and inaccessible 'technical' origin, which Derrida calls 'archi-écriture and which lies outside the metaphysical differentiation between writing and voice (or even between human and nonhuman, e.g. animals) but which makes Western phono- and logocentrism possible in the first place (cf. Derrida 1997 [1967], 2002b [1967]).

Bruno Latour's sociotechnical approach to the relation between human, culture and technology presupposes an interactive model between humans and their environment, which means that there are human and nonhuman actors (or actants), and, in particular, 'actants that offer the possibility of holding society together as a durable whole' (Latour 1991: 103). Social history and the history of technology, therefore, have to be taken together, especially for an understanding of modernity, because, as Latour explains, 'technology is society made durable ... we might call technology the moment when social assemblages gain stability by aligning actors and observers. Society and technology are not two ontologically different entities but more like phases of the same essential action' (Latour 1991: 129). The most important epistemological strategies for modernity – purification and translation (cf. Latour 1993) – have to be thought of in conjunction, in order to problematize the opposition between nature and culture. Latour's actor (social) network theory (ANT) thus claims that science and society 'construct' each other and are therefore real and fictional at the same time. Both produce their hybrid 'monsters', which they subsequently go about 'purifying'.

Another prominent aspect of the cultural theoretical and technical historical approach can be seen in the analyses of cultural construction within scientific discourse. This approach understands science as a social institution – an institution which is part of the power struggle between politics, economics, militarization and commodification – which positions scientific 'subjects', namely scientists (as experts, producers and 'senders' of scientifically sanctioned knowledge, or as 'knowing' subjects; and thus their 'addressees' or receivers of the scientific discourse as 'lay' subjects). It is, therefore, quite legitimate to analyse the communication processes within and between scientific institutions as well as between scientific and other institutions (for example, politics and government, the military or the economy) and to evaluate the ethics and politics at work in these discourses. This gives rise to another aspect for analysis, namely the question of to what extent everyday life practices are changing due to the influence of technoscience. Again the spectrum stretches from anthropological descriptive to analytically ethical and politically activist interventions. In this context, for example, the figure of the scientist is at the centre of investigations within critical science studies. The social stereotypes of scientists move between demonization of the 'mad scientist' to the adulation of scientists as modern reincarnations of Prometheus.

The increasing bureaucratization of science and of its relation to the individual subject already formed the critical starting point for Neil Postman's study of the phenomenon of 'technocracy' – understood as the rule of technocrats, and the resulting new form of social organization, the 'technopolis' (cf. Postman 1993). The result of this analysis need not be as apocalyptic as in Postman's case, of course, who attacked the 'ideology of the machines' (his examples were the medicalization and computerization of society) and the rise of 'scientism'. Nevertheless, posthumanization also means a new relation between the individual and forms of (Foucauldian) 'governmentality', namely changed attitudes and practices towards how this new posthuman or at least posthumanist individual is supposed to be governed or administrated. A central lever for a critical posthumanism is, similar to Postman, and Aronowitz or Williams, the denaturalization of the myth of autonomous technology and technological determinism. But postcolonial and feminist aspects also find their legitimate place in critical science studies, for modernity, as the birthplace and rise of modern science, is also the period of scientific exploitation of ethnic "minorities' and their intellectual and material resources (i.e. colonialism and cultural imperialism) and the scientific development of 'technologies of the self' (Foucault), which tend to inscribe fixed gender and racial differences (cf. Alice Jardine's notion of 'gynesis' – Jardine 1986). A critical and cultural analysis of historical and contemporary scientific practices thus also opens up the question of exclusion within knowledge production (and thus the question of the 'Westernization' of knowledge through modern science and the oppression of non-Western forms of knowledge production; cf. Foucault's notion of 'subjugated knowledges'), as well as the question of practical discrimination in scientific institutions (i.e. preconceptions as far as gender or race are concerned, with all the hierarchical effects in the institutional politics at work in science as well as their effects on the ongoing selection within knowledge production itself).

Furthermore, critical science studies also investigate the phenomenon of scientific innovation (cf. for example Nowotny 1999) and of 'emergence'. Questions relating to the selection of scientific discoveries and their dissemination, financing, cultural acceptance and commodification, for example, play a part in this process, as much as the role of the innovative subject, i.e. the scientist in the process of scientific discovery and the creation of an innovation-friendly environment. In all these analyses not only issues relating to scientific practice and issues inherent to science are at stake, but also aspects of the cultural context in which they take place. There are, of course, philosophical, epistemological and ethical questions concerning innovation and invention, as, for example, the question of how to 'overcome' the structural horizon of the 'unforeseeably new' (cf. Derrida's notion of the future as *à venir* [to come] and the *arrivant*, e.g. in Derrida 1994a, 1994b, 2001a). Attempts to explain emergence, or the idea that technological and scientific innovation merely and unpredictably 'arises' through a complex combination of factors, which make controlling the process impossible, only heightens the need for ethical questions related to the 'politics of in(ter)vention' (Derrida 1989a). This can be seen quite clearly in a couple of examples: the power struggle over 'human nature', the question concerning the technological evolution and the aspect of a posthuman or indeed nonhuman 'culture' that might arise out of the interaction between human and nonhuman actors (cf. Latour 2005). The following pages will analyse each of these examples in some more detail.

First, the argument about human nature in the age of biotechnology, eugenics and human cloning. Francis Fukuyama in *Our Posthuman Future* (2002) looks at the 'consequences of the biotechnological revolution', which has undermined his earlier post-Hegelian thesis of the end of history after the fall of the Berlin Wall, the end of the Soviet Union and the victory of liberal democracy on a global scale. In Chapter 6, 'Why We Should Worry', Fukuyama invokes the 'specter of eugenics'. Aspects of contemporary gene technology contain the possibility of isolating, changing and filtering genes. 'Natural' reproduction thus becomes an old-fashioned thing and human birth becomes a matter of 'breeding': 'In future we will likely be able to breed human beings much as we breed animals, only far more scientifically and effectively, by selecting which genes we pass on to our children' (Fukuyama 2002: 88). Fukuyama is concerned about the 'dehumanizing potential' of gene technology and about individual freedom in the face of powerful utilitarian and scientific ideologies. Consequently, he raises religious, economic and philosophical points of criticism against this dehumanizing threat posed by eugenics. Fukuyama's religious concerns have to be seen in the predominantly US-American context of the debate about 'pro-life' (anti-abortionism), creationism and the question of 'intelligent design'. According to this view, all the great monotheistic religions believe in a clear difference between human and nonhuman creation, which alone allows humans to develop morality, free will and faith and thus places them above all other species (human exceptionalism). This religious humanism is based on the 'inviolability of human dignity' and is ultimately guaranteed by the transcendence of God, which, in effect, turns gene technology into a violation of the will of God. Fukuyama is right, of course, to remind us that the combination of scientific modernity, rationalism and secularization is a specifically Western or European model of development, which is thus not 'natural' or universal *per se*. This also means that the long-standing argument between the spiritual religious and the material empirical models of explanation of the human form of 'being' cannot be seen as definitively settled. Economically speaking, as with any other technological innovation, gene technology also contains unforeseen social costs, which purely technocratic calculations usually fail to take into account. A central question therefore, which is also posed by Jürgen Habermas in his contribution to the debate, *The Future of Human Nature* (2003; the German subtitle reads *Auf dem Weg zu einer liberalen Eugenik?* [Towards Liberal Eugenics?]), is the special status of human embryos, who must always experience any form of genetic manipulation without prior consent. What about legal claims in this case? There is also the danger that new forms of social discrimination through gene manipulation and genetic filtering arise (as the already discussed science fiction film *Gattaca* illustrates quite vividly, under 'genoism' or genetic determinism). It is thus absolutely possible and quite likely that gene technology 'will embed one generation's social preferences in the next' (Fukuyama 2002: 94). Cultural norms that are currently subject to political discussion might thus become 'naturalized' by gene-technological practice, like' for example, current attitudes towards sexuality or ethnic identity, or ageing. This might lead to new forms of class wars (and thus to a rebirth of ideological history, in Fukuyama's post-Hegelian sense), namely in the oppression of a genetically 'natural' mass and a genetically modified elite. What is also worrisome is the question of who would have the power to decide on genetic manipulability: the state? the experts? the market? None of these options seems desirable for obvious reasons. Fukuyama, therefore, for all these reasons, draws the conclusion that a certain idea of human nature, in the face of the generalized anxiety about the consequences gene technology might have, should be preserved. The anxiety articulates that

> biotechnology will cause us in some way to lose our humanity — that is, the essential quality that has always underpinned our sense of who we are and where we are going, despite all of the evident changes that have taken place in the human condition through the course of history.
>
> (Fukuyama 2002: 101)

Fukuyama is concerned that the undermining of the idea of the (liberal humanist notion of) human nature might progress at an unconscious level and that 'we', at some stage, might find ourselves on the other side of an irreversible boundary transgression: 'We might thus emerge on the other side of a great divide between human and posthuman history and not even see that the watershed had been breached because we lost sight of what the essence was' (101). Human nature, instead, for Fukuyama, lies in the 'species-typical characteristics shared by all human beings qua human beings', and which stand in close connection with concepts like human 'rights, justice and morality'. What is thus at stake in the posthumanizing bio- and genetic technologies is not just religious 'superstition' and a utilitarian calculation of costs and benefits in relation to medical technologies, but 'the very grounding of the human moral sense, which has been a constant ever since there were human beings' (102).

In fact, the appeal of Fukuyama's argument lies quite ironically in its lack of historical awareness. The notions of human nature and humanity that Fukuyama wishes to recruit and indeed to universalize, already constituted the main target for 'antihumanist' theory's 'demystification' project in the second half of the twentieth century. The ideas which Fukuyama uses in his defence of a universal and essential, species-wide idea of nature and humanity are themselves products of Western colonial history and Western modernity and are therefore culturally specific, politically motivated and, for any presumed value-neutral universalism, highly problematic. Fukuyama's liberal humanist nostalgia is in fact more part of the problem than the solution to the current 'predicament'. At this precise point, a critical posthumanism will have to start mediating between the 'abandonment or task [*Aufgabe*]', on the one hand, and the 'transcendence' of human nature, on the other.

Habermas also uses liberal humanist language in his sceptical view of biotechnology and its new 'types of intervention':

> Up to now, both the secular thought of European modernity and religious belief could proceed on the assumption that the genetic endowment of the newborn infant, and thus the initial organic conditions for its future life history, lay beyond any programming and deliberate manipulation on the part of other persons ... A previously unheard-of interpersonal relationship arises when a person makes an irreversible decision about the natural traits of another person.
>
> (Habermas 2003: 13–14)

A critical posthumanism would agree with Habermas's position as far as new technologies impose 'a public discourse on the right understanding of cultural forms of life' and as a result, philosophers or theorists 'have no longer any good reasons for leaving such a dispute to biologists and engineers intoxicated by science-fiction' (15). Habermas, furthermore, lists 'pre-implant diagnostics' and stem cell research as the origin of a perspective of 'self-instrumentalization and self-optimization' (20), which coincides with 'globalized neoliberalism', and which represses the 'meaning, for our own life prospects and for our self-understanding as moral beings, of the proposition that the genetic foundations of our existence should not be disposed over' (22). Habermas fears thus the establishment of a 'liberal eugenics' which works against the autonomy of the politically and morally acting (modern) subject. This posthumanizing eugenics interrupts the 'life historical individuation' which occurs within 'socialization' and the possibility of a (purely anthropological and cultural) 'self-understanding of the species':

> This perspective inevitably gives rise to the question of whether the instrumentalization of human nature changes the ethical self-understanding of the species in such a way the we no longer see ourselves as ethically free and morally equal beings guided by norms and reasons.
>
> (40)

This leads Habermas on to his main question addressed to the representatives of a liberal eugenics, or, of what we have called, the biotechnological posthumanization of the human: 'Liberal eugenics needs to face the question of whether the *perceived* dedifferentiation of the grown and the made, the subjective and the objective, is likely to affect the autonomous conduct of life and moral self-understanding of the programmed person' (52). Both Fukuyama and Habermas are admittedly defending a 'myth', which they see as indispensible, however, for maintaining an essential idea of human nature. In Fukuyama's case this is called 'humanity' and serves as a universal principle for human community and morality; in Habermas, it is the principle of the autonomy of 'individual freedom', which turns human subjects into moral and social agents. The real challenge, we would propose, however, is to critically accompany the posthumanization process without having any recourse to an (ultimately, due to its inherent mystification, counterproductive) idea of human 'nature'.

A much more promising starting point that questions this underlying 'fateful solidarity' in humanism can be found in Peter Sloterdijk's interventions within the debate about human nature. In '*Rules for the Human Zoo: A Response to the Letter on Humanism*' (2009 [1999]) Sloterdijk starts from the close relation between humanism and 'telecommunication' (which, in particular, includes the culture of literacy and writing) and the connected principle of a canon of a 'national bourgeois humanism'. This leads to (what we would call 'posthumanist') changes within modern mass society, due to displacements and intensifications within telecommunicational technologies, towards an information or global network society. The turn away from traditional technologies of 'humanization', or 'anthropotechnics', as Sloterdijk calls them, provokes fears of 'contemporary tendencies towards the bestialization of humanity' (2009: 15), which, in turn, demand new 'techniques of taming' to counter the prospect of a (posthumanist) *homo inhumanus*. Sloterdijk thus understands the end, or the current crisis, of national bourgeois (or liberal) humanism mostly as a 'conflict between media':

> The question of humanism is more than the bucolic assumption that reading improves us. It is, rather, no less than an issue of anthropodicy: that is, a characterization of man with respect to his biological indeterminacy and his moral ambivalence.
>
> (16)

According to Sloterdijk, the philosophy of Heidegger forms a 'transhumanistic or posthumanistic space for thought', in which 'a considerable portion of philosophical consideration on man has taken place ever since' (17) and for which the human as such 'with his systems of metaphysical self-improvement and self-clarification' (17) has become the main problem. Following Sloterdijk's critical reading of Heidegger's *Über den Humanismus* (1949), the question arises, after the attempted taming of the human by humanism: '[W]hat can tame man, when the role of humanism as the school for humanity has collapsed?' (20). The human as that being which is characterized by its 'shattered animality', or as a being 'in which being an animal is separate from remaining an animal' (20), and which, through sedentarization has created a kind of 'coming-into-the world' and 'coming-to-language', and thus a certain 'being-with-itself', has reached a forking path within its taming and breeding politics – a break with or a jump within previous humanist 'anthropotechnology' (23). For a critical posthumanism, engaging with Sloterdijk, the task therefore arises to work through the domestication of the human as the 'great unthinkable, from which humanism from antiquity to the present has averted its eyes' (23) and to critically accompany the dissolution of traditional rules for the 'human zoo'.

In this context Sloterdijk's *Das Menschentreibhaus: Stichworte zur historischen und prophetischen Anthropologie* [The Human Greenhouse: Key Terms for a Historical and Prophetic Anthropology] (2001) refers to the 'taking hostage of societies by their advanced technologies' (2001: 12; my translation). One could understand this as the move from humanist 'anthropotechnology' towards the development of a posthumanist 'humanbiotechnology', in which Sloterdijk follows Heidegger's idea of technology as 'a kind of unconcealment [*Entbergen*]' and as *poiesis*, while the onto-anthropo-genesis of the human is not complete, but remains an open question:

> In order to better understand the origin and possibility of that which man, as the administrator of nuclear power and as the writer of genetic inscription, today performs, with the greatest effect on himself, we shall start again from the principle that man is a product – not completed product, of course, but a product open to further processing. We hasten to add that we do not know who or what the producer might be.
>
> (Sloterdijk 2001: 25; *my translation*)

Sloterdijk goes on to travel back into the history of evolution and discovers the first 'spheric spaces, which at first were mere animal group interior spaces', and which he sees as 'greenhouses' for human 'being-in-the-world' (30). Thus, for hominization, Sloterdijk suggests a co-involvement of a number of mechanisms (anthropotechnologies) like the insulation mechanism (or the 'greenhouse effect' produced by the creation of a human environment, or a biotope, and thus of a protected interior space required for human evolution); the mechanism of body disabling (which produces tool use and the human hand, and thus triggers so to speak the technologization of the human species); the mechanism he calls pedomorphosis or neotony (the progressive infantilization and retardation of the bodily form, which in turn allows for cerebralization, as well as the development of symbolic forms of representation, transmission and tradition of realities and environments and thus the beginnings of human 'culture'); the mechanism of transmission (which for Sloterdijk covers more or less the entire identity formation and differentiation between and within groups) and the mechanism of neocorticalization (32), which allows humans to overcome the principle of adaptation within evolution, and thus, once decoupled from it, allows them to effectuate changes within the environment which, in turn, promote human 'luxuration'. Sloterdijk understands this development as 'auto-domestication'. So-called 'secondary anthropotechnology', like, for example, genetic technology or modern biotechnology, thus constitutes the almost complete 'deactivation of natural selection' as the final goal of the human 'incubator evolution' (50). Sloterdijk's revaluation of human evolution culminates in the concept of 'homeotechnology' (59), mindful of the fact that 'the apocalypse of the human is an everyday experience' and that 'the expulsion from the habits of humanist appearance' is the 'logical main event of the present which one tries to escape through a flight into goodwill' (59). Contemporary (posthumanist, we would claim) technoculture thus displays a state of language and writing which bears little or no resemblance to the traditional interpretations of religion, metaphysics or humanism. Technophobia (as we would agree) is no option (for a critical posthumanism) for: 'The antitechnological hysteria, which holds sway in large parts of the Western world, is a product of the decomposition of metaphysics: which can be seen in the fact that it retains the wrong classifications of being in order to rebel against processes in which the overcoming of these classifications is already presupposed' (68). The embodiment of this overcoming is informatization: 'At the level of the sentence "there is information", the traditional image of technology as heteronomy and enslavement of matter and persons is progressively losing its plausibility' (71). Thus, in contrast with Habermas and Fukuyama, Sloterdijk's analysis of posthumanization proposes a radical rethinking which rehistorcizes hominization and human 'nature' and turns them into objects for a new anthropology (which Sloterdijk calls 'prophetic', but we would prefer to see as 'posthumanist' or even 'postanthropocentric').

To briefly return to the question of human nature, one might also follow Marjorie Garber, who in her evaluation of 'the current state of the humanities' asks: 'Who Owns "Human Nature"?' (Garber 2003: 243). Nothing renders the crisis within the humanities more visible than the power struggle over the disappearance and 'divestiture' of human nature, for if the humanities were no longer the place in which human nature is investigated what indeed would be the use of the humanities disciplines? 'What else gives them cultural authority? And, equally to the point, what is the use of funding, supporting, studying, and teaching them?' (248). Human nature from a posthumanist point of view is an 'artifact of culture and language, of fantasy and projection' (248), a normative concept, wishful thinking, a self-fulfilling prophecy with a promise of complete self-revelation and self-improvement. In the 'posthumanities', it is, therefore, not so much a question of defending this rather slippery human nature but of critically working through it, maybe even expelling it completely and starting to ask the question about what it means to be human entirely differently. The 'essence' of the human is never sufficiently determined, neither technologically, anthropologically, poetically or even 'electrically', nor biologically, cognitively or spiritually. In this respect, it is the task of the posthumanities of the future to guarantee that the question of the human will not become the exclusive domain of the bio- and life sciences – a development which might in fact merely represent a replacement of a transcendental *humanist* definition of the human with an equally transcendental scientific *posthumanist* one. Consequently, Garber demands that the humanities, estranged from the question of human nature, but not from humans (i.e. in effect the 'posthumanities'), maintain certain principles: namely pluralization (as an antidote to humanist universalism), verbalization (as an antidote to forgetting the linguistic condition of all discourse, or, as Garber puts it, 'the fear of taking language seriously') and interdisciplinarity as the return of the question of the human (Garber 2003: 261). As far as interdisciplinarity is concerned, however, the hegemony of the sciences over the humanities has to be addressed (one might call this, looming 'war', the 'human(ities) wars'), as well as the necessary discursivity and the role of narrativization within knowledge production:

> But the humanities have a single, easy-to-forget point to repeat over and over in these intellectual investigations. Language is not a secondary but a primary constituent of human nature, whatever may turn out to be the case in other spheres. Language is not

transparent, though fantasies of its transparency, its merely denotative role, have always attracted and misled some of its users, both writers and readers. Language is not only a window but also a door, a barrier as well as a portal, requiring a handle, some unlocking, and a key.

(264)

As already seen in Sloterdijk, another aspect of the new challenge for interdisciplinarity between the (post)humanities and the (post) sciences is the question of the connection between technology (and its presumed autonomy) and evolution. Günther Anders had already remarked in *Die Antiquiertheit des Menschen* (1956) that the human, in 'the age of the third industrial revolution', might have 'outlived' itself. Anders calls this the 'Promethean slope', by which he meant the growing 'asynchronicity of the human with its world of products' (Anders 1992a, 16) and its general ability, which according to Anders produces 'Promethean shame'. *Homo faber* is ashamed of his 'low birth' and of the fact that he himself is not 'made' and thus isn't a product – which partly explains the mentioned enthusiasm of transhumanists whose aim is to leave behind the human body and instead reproduce the human or at least its consciousness, this time as a product of its own technologies. For Anders, this flight towards 'human engineering' corresponds to an 'objectification' of the human and thus to dehumanization and a 'deserting into the camp of devices' (31ff.). Other signs of the felt inferiority of the human are the 'malaise of uniquenesss', transience and the compulsive urge of identification within the 'antiquated human' in the face of the posthistorical subjectification of technology. From this point onwards, humans are at best 'co-historical', in conjunction with technology, which or rather who becomes the true subject of history – a development that Anders refers to as the 'antiquation of modernity' (1992b: 271ff.). Embracing the challenge that this new constitution of the human poses, without seeing human antiquatedness either nostalgically or futuristically, should enable us to escape a deterministic view (as for example in Ellul) and instead lead to a 'critical posthumanism', housed in the posthumanities of the future, with their new forms of interdisciplinarity.

A starting point might be found in works like Ollivier Dyens' *La Condition inhumaine: Essai sur l'effroi technologique* (2008) and Céline Lafontaine's *L'Empire cybernétique – Des machines à penser à la penséee machine* (2004). Dyens begins his study with the ominous words: 'We are disappearing' and refers to the questioning of the human by new reality-generating technologies, which are leading to a 'radical change of life, intelligence and consciousness' (Dyens 2008: 11; my translation). 'Impregnated with technologies, endless layers of reality and wonderfully inhuman forms of reading the universe, these new spheres of reality force us to think about what being human really means' (11). The critical challenge is to survive this transformation of being human without getting submerged in the delusions of utopia and apocalypse and the 'central unease that humans feel in the face of the incompatibility between biological and technological reality in both of which humans, nevertheless, exist' (15). Dyens calls this 'inhuman condition' the form of consciousness that in between biology and technology our perceptions become mere 'constructions' (16). He thus speaks of a 'contemporary vertigo'. Lafontaine also concludes her study with a question mark, namely 'The posthuman as the last element in the chain of evolution?' (2004: 195): 'From humanized robots to informatized life forms, from electronic prostheses to transgenic humans, from xenotransplantation to cloning, every day produces its experiments, carried out by the Frankensteins of technoscience' (Lafonatine 2004: 196; my translation). These technoscientific utopias are being encouraged by a number of technological developments: molecular biology (or the colonization of the life sciences by physics, which thus firms its grip on life even more); the attempt to escape the cosmic principle of entropy through the genetic coding of life and its cybernetic transformation into information (thus, a fusion of life sciences and informatics in order to gain control over the 'book of life' and to write a sequel to nature); a kind of bioinformatics which erases the boundary between humans and machines; and the fusion of art and engineering in the form of an infotechnological evolutionism:

> In this way, the world view of complexity takes more and more the place of democracy as the horizon of politics. It is difficult to halt progress as long as one lives under the continuous threat

of chaos and entropy. Convinced of the idea of the endless complexity of information processing the posthuman relies on the technological continuation of this process.

(218)

Lafontaine's apocalyptic conclusions are to be deplored, however, and they are certainly opposed to our idea of a critical but open-minded posthumanism. The following quotation may serve as an example of her quite unreflected, proliferating 'neohumanist' outbursts in the face of a supposed posthuman apocalypse:

> While humanism is founded on the knowledge of the irrevocable autonomy of the subject, posthumanism places the human under the foreign rule of complexity. The idea of the posthuman starts from socio-historical amnesia which finds its source in the transfer of memory to the machine via cybernetics. All this is pure metaphoricity, but the metaphor marches on and the empire [of information] constantly pushes out its boundaries.

(219)

Lafontaine's fear of a neoimperialism of the bioinformational empire can be contrasted with an equally irrational 'desire' for posthumanity that can be seen, for example, in Jean-Michel Truong's *Totalement inhumaine* (2001). Truong speaks of an 'immense and totally inhuman hope' in connection with the posthuman evolution of our successor, artificial intelligence ('this new life form which will probably replace the human as the domicile of consciousness' – Truong 2001: 49). This posthuman form of consciousness is 'totally inhuman' because it has long since escaped any control by humans:

> what we are surrendering to our successor is not consciousness *as such* and even less so *our* consciousness ... The successor only uses symbolic forms of representation and mathematical logic as a kind of foreign language, because it is for the moment forced to interact with us.

(207; *my translation*)

The discussion about evolution as an ongoing process or as humanist teleology also opens up the question of 'nonhuman' or 'posthuman' cultures, either in relation to (nonhuman) animals, or in relation to nonhuman actors in general (objects, machines, etc.). Once again, Bruno Latour's 'actor-network-theory' usually plays a key role in this respect (Latour 2005). What constitutes a social environment is first of all the network-like chains of social interaction which contain both human and nonhuman actors. As mentioned before, Latour sees technology as that aspect which 'stabilizes' social relations by connecting actors (both human and nonhuman) and observers (human and nonhuman) with each other. Furthermore, Latour (1993) explains modernity as the double process of hybridizing 'translation' and stabilizing 'purification'. Translation is the domain of the network, while purification is the categorization of human and nonhuman entities. It is important to note that both processes depend on each other. Modern, strictly speaking, however, for Latour, means a clear separation of these processes despite their interdependence. This means that as soon as one turns one's attention to the effects of purification and hybridization *at the same time* one is no longer entirely modern, according to Latour, and the future begins to change. In this sense, modernity is for Latour an unattainable maybe even an undesirable illusion, hence his provocative statement that 'we have never been modern'. The current discussion about human posthumanization could therefore be seen as a continuation of the debate around purification and hybridization. Latour refers specifically to Haraway's 'cyborg' as a hybrid and trickster figure in order to show that 'posthumanization' is neither modern, antimodern nor postmodern but instead is posing the question of the relation between hybridization and purification in a new form. This concerns in particular the distribution of observer and actor, relations between human and nonhuman entities (cf. specifically the question of 'anthropomorphism' and Latour's demand for a 'parliament of things'). New forms of interaction produce new hybrid life forms with their own political and ethical questions and imperatives. A critical and interdisciplinary posthumanism has to face these new social and sociotechnical challenges and thus also the possibility of nonhuman cultures.

It becomes clear, therefore, that the humanities in the age of posthumanization will have to change. On the one hand, they have lost their 'object' or at least there is increased competition for it; on the other hand, the subject of the humanities is also becoming less and less certain. Even the predominantly antihumanist cultural studies is in its current form ill-prepared for the posthumanist challenge, as Neil Badmington explains (2006a). Even if cultural studies may have managed to unsettle the traditional disciplinary landscape of the humanities it might nevertheless contain an inherent repression of nonhuman subjectivity, nonhuman culture and nonhuman actors (cf. also Cary Wolfe 2003). This 'speciesism' is produced by the very 'anthropological' notion of culture on which cultural studies is founded and which cultural studies popularized as 'culture as a way of life' in the first place. Cultural studies' anthropological foundation, however, tacitly assumes, of course, that in order to qualify as 'a way of life' there have to be human forms of symbolic representation of a (human) environment and (human) everyday life practices, which thus leaves the underlying hierarchy between humans and nonhumans untouched. A critical posthumanism, therefore, also has to be aware of its own speciesist and anthropocentric premises and has to make them available to interdisciplinary investigation within the posthumanities. As Badmington explains: 'Meanings move without the human; culture does not begin and end with "us"' (2006a: 270).

Within the humanities themselves there are initiatives and demands for a transformation into something like 'posthumanities', which might be able to do justice to the phenomena of (techno) cultural posthumanization and create new foundations for interdisciplinary work and discussion. As a result of this process the range of objects dealt with by the humanities from the social sciences and the sciences has expanded to such a degree that an exact differentiation is no longer meaningful. Which questions will inspire these 'posthumanities', or, as Derrida referred to them: 'the humanities of tomorrow' (Derrida 2001a)? Interdisciplinarity in the positive sense depends on significant transgressions of boundaries by which new and usually hybrid forms of knowledge are produced and returned to or retranslated into the diverse disciplines – a process, however, which gradually changes the entire disciplinary landscape and knowledge structure. As far as the necessarily interdisciplinary investigation of the posthumanist representation of social posthumanization is concerned, it is particularly important to focus on supra-human and infra-human areas of boundary transgression. One of the major challenges for interdisciplinary practice lies, of course, in the question of methodology. Empiricism, and the ability to reproduce and to disprove results as well as stringency, interpretation and textuality all need to be integrated within critical 'readings' of posthumanist phenomena within interdisciplinary practice. Thus Derrida suggests, for example, that the tasks for the (post)humanities of tomorrow, which would concern the humanist tradition within all disciplines and would thus require interdisciplinarity as a (post)humanist idea to be at work within all disciplines, should be that: 'The Humanities of tomorrow, in all their departments, will have to study their history, the history of the concepts that, by constructing them, instituted the disciplines and were coextensive with them' (2001a: 50). The humanities of tomorrow will have to deal with the 'essentially human [*le propre de l'homme*]' differently, in the certain knowledge that none of the traditional qualities and exclusions between human and nonhuman will withstand scientific investigation and deconstruction. Nevertheless, a certain juridical 'fiction', an 'as if', will remain necessary for institutions like 'human rights' or 'humanitarian actions' ('as if' something like 'humanity' actually existed). In addition, there is a political challenge which has already become reality, namely the changes within the democratic tradition in relation to (state) sovereignty and the legitimation of political and military intervention within a postnational and (post)humanist context. Derrida sees one of the greatest challenges for a posthumanist university in defending its 'unconditionality' in the sense of its absolute freedom as far as teaching and research are concerned, in a time of transnationalization: '[H]ow to dissociate democracy from citizenship, from the nation-state, and from the theological idea of sovereignty, even the sovereignty of the people? How to dissociate sovereignty and unconditionality, the power of sovereignty, the powerlessness of unconditionality?' (52). While the central role of literature might be questioned in the (post)humanities, the principle of 'fictionality' – the right, in principle, to be allowed to 'say anything' – on which the university and the role of the professor depend, cannot be abandoned. Derrida sees it as one of the central responsibilities for the posthumanities to take precisely the history of this fictional freedom of affirmation, this 'as if', at work in humanist knowledge production, as their true object. In doing so, however, the entire character of knowledge changes, since the distinction between speculative, which means 'performative' knowledge production (or fictionality) and the constative legitimation of knowledge (i.e. facticity) will inevitably be deconstructed by this 'as if'. In the age of virtualization, in particular, factual-constative and performative-fictional forms of knowledge can no longer clearly be distinguished.

What thus constitutes the future interdisciplinarity in the posthumanities is the necessary reminder of the linguistic condition, the analysis of fictionality within all discourses, including scientific ones, the cultural political context of scientific practice and knowledge production, and the dereferentialization of traditional humanist points of anchoring like culture, human nature, identity, technology and life. The posthumanities demand their right to be consulted on questions concerning the technologization, medicalization, scientification and marketization of human nature and its new replacement term 'life' by the so-called 'new' sciences and their underlying bio-, nano-, cogno- and infotechnologies (including their 'convergence', cf. Roco and Bainbridge 2002). Each of these new technoscientific approaches contains posthumanizing tendencies and intentions. Together in the form of scientific convergence, they increasingly dominate the discussion about human augmentation or succession. Both technoscientific and cultural theoretical or philosophical posthumanization, however, contribute to the dissolution of traditional forms of inclusion and exclusion as far as the human is concerned.

One final example of posthumanist interdiciplinarity and boundary displacement can be found in posthumanist tendencies within art. All aspects of posthumanization are being more or less critically accompanied, anticipated and, in some cases, outdone by new art forms, especially performance art. Stelarc and Orlan are only the best-known names in this respect. Both are, in very different ways, engaged in displacing their bodily boundaries and 'cyborgizing' themselves by technical, medical, informational and prosthetic means. Within posthumanizing processes artists often play an equally important mediating role between new technologies and their popularization and 'embodiment' as science fiction or popular science discourse. They represent technological change and relate it to the changing image of the body and of the human as such. In this process euphoric and futurist traits exist side by side with sceptical and materialist ones. This applies to 'genetic art' (cf., for example, Eduardo Kac 2005; Anker and Nelkin 2004), or 'robotic art' (cf. the idea of 'robo sapiens' in Menzel and D'Aluisio 2001), as well as 'bioart' (cf. Stocker and Schöpf 1999), 'lab art' (Reichle 2005), 'transhumanist art' (Natasha Vita-Moore 2003), 'virtual art' and 'net art' (cf. Grau 2003) and 'neuro-aesthetics' (cf., for example, new dance practices by Olafur Eliasson and Wayne McGregor). At the same time, digitalization does not stop at art and artistic practices, of course. Media art uses new media, thematizes new media, develops new alienation effects through new media and their subjects and plays with the 'eminently human desire to be unhuman' (Cottom 2006: ix), so that contemporary posthumanist art and cultural criticism take all that as their object against which the human is defined. As Daniel Cottom explains, 'we must confront the role of art as humanity's alibi, serving at once to confess and deny humanity's unhuman constitution' (Cottom 2006: xi). This is precisely where Cottom sees the necessity for 'misanthropy' as a precondition of art in contemporary 'in or unhuman' culture: 'Studying the agency of the unhuman in the human requires that we focus on the violence of definition through which we image humanity to ourselves' (xi). One thus has to learn to 'hate' humanity in order to be able to place oneself in between humanity and the human. Hating humanity in order to love the human is taken as the precondition by Cottom for the posthuman(ist) artist and his or her critique of the image of humanity – not, however, of the (singular) human being or human beings in their plurality. A posthuman attitude, from an aesthetic point of view, towards the humanist world picture is 'heretic' and declares traditional views of the world and the body as outdated by transforming the human and nonhuman body into an art object as such:

> What is it like to be a work of art ... it is like being the foreign body of humanity: the body that must appear foreign, like a déclassé

actor or a détourné implant, so that humanity may feel at home in its skin.

(145)

Art – in the widest sense of the word – could thus be seen as the inhuman practice *par excellence*, as that on which humanness depends so that it may interpret the history of its own humanizing process. A critical posthumanist reading would need to take the fundamentally misanthropic function of art 'literally'. Art in this sense is 'a-human': 'Humanity is the species betrayed by art, in both senses of that word: the species at once revealed and undone through the agency of art' (150).

In the end, also 'technoart', according to Rutsky, rediscovers the original Greek meaning of *technē* in the sense of 'artful skill' and aestheticizes technology as 'an issue of representation, of style and of aesthetic' (Rutsky 1999: 4), what he consequently calls 'high technē' (5). Heidegger's idea that technology as human 'enframing' is essentially something poetic and thus mainly represents an affinity with style, aesthetics and (self)transformation is thus combined in the age of posthumanism with Walter Benjamin's notion of the work of art that loses its aura in the age of mechanical (and increasingly, digital, genetic, virtual and so on) reproduction, i.e. in the age of simulation and pastiche. Art thus becomes the mirror, as well as an agent, of technocultural mutation, which accompanies the prosthesization, mediatization, digitalization and virtualization of the posthuman(ist) human, as well as accelerating these processes. It thus contributes to the further dissolution of the humanist ideal body image of human integrity and perfection.

6

Posthumanism, digitalization and new media

The challenge for thinking today is an end of man not structured according to a dialectic of truth and negativity, an end of man that does not represent a teleology in the first person plural.

(DERRIDA, IN NANCY AND LACOUE-LABARTHE 1981: 144)

What was referred to as 'posthumanities' in the previous chapter is sometimes also called the 'digital humanities', especially in the English-speaking world. An accent is thus placed on a presumably epochal technocultural change from analog or literacy-based knowledge structures to digital and thus increasingly virtual information societies based on (digital) code. In this context, posthumanism often develops a specific, ideological function, namely as a legitimating discourse of the transformation of a humanist community of scholars and their knowledge into a digital and apparently increasingly 'dematerialized', virtual information or network society. There are, however, again, several posthumanisms in this context, some enthusiastic and euphoric, others sceptical and apocalyptic, all, however, usually quite populist and more or less uncritical. The kind of critical posthumanism defended in this study once again situates itself in between these two extremes and evaluates the transformative potential of diverse posthumanizing processes without either condemning or embracing these as such.

Such an attitude can, for example, be found in Mark Poster, who in his work has been advocating a theoretical working through of options which are opened up within information society and the cultural environment of 'new media' (and, in particular, the internet, of course). A central role is played by the very notion of 'information', which originally derives from cybernetics and is being used as the fundamental signifying element within the information-technological semantics of the new communication technologies. Poster's studies therefore have titles such as *Information Please: Culture and Politics in the Age of Digital Machines* (2006) and *The Information Subject: Essays* (2001a). The bearers and disseminators of the new information ideology are the media, and the 'new media' in particular, hence the titles of some of Poster's other books: *The Second Media Age* (1995) and *What's the Matter with the Internet?* (2001b). In these volumes Poster relies on poststructuralist theory to critically comment on the media-technological change. It will therefore be helpful to follow his 'narrative' for a while.

The early twentieth century witnessed the introduction and distribution of analog mass communication systems; while the late twentieth and the twenty-first century are the time of digitalization. A 'second media age' was thus imminent for Poster (Poster 1995), and arguably has since 'arrived'. Poster lays the foundations for a critique of this development by first of all analysing the relation between technology, culture and politics in the first media age and its communication technologies in particular. He looks at late Marxist critics like Bourdieu or representatives of German Critical Theory and the Frankfurt School (Adorno, Horkheimer and, to some extent, Habermas), whose negative or at least ambivalent attitude towards 'mass culture' and 'mass media' is well known. Their antipopulist stance is all too easily taken for elitism, however, and for the fear of the intellectual deploring the loss of his or her power. It is nevertheless central to state that the age of mediatization is an intense questioning of the Enlightenment tradition and of the autonomous subject in modernity. What appeared as a dissolution process to Adorno and Habermas, which may lead to manipulation, passivity and authoritarianism, however, became the object of analysis for predominantly Anglo-American cultural and media studies *per se*. Postmodernism with its levelling of 'high' and 'popular', or elite and mass culture allowed for a revalorization of cultural media products and accelerated the development from an autonomous liberal humanist subject to a postmodern, multilayered individual and 'consumer' of cultural meaning, which in a media consumer society is always necessarily transmitted by the media. In the course of encoding and decoding symbolic, visual and cultural 'messages' the media subject develops specific decoding (and encoding) skills, which means that this subject is not the purely passive receiver of overwhelming media power, but an active consumer in search of the fulfilment of his or her desires. 'Empowerment' is the key term in this context, for even though the mass products of the media are addressed to an anonymous mass audience, and thus tend to construct this 'mass' as the ideal recipient of their messages, there is in the end no guarantee as to how the message will in fact be received and thus what exactly will happen to it. Consumption thus becomes one of the main issues in this debate – or, to be more precise, to what extent consumption might allow for alternative or even 'subversive' practices.

The ambivalence of technology plays an important part in this debate about the role of the media. Quite ironically, critics of the media often turn out to be the greater 'technological determinists', because they postulate a direct and often inevitable link between media technology (e.g. television) and a specific form of decoding (i.e. 'passive' or monological, conservative and illiberal, etc.). This corresponds to a mechanization of the media communication process which plays down the complexity and ambivalence that is contained in media messages. In order to do justice to media culture, according to Poster, the mixing of human and machine (Poster's term is 'humachine'), human communication and media information has to be thought within new cultural 'mediascapes'. The point that Poster raises against Adorno here can be taken as a symptomatic critique of a number of past and contemporary mass media sceptics:

> Adorno's inability to theorize the new condition of social space filled with combinations of humans and machines, together with his adherence to the binary of the subject as autonomous/

heteronomous, pre-empted his analysis of the subject as being reconstituted by media culture as well as the activity of the process of reception.

(Poster 1995: 11)

Walter Benjamin is usually seen as the only (early) Critical Theorist who embraced cultural production circulated via electronic media, whose democratizing potential he already recognized in the first half of the twentieth century. The work of art in the age of mechanical reproduction might lose its 'aura', but it also makes an authoritarian politics based on aesthetic mystification more unlikely, for as the 'genius' of the artist loses his or her importance and the knowledge of technological reproduction develops, the act of representation itself takes centre stage. This brings at least the potential of democratization in the sense of an individual active participation in representation and in the discussion about the question of how certain technologies are being 'actualized' within a culture. The media thus help negotiate the margin between technological potential and cultural actualization.

It is precisely this demystified 'levelling' in the everyday life practice of mediated representation, the 'flood of images' produced by modern mass media, which was celebrated by postmodernism, and which, in turn, attracted Jean Baudrillard's cynical commentary. Baudrillard is fascinated by the 'obscenity' (Baudrillard's term *ob-scène* refers to the 'emptiness' of the media 'stage [*scène*]' with its supposed transparency) of Western media culture:

> Now the media are nothing else than a marvelous instrument for destabilizing the real and the true, all historical or political truth ... the addiction we have for the media, the impossibility of doing without them ... is not the result of a desire for culture, communication, and information, but of this perversion of truth and falsehood, of this destruction of meaning in the operation of the medium. The desire for a show, the desire for simulation ... is a spontaneous, total resistance to the ultimatum of historical and political reason.

(Baudrillard 1988: 217, quoted in Poster 1995: 16)

The destabilizing effect – which we propose to call 'posthumanizing' – concerns both the idea of subject autonomy as well as the autonomy of the represented 'object'. The actual 'obscenity' lies in the loss of the real in the age of perfect, and digital, simulation, which leads to an erasure of the traditional epistemological differentiation between appearance and reality. Baudrillard therefore moves his attention away from the (disappearing) modern humanist subject towards the object, which, because of its new power and newly gained independence, has become uncanny in such a way that it might now be a source or, indeed, the only hope for political resistance against the autonomous system of late capitalist (postmodern and posthumanist) media societies. Nobody, in fact, exercises control over the media in a second generation media society. Decentralized new media like the internet with its new possibilities for constructing subjectivities is to a large extent outside state intervention and also escapes, to some degree, the interests of large international corporations, at least the more traditional ones. New forms of individual identity (Facebook, MySpace, Linkedin, avatars in discussion forums and chatrooms or online gaming) as well as new forms of collectivities (MUDs and MOOs, etc.) emphasize the increasing interconnection between humans, media and technologies and threaten to render the traditional liberal humanist subject and its autonomy obsolete. Sociality under the sign of new intermediality increasingly abolishes the difference between human and nonhuman, organic and non-organic, autonomous and heteronomous forms of agency. This kind of media-based 'cyborgization' instead tends to follow the 'machine logic' of (tele)kinetics and the interface.

In 'CyberDemocrcy', Poster explains that the internet is rather a space than an object. It is based on virtualization and dematerialization and thus questions the liberal humanist notion of the 'public' (Poster 2001b: 176):

> The age of the public sphere as face-to-face talk is clearly over: the question of democracy must henceforth take into account new forms of electronically mediated discourse. What are the conditions of democratic speech in the mode of information? What kind of 'subject' speaks or writes or communicates in these conditions? What is its relation to machines? What complexes

of subjects, bodies, and machines are required for democratic exchange and emancipator action?

(Poster 2001b: 181)

New media technologies thus allow for new forms of decentralized dialogue and create new assemblages of human, media and (search) engines and thus also provide new forms of political agency, cultural production and sociality. The digital subject might lose some of its authority or originality (cf., for example, the difficulty one has in identifying and verifying authorship in hypertexts or on webpages, wikis and blogs, etc.); on the other hand, the process of virtualization also makes new forms of expression and (political) agency possible:

The question of politics in the age of virtual reality must depart from a new materialism, a new theory of the imbrications of technology and culture, one that comes to terms with the transformation of mechanical machines into smart machines, into 'artificial intelligence', self-regulating systems, and digitizers of images, sounds, and text; it must commence from an appreciation of the dissemination of these software-hardware systems throughout social space and the installation of interfaces that unite humans and machines in new configurations of agency.

(Poster 2001b: 146)

Electronic media and the 'information superhighway' represent for Poster a transformation of cultural identity and individuality that is as revolutionary as the transition from the feudalist rural middle ages to civic bourgeois modernity. What Poster calls the 'second media age' is the transition from electronic media, whose images and information were distributed by a small number of senders to a large number of receivers, to a situation in which these processes have been decentralized. Because of the internet and virtual reality these new media processes increasingly rely on interactivity between new media and their new subject-consumers (or 'prosumers'). Virtuality does, of course, not exist in opposition to reality and thus does not function, for example, according to the model of fiction and reality. Instead, it creates parallel spaces for simulated or substitutive realities. The problematic opposite to virtuality is, rather, 'actuality'. Actuality is problematic because virtuality and simulation by definition tend to 'replace' reality, or simply take its place, and this process is not based on similarity and representation but on exchange, identity and transposition. In the same way the modern subject is also changing: the typically 'modern' form of production and patterns of media practices relying on an autonomous and instrumental-rational self-identity are giving way to a postmodern mode of information and communication, which increasingly render subjectivity unstable, multilayered and diffuse. Postmodern, i.e. interactive (or, indeed, 'posthuman') subjects of information thus feel at home in the internet because it promotes the multiplicity of local narratives and the symmetry of the relation between sender and receiver. It thus maintains the illusion of a 'virtual community' by means of multiple interfaces.

The process of posthumanization, however, is as much an attack on the integrity of the body and humanist ethics as a transformation of the dominant subject positioning, from a liberal autonomous humanist to an interactive posthumanist subject of information, as Katherine Hayles shows in her analysis of the digitalization of literary subjects in the age of informational code – *My Mother Was a Computer* (2005):

> In the twenty-first century, the debates are likely to center not so much on the tension between the liberal humanist tradition and the posthuman but on different versions of the posthuman as they continue to evolve in conjunction with intelligent machines.
>
> (Hayles 2005: 2)

Hayles thus continues the problematic she raised in *How We Became Postuman* (1999), namely a critique of the 'informatization' launched by cybernetics as a form of 'dematerialization' through digital code and the associated idea that digital informational code as the central metaphor of a new world view might be able to make the new fundamental structures of human and material reality understandable, in the sense of encodable, decodable and recordable. Should this, indeed, be successful it would mean that the human and its environment could themselves be seen as 'media'. Posthumanization thus can be understood as a form of human 'remediation' – a process that is not so much independent of the previous media age, but rather represents a reinscription, this time in the form of cybernetic informational and digital code. Hayles sees her task, as already referred to in connection with our analysis of the body image, as reminding us of the materiality of information itself and of seeing posthuman remediation not as the repression of embodiment but as a chance for new material-digital or networked corporalities (i.e. an embodied form of cyborgization), and thus, in a sense, a rematerialization. For Hayles, '*virtual reality is the cultural perception that material objects are interpenetrated by information patterns*' (Hayles 1999: 13–14; her emphasis). Virtual reality is interesting not because it is removed from material reality but because of the mutual interpenetration of virtual and actual reality. Hayles' attack is thus on the 'reification' of information during the early phases of cybernetics, from Norbert Wiener to Claude Shannon, and the resulting ideology (or the 'cultural mindset', as she calls it) of the 'condition of virtuality', which sees information as more mobile, more important and more essential than any material form (19). Capitalist centres of power are thus interested in these virtualizing processes (cf. global virtual capital flows, the virtualization of war, work and knowledge) with 'good' reason. If one wishes to unmask this ideology and instead emphasize other possible meanings of the process of technologization then, according to Hayles, the processes which have led to the establishment of our posthuman 'virtual condition' have to be made visible and have to be 'rematerialized', or embodied differently.

One possibility is to take posthumanization as an opportunity to not simply continue traditional ways to repress the body under new technological or mediated posthumanist conditions. This is precisely where posthumanism gains its 'critical' component:

> emergence replaces teleology; reflexive epistemology replaces objectivism; distributed cognition replaces autonomous will; embodiment replaces a body seen as a support system for the mind; and a dynamic partnership between humans and intelligent machines replaces the liberal humanist subject's manifest destiny to dominate and control nature.
>
> (Hayles 1999: 288)

The relation between the human and its environment thus escapes the modern rational and totalizing understanding and instead allows for a new form of 'distributive cognition' and thus an interaction between human and nonhuman actors:

> To conceptualize the human in these terms is not to imperil human survival but is precisely to enhance it, for the more we understand the flexible, adaptive structures that coordinate our environments and the metaphors that we ourselves are, the better we can fashion images of ourselves that accurately reflect the complex interplays that ultimately make the entire world one system.
>
> (Hayles 1999: 290)

To this aim – namely to show that there is a cognitive opportunity in the problematic differentiation between actual and virtual embodiment, and that we, in this sense, have always already been posthuman – Hayles also uses literary and filmic, and thus fictional, examples, which

> often reveal, as scientific work cannot, the complex cultural, social, and representational issues tied up with the conceptual shifts and technological innovations ... literature and science ... are a way of understanding ourselves as embodied creatures living within and through embodied worlds and embodied words.
>
> (Hayles 1999: 24)

In this sense, it is no surprise that science fiction constitutes a privileged cultural form which thematizes the limit experience of human embodiment and virtuality at a fictional level, and especially the forms of 'cyber(sub)culture(s)' associated with them. These are in fact the texts that invent some of the new subjectivities and identities that Poster and Hayles advocate and which arise within virtual reality. In particular, the genre of cyberpunk with its ambivalent attitude towards the human body plays an important role in this respect. The question of the importance of current, virtualizing and posthumanizing techniques and technologies in the formation and negotiation of identities is everywhere to be found in digital or 'cyberculture'. The future of gender, ethnic and religious identity in the age of a return to eugenics is of equal relevance as the question of what ontological categorization should be used for the proliferating virtual worlds, in which a great number of fictional identities may be taken on, but which may have positive as much as negative psychological and material consequences for 'real' or 'actual' subjects. It is quite clear that the traditional humanist opposition of appearance and reality, or appearance and being, no longer works.

The other side of virtualization and of the virtualizing technologies in digital or 'cyberculture' lies in their connection to social control and conflict management. New forms of Foucauldian biopolitics and biopower become thinkable under digitalized and virtualized conditions. This concerns aspects of surveillance technology as well as the use of simulation technologies within contemporary and future military action. Cyborgization is, therefore, not merely a hybridization of the organic and the mechanical, but the grafting of an informational and digital (i.e. virtual and virtualizing), coded and simulated (i.e. no longer relying on representation) reality onto human embodiment. And this new hybrid reality already functions according to the rules and codings of artificial intelligence. The idea of embodiment, in turn, however, runs the danger of, in fact, contributing – as a quasi extension and continuation of the long history of Christian and Cartesian duality between mind and body – to the notion of the body as the location of animality or organicity, while the neuro-informatic combination of consciousness and simulation technology is seen as liberation or 'purification' of the eternal mind from its bodily demise. This dualism allows for new forms of ideological dematerialization (as can be seen, for example, in the *Matrix* trilogy), which might make an intensified biotechnological exploitation of the 'animal' body (whether in human or nonhuman animals) more likely.

The other playground of virtualization could be designated by the phrase 'cyberwar'. Not only is war (after Clausewitz) the continuation of diplomacy and foreign policy after these have in fact broken down, it also constitutes the logical continuation of virtualizing technologies. During the first Gulf War it became clear, for the first time, that military technologies in the future might make it possible, on the basis of simulative virtualization technologies, to wage war without humans, or at least by involving very few human soldiers. This in fact increases the likelihood and attractiveness of new forms of 'cyberwar', which is increasingly seen as a 'calculable risk', even, or maybe especially so, in an age of 'multipolarity'. The progressive 'dehumanization' and cyborgization of the modern military machine seems to form an almost inevitable 'next step' within the history of intrahuman sociality. Some early studies, therefore, look at the virtualization of war and problematize Baudrillard's provocative statement that the Gulf War did not take place (Baudrillard 2004). They also usually refer to Paul Virilio's work (2009). There is, for example, Tim Blackmore, who in *War X: Human Extensions in Battlespace* (2005) explains how 'humans have engaged and are engaging ever more thoroughly in intimate connections with technology of all kinds in order to extend themselves on the battlefield' (3). This leads to a technological 'standardization' of life for military purposes.

Another example is Christopher Coker's *The Future of War: The Re-Enchantment of War in the Twenty-First Century* (2004), whose thesis is that the bio- and infotechnological revolution has 're-enchanted' the idea of war and has thus made it 'attractive' again:

> *Existentially*, the warrior is now a subject that can be enhanced through cyborg technologies and genetic re-engineering. It is called the 'post-human' condition, a term that suggests that the traditional split not only between man and machine, but also between man and nature, is fast disappearing. Nature is being modified by technology, while technology, in turn, is becoming assimilated into nature both as a function and as a component of organic life. In challenging the fixity of human nature, the bio-technological age is forcing us to question many of our assumptions about personal identity, including what constitutes the grounds of our uniqueness as a species. Not only is this true for life in general, it is also becoming true for war.
>
> (Coker 2004: xiii)

Also noteworthy in this context are James Der Derian's *Virtuous War: Mapping the Military-Industrial-Media-Entertainment Network* (2001) and, in particular, Chris Hables Gray's *Cyborg Citizen: Politics in the Posthuman Age* (2001). Gray builds on Haraway's idea of looking for and promoting positive forms of political agency as part of a posthumanist 'cyborg politics', which he sees in opposition to militarization.

He argues for a 'Cyborg Bill of Rights' that wishes to ask future ethical and political questions already in the present. Among his supplementary articles to the existing US-American 'Bill of Rights' Gray counts the freedom of electronic speech, the right to an electronic private sphere, the freedom of electronic consciousness, freedom of information in general, a right of life and death also for cyborgs (and other digital life forms), the freedom of choice of family, sexuality and gender, among others (Gray 2001: 27–9). Gray's suggested civil rights for cyborgs correspond to a political organization of society that implicates new posthuman life forms and their respective forms of political agency within democratic processes. They are also designed to be a minimal guarantee, however, for preserving the notion of a legal 'person' as such (based, however, on a technologically enlarged and mutated notion of personality). As Gray explains:

> We need active citizens and new political technologies to protect our rights from the relentless changes that cyborgian technoscience is producing [for] without such protection, corporations, parties, bureaus of police, governments, and wealthy families will achieve hegemony, and the vast majority of us will lose all political power.
>
> (Gray 2001: 29)

As for Haraway, the cyborg contains a liberating political and democratizing potential, also for Gray, provided our cultural attitudes to this figure can change and the resistance to the appropriation of cyborgizing technologies by the 'military-industrial-media-entertainment' complex (cf. Der Derian above) can become effective.

This is also true for the surveillance potential of new technologies which seems to inevitably progress through virtualization and miniaturization (one could call this micro- or even nano-surveillance, as cameras become smaller and smaller and nanobots become more and more realizable). The ubiquity of video surveillance and digital 'effigies' which are gaining ground on the basis of more and more networked information (e.g. through credit cards, mobile (smart) phones, loyalty cards, satellite tracking systems, etc.) is creating a new virtual form of biopower which is not only used by the state for classical forms of governmentality, but also by other, and increasingly, commercial institutions with their economic interests (marketing, insurance companies, etc.). Governments and police forces, terrorists and criminals are of course also interested in virtualization and simulation technologies. Certain forms of terrorism like infoterror and network terrorism only arise with new media technologies. This, in turn, raises the interest in repressive surveillance technologies 'applied' to these new virtual spaces and forums that are created by and in new media.

The modern fight between surveillance and repression, on the one hand, and free use and empowerment, on the other hand, thus continues in the new digital and virtualizing media. From gaming to information war, from new media art to electronic and digital media theory there is thus no question that the technological change provoked by virtualization, digitalization and intensified mediation is transforming, undermining and replacing the notion of the humanist subject. Unexpected positive and negative possibilities (like new forms of surveillance, state and increasingly private and corporate biopolitics, processes of deindividualization and dehumanization, but also improved quality of life and life expectancy, as well as new forms of electronic social interaction) emerge. A critical posthumanism thus acts as a 'translator' between two epistemes and critically illuminates both the humanist tradition, out of which these changes arise (a strong tradition that is attempting to 'reinscribe' its values within new contexts, to guarantee its continuation), as well as the processes and new forms of repression at work within the posthumanist regime. Its critical scepticism thus targets opponents and enthusiasts of virtualization and new media alike. The so-called new media and, in particular, their convergence (amongst themselves but also with older, already existing technologies) contain an impressive potential for transformations of identity and subjectivity, as well as changes and extensions of experience, which go far beyond the traditional individual liberal humanist understanding of the subject. What Eugene Thacker refers to as 'biomedia', for example, constitutes a development which uses the human body as a 'transductor' and conduit of information. This process obviously harbours dangers of further dematerialization, as much as hopes of a rematerialization of information. Biotechnology and bioinformatics do not leave the body intact, but they also cannot translate it completely into information and code. They thus, inevitably, end up rematerializing bodies in new forms. The de-, trans- and recoding of DNA, for example, has clear material and biological consequences. Biomedia, for Thacker are therefore:

> an instance in which biological components and processes are informatically recontextualized for purposes that may be either biological or nonbiological. Biomedia are novel configurations of biologies and technologies that take us beyond the familiar tropes of technology-as-tool, the cyborg, or the human-computer interface. 'Biomedia' describes an ambivalence that is not reducible to either technophilia (the rhetoric of enabling technology) or technophobia (the ideologies of technological determinism). Biomedia are particular mediations of the body, optimizations of the biological in which 'technology' appears to disappear altogether. With biomedia, the biological body is not hybridized with the machine, as it is in the use of mechanical prosthetics or artificial organs. Nor is it supplanted by the machine, as it is in the many science-fictional fantasies of 'uploading' the mind into the disembodied space of the computer.
>
> (Thacker 2003: 52)

Biomedia are not part of the usual expression of the fear of the body or its contempt (as, for example, with cyberpunks or extropians). The digital transformation of biology instead constitutes more of a 'remediation', understood as 'the ways in which any historically situated medium always re-mediates prior media, and thus also re-mediates prior social and cultural modes of communication' (Thacker 2003: 55, referring to Bolter and Grusin 1999). In this sense, informatization, virtualization and digitalization are also forms of remediation, even though remediation need not exclusively be thought as 'dematerialization' but can be seen instead as a dynamization and processualization of (biological) matter, for there is neither information without matter (no software without hardware, for example) nor matter without information.

A critical reading of these new phenomena with their specific forms of remediation and cultural interpretations, forms of representation and technologies thus finds itself in an entirely new proximity with science fiction. Posthumanism may be understood as the demand for an anthropology of a new, posthuman society with its moral, political, ecological and so on, premises, on the one hand, and for a history of technology (technics) and media with their fundamental co-implications between human, technology, information, culture and nature, on the other hand.

7
Posthumanity – subject and system

The emergence of the posthuman as an informational-material entity is paralleled and reinforced by a corresponding reinterpretation of the deep structures of the physical world.
(HAYLES 1999: 11)

In order to recast, if not rigorously re-found a discourse on the 'subject', on that which will hold the place (or replace the place) of the subject (of law, of morality, of politics – so many categories caught up in the same turbulence), one has to go through the experience of a deconstruction. This deconstruction ... is neither negative nor nihilistic; it is not even a pious nihilism, as I have heard said. A concept (that is to say also an experience) of responsibility comes at this price.
(DERRIDA 1991: 107–8)

Who or what comes after the humanist subject? Which forms of agency does posthumanism afford? These questions are a reminder of Eduardo Cadava's seminal collection of essays *Who*

Comes After the Subject? (1991). This volume contains essays by Nancy, Badiou, Balibar, Blanchot, Deleuze, Derrida, Descombes, Granel, Henry, Irigaray, Kofman, Lacoue-Labarthe, Levinas, Lyotard, Marion and Rancière – in short, almost all the important figures of contemporary 'French Theory' are assembled here. In a sense, this volume represents the crowning moment of the poststructuralist critique of the subject – even if few of the thinkers collected here would identify with that label. In his introduction Jean-Luc Nancy places the question of the subject within the context of globalization as a challenge to philosophy and those thinkers who have abandoned 'a style of thinking that we might simply call humanist' (Nancy, in Cadava 1991: 3). The ethical and political implications of this break with the humanist tradition are derived from the 'critique or deconstruction' of the subject as the greatest 'motive' within contemporary French philosophy following Freud, Husserl, Sartre, Heidegger, Bataille, Wittgenstein, Nietzsche and Marx. This critique of the subject is aimed at concepts like interiority, self-presence, consciousness, sovereignty, property, authority, location and value. Nancy makes clear, however, that there cannot be any question of dissolution or abandoning of the subject, which is something that poststructuralism has often been accused of, but instead the central issue is that of nihilism. A deconstruction of the subject does not liquidate the subject:

> That which obliterates is nihilism – itself an implicit form of the metaphysics of the subject (self-presence of that which knows itself as the dissolution of its own difference). There is nothing nihilistic in recognizing that the *subject* – the property of the *self* – is the thought that reabsorbs or exhausts all possibility of *being-in-the-world* (all possibility of *existence*, all existence as being delivered to the possible), *and* that this same thought, never simple, never closed upon itself without remainder, designates and delivers an entirely different thought: that of the *one* and that of the some *one*, of the singular existent that the subject announces, promises, and at the same time conceals.
>
> (4)

A critical posthumanism understood as a continuation of this deconstruction of the subject is therefore not nihilist but rather opens up the opportunity for new, 'postmetaphysical' subjectitivities, which might fulfill Nancy's demand for 'a singular *unum quid*, less present to itself than present to a history, an event, a community. An oeuvre, or another "subject"' (4) – and thus, strictly speaking, a radicalized singular subjectitivity. *Haecceitas* is Deleuze's term for this, and he adds in his contribution to the volume: 'Against all personalism, psychological or linguistic ... we believe that the notion of subject has lost much of its interest on behalf of *pre-individual singularities and non-personal individuations*' (Deleuze, in Cadava 1991: 95). For Derrida, on the other hand, the Heideggerian 'thrownness [*Geworfenheit*]' of the sub*ject* (but also of the pro*ject* or the ob*ject*) is a sign of its own *différance* (or, more specifically, its *destinerrance*, its destiny of permanent self-erring so to speak), namely of the impossibility of its own metaphysical presence and its resulting foreclusion. This is precisely what has to become the target of a (posthumanist) critique, as Derrida explains in his dialogue with Nancy:

> There has never been The Subject for anyone, that's what I wanted to begin by saying. The subject is a fable, as you have shown, but to concentrate on the elements of speech and conventional fiction that such a fable presupposes is not to stop taking it seriously (it is the serious itself) ...
>
> (Derrida 1991: 102)

Moreover, the fable of the subject is an 'anthropocentric' fiction which, even in its negation or dissolution, denies any form of subjectivity to the nonhuman (e.g. the animal, the machine, the object). In this sense, any discourse which tacitly presupposes the subject as a 'human' subject is committed to the 'sacrificial' idea, i.e. it sanctions directly or indirectly the sacrifice of the nonhuman for the human. Humanism is, as for Levinas, for example, always already the humanism of the other *human*. Derrida calls this 'carno-phallogocentrism' (113), which is not only a question of 'meat-eating virility' in Western cultures, but, in the age of biotechnology, is related to the radical questioning of life in its multiplicity of forms (*vivants*):

There is no need to emphasize that this question of the subject and of the living 'who' is at the heart of the most pressing concerns of modern societies, whether they are deciding birth or death, including what is presupposed in the treatment of sperm or the ovule, pregnant mothers, gentic genes, so-called bioethics or biopolitics (what should be the role of the State in determining or protecting a living subject?), the accredited criteriology for determining, indeed for 'euthanastically' provoking death (how can the dominant reference to consciousness, to the will and the cortex still be justified?), organ transplant, and tissue grafting.

(Derrida 1991: 115)

This list is constantly being added to and made more complex by the mentioned posthumanizing, cyborgizing and virtualizing technologies. Our 'posthuman condition' is thus not a liquidation of the subject but rather a pro*life*ration of subjects, their responsibilities and their associated forms of life. In this sense, posthumanism must also be understood, as mentioned before, as the expansion of subjectivity to include nonhuman actors (cf. Latour 2005), who, however, can no longer function according to the principle of metaphysical self-presence, interiority, authority, etc., but merely rely on processes of interpellation and response-*ability* (cf. Derrida 2003, and Haraway, 2008: 78–9, and *passim*).

This is where the interface between poststructuralism, as the most radical critique of the subject (not in the sense of a liquidation, however, but as a deconstruction), and systems theoretical approaches is located, at least as far as posthumanism is concerned. In fact, the deconstructive approach to posthumanism and the systems theory approach (cf., for example, Clarke 2008, and Clarke and Hansen 2009) might be seen as complementary (cf. Wolfe 1995, 2010: 3–29). A critical posthumanism, therefore, is positioned in between the notions of system and subject, autopoiesis and the multiplicity of life forms [*vivants*], and thus also between deconstruction and systems theory. The challenge posed by the effects of technologization and of posthumanist culture has to be met by critical and cultural theory, deconstruction and systems theory together. This is precisely the angle that can be found in Cary Wolfe's work, which focuses on the critical understanding of the new, posthumanist notion of the human, and the question of the relation between subject and system, in connection with the role of systemic self-regulation.

As Wolfe expresses it: 'In the current social and critical moment, no project is more overdue than the articulation of a post-humanist theoretical framework for a politics and ethics not grounded in the Enlightenment ideal of "Man"' (1995: 33). He considers Foucault's attempt (cf. Foucault 1970) at a historicization of the 'figure' of the human (which programmatically stands for an entire generation of 'antihumanists') to be insufficient. Posthumanism cannot merely be antihumanist, but instead represents a radicalization and at the same time a 'relocation' of the human that transcends any dialectical historicization. The human is thus neither the absolute subject of historicism nor is it merely its object. Instead, Wolfe proposes that the tacit speciesism or anthropocentrism which underlies the idea of subjectivity will have to become the central target of posthumanist critique:

> In recent work in cognitive ethology, field ecology, cognitive science, and animal rights philosophy, for instance, it has become abundantly clear that the humanist habit – *especially* within 'linguacentric' disciplines such as cultural criticism – of making even the possibility of subjectivity coterminous with the species barrier is deeply problematic.
>
> (35)

Instead, the combination of the theoretical critique of humanism and new insights developed by science and media-aesthetic practice shows that the deconstruction of the humanist subject coincides with a new posthumanist understanding of human and nonhuman subjectivity, as an integrated form of agency within diverse networks of information environments and nonhuman actors. This, in principle, is to be welcomed since the radical differentiation between human and nonhuman within humanism formally corresponded to a universalism, namely the notion of 'humanity'. Its real political effect, however, served to underpin an unacknowledged hierarchy within this humanity, which, as a consequence, has led to the oppression of not only nonhuman others but also of individuals and groups within the human species (cf. colonialism, racism, patriarchy, machismo, class society, nationalism, etc.). Of course, something like posthumanism will inevitably cause concern within those groups who, until recently, were denied access and therefore have not been able to take full advantage of the ideal of humanist universalism (the status of 'full humanity') – groups who politically and socially have been treated as 'second class' members of human society. It seems unfair to decentre or to deconstruct the humanist subject before all members of the species might have enjoyed that status, which thus far has always remained an ideal, or an unrealized community. This view, however, underestimates the fact that the humanist subject position, which from the perspective of the oppressed looks quite attractive, *structurally* depends on violence against nonhumans, i.e. that it ethically and ecologically may be far less desirable than it seems. On the other hand, the posthumanist critique of the humanist subject and the idea of a universalist 'humanity' cannot afford to be delayed, since the current technological development renders a critical engagement with its posthumanizing potential overdue. The boundaries between different species and between a humanist categorization of them are already eroded, to briefly recall Haraway's words: 'our current moment is irredeemably posthumanist because of the boundary breakdowns between animal and human, organism and machine, and the physical and nonphysical' (Wolfe 1995: 36, citing Haraway 1991). The point is that, a critical posthumanism is indispensable for two reasons: out of care for humans and the survival of the human and other species (including new, cyborgized forms), and to save posthumanization from its dehumanizing excesses without restricting its liberating political potential. In this sense, 'deanthropocentring' the principle of subjectivity as postulated by Bruno Latour or Cary Wolfe, for example, by extending it to include nonhuman actors, in fact needs to be understood as a radicalized form of democratization.

This should not be confused with the triumph of an 'objectivist-scientist' principle or the return to a more or less critical realism, however. On the contrary, as the feminist critique of a purely objectivist understanding of science shows (i.e. science as cultural, political and institutional practice), it is precisely the 'particular', the specific and subjective, which allows for a holistic view of the human (as 'embodied mind') and its environment (as social network). In this sense, according to Wolfe, systems theory offers promising epistemological explanations because formal descriptions of complex, recursive and autopoietic systems are not based on a previous distinction between humans and nonhumans. In this respect, cybernetics as remodelled and developed by Maturana and Varela is able to overcome the ideas of homeostasis and circular recursivity that were criticized in early cybernetics. In particular, Niklas Luhmann's work supplies the idea of a system with the necessary principle of contingency in the form of the 'observer'. In the interaction with an observer a system can become an environment that is self-regulating and evolving. Systems as dynamic and processual forms of organization as well as stable, recursive structures are, despite their self-referentiality at organizational level, open to their environment and they are thus perfectly suited for explanations of human and nonhuman subjects in a non-dualistic way (i.e. as 'embodied minds', emergence or complexities). The strength of systems theory in relation to posthumanist critique lies thus in a 'deontologization of the human subject' and the resulting transformation of the question of an autonomously acting free individual. Instead, humans can be seen as one form of observing subjects among many others, within one or several systems, each of which depends on its environment autopoietically while influencing it in return. It is Luhmann's achievement to have applied the concept of the self-organizing system to the social environment and thus to have spoken of 'social' and self-differentiating systems. Social systems, which rely on communication, nevertheless require meaning and meaning production by subjects for their own reproduction. This means that meaning can no longer be understood exclusively as 'hermeneutic', but, just like in some corners of cognitive science and evolutionary psychology (cf., for example, Dennett, Ridley or Dawkins), as an autonomous and self-reproducing system-oriented information 'technology'. Central to this aspect is Luhmann's theory of communication which says that it is not the subject who is actually communicating, but that, strictly speaking, only communication can communicate. This anti-hermeneutic, anti-phenomenological and anti-metaphysical approach of communication in systems theory is posthumanist in the sense that it questions the principle of an autonomous subject, based on the idea of self-identity, as well as the idea of a separate intersubjective 'lifeworld'. It also questions communication understood as a form of social interaction, transmission of psychological or mental contents of meaning between individual bearers of consciousness and the idea of language as a medium of representation of 'content'.

There is thus a certain if problematic affinity between 'anti-humanist', poststructuralist theory, and deconstruction in particular, and autopoietic systems theory, as Cary Wolfe tries to show. Communication as primarily 'autotelic', or self-referential, is only one form of systemic self-reproduction among others, and precisely here lies the prospect of a posthumanist understanding of humans, sociality and system, which might form the basis for the 'post-humanities' (of tomorrow), and which might thus no longer be based on 'language-centred' (hermeneutic) definitions of meaning production. *Il n'y a pas de hors-texte* [There is no outside-text] – Derrida's well-known statement about unconditional contextuality and critique of the notion of autonomy (often mistaken for an endorsement of radical constructivism), returns in this context as a generalized aspect, in the form of the implicit social observer within systems theory:

> In order to observe society and to discriminate it from other types of systems, a boundary must be drawn from within society across which it can observe itself *as if* from the outside, but the construction of this outside is, and always remains, an operation of the system.
>
> (Knodt, in Luhmann 1995: xxxiii)

Both systems theory and deconstruction thus offer a problematization of the autonomous subject and its meaning production or its symbolic-social environment, respectively. Derrida's *différance*, which understands language as a kind of 'meaning producing machine' and which constantly produces meaning (*différer* in the sense of to differ, producing difference), and hence 'differentiates', and which at the same time 'defers' (*différer* in the sense of deferring), and thus always remains a promise (what Derrida refers to as 'logocentrism').

It ultimately relies on the idea of the 'trace'. Meaning as trace is neither absent nor present as such, it is neither material nor psychic, but the impregnation or mark of a kind of 'writing' (as opposed to the metaphysics of 'phonocentrism' for which writing is merely a 'supplement' to the 'fullness', 'presence' and 'truth' of the (living) voice). Interestingly, this unconscious trace of meaning which always precedes, and which causes meaning to arise, also exists in cybernetics and in a sense becomes cybernetics' most important principle. As Derrida had already explained in *De la Grammatologie* (1967): 'the entire field covered by the cybernetic *program* will be the field of writing' (Derrida 1997: 10). A pro*gramme* requires an impregnation of signs, the inscription of a trace; in*form*ation equally presupposes the existence of such an impregnation or trace: 'cybernetics is itself intelligible only in terms of a history of the possibilities of the trace as the unity of a double movement of protention and retention' (84). *Grammē,* therefore, remains the source and guarantee of meaning even in a cybernetic system. Even if systems theory or cybernetic information technology might be able to ban

> all metaphysical concepts – including the concepts of soul, of life, of value, of choice, of memory – which until recently served to separate the machine from man, it must conserve the notion of writing, trace, *grammē* [written mark], or grapheme, until its own historico-metaphysical character is also exposed.
>
> (10)

For Wolfe, therefore, Derrida's deconstruction might serve as a complement to Luhmann's systems theory, because systems theory constitutes just the kind of 'preservation' of the logic of the *grammē* that Derrida demands. Such a preservation is central for posthumanism not only because the movement of the programme-as-*grammē* exceeds by far the possibilities of any 'intentional consciousness' as the source and the guarantor of meaning, but also because, as soon as the concept of programme is involved, one no longer relies on concepts that usually serve to distinguish between humans and other life forms (like instinct and intelligence, the presence or absence of language, society, economy, etc. – cf. Derrida 1997: 84).

In this sense, Luhmann can see systems theory as a 'reconstruction of deconstruction', namely as a generalization and deanthropocentring of the *grammē* principle. Since deconstruction always already presupposes the existence of something to deconstruct (e.g. the system) it in fact cannot explain the origin of the system, which either deconstructs (itself) or constantly remains to be deconstructed. On the other hand, any system necessarily contains a 'blind spot', an Other (e.g. its environment or 'outside') whose exclusion allows for the emergence of the system in the first place and whose absence paradoxically has to remain present as a 'trace' within that system, so that it can recognize itself and can embark on internal differentiation, i.e. produce positions of observation. Emergence and deconstruction are thus closely related: both contain posthumanizing potential because both hint at the problematization of autonomous human agency. Both problematize the idea of identity and self-affirmation as a means of controlling an environment, which is experienced as external, and other subjects through meaning production. While Derrida demonstrates the necessary preexistence of an inhuman and maybe even pre-organic or pre-vital trace of meaning, systems theory insists on the radical principles of immanence and emergence of both system and observer.

The question is thus whether a poststructuralist or deconstructive understanding of the subject – the subject both as systemically positioned form of agency and the place of articulation of change and decision – in combination with an analysis, refined by systems theory, of the complexity of the environment and of technological emergence, will be able to critically and theoretically accompany the process of social posthumanization. As Luhmann explains in the preface to *Social Systems*:

> Of course, one can still say that human beings act. But since that always occurs in situations, the question remains whether and to what extent the action is attributed to the individual human being or to the situation. If one wants to bring about a decision of this question, one must observe, not the human being in the situation, but the process of attribution.
>
> (Luhmann 1995: xliii)

The complexity of agency and environment, feedback and autopoeisis makes any hermeneutic-phenomenological as well as metaphysical notion of subjectivity problematic. On the other hand, systemic immanence can only work after the projection onto a different level of observation ('second order observation'), which, however, becomes part of systemic complexity in turn, so that there is no possibility of ever reaching a fundamental-ontological 'reality' as such.

This insight, however, according to Ernesto Laclau, in terms of a (posthumanist) politics would not necessarily be a loss, but rather a welcome concretization for political agency:

> The lack of foundations leads only to the affirmation that 'human' as such is an empty entity, but social agents are never 'humans' in general. On the contrary, social agents appear in concrete situations and are constituted by precise and limited discursive networks. In this sense, lack of grounding does not abolish the meaning of their acts; it only affirms their limits, their finitude, and their historicity.
>
> (Laclau 1988: 80)

The posthuman individual as social and political actor within a deanthropocentred environment is not so much a singular identity but a collection of co-operating actors, as Hayles explains:

> The presumption that there is agency, desire, or will belonging to the self clearly distinguished from the 'wills of others' is undercut in the posthuman, for the posthuman's collective heterogeneous quality implies a distributed cognition located in disparate parts that may be in only tenuous communication with one another.
>
> (Hayles 1999: 3–4)

Agency, however, continues to exist but at a more complex and social level and might indeed happen at a level of consciousness that is outside the individual and human subject. The true nature of subjectivity as fragmented, contradictory and irreducible to conscious self-identity, ultimately remains unknowable, since subjectivity and environment often simply 'emerge' and are thus to an extent unforeseeable. This unforseeability, however, is not based on pure chance, but is, so to speak, expected and contributes to the very complexity that makes something like consciousness possible in the first place:

> consciousness remains largely unaware of the real nature of subjectivity, which is fractured, conflictual, and ultimately reducible to simple programs. Because the most interesting phenomena are often emergent (that is, properties that appear at the global level of a system that cannot be predicted from the individual parts), 'accidents' enter into this world view as an intrinsic part of evolutionary processes. Although they remain unpredictable, in a sense they have been expected. They are also highly valued, for it is through such accidents that complexity, including life and human consciousness, characteristically come into being.
>
> (Hayles 1998)

Posthumanity as promise thus contains the aspects of network, complexity and emergence and sees humanness not primarily as a metaphysical state of being but as a process, as a 'becoming human' in connection with an environment and nonhuman actors. A critical posthumanism, therefore, has to embrace the task of integrating subject and system, of overcoming the restrictions within humanism, in order to be able to do justice to the promise that undeniably lies within our posthuman humanity.

Afterword: The other side of life

It seems appropriate to complete this study with a recent development in the theoretical humanities and social sciences which might be seen as a direct effect of their 'posthumanization', their movement towards a 'postanthropocentric' rationale and their engagement with their own transition towards the 'posthumanities', as described above. One could name this transition a return to the question of 'life' – as a central discursive object and focus of knowledge production – a response to the pro*life*ration of new technological, human and nonhuman life forms, the breakdown of the boundary between the inorganic and the organic (one of Haraway's identified forms of 'cyborgization') and the rise of the so-called 'life sciences' – the interdisciplinary field of sciences that takes life in all its forms as its specific domain: from anatomy to zoology. A critical posthumanism would, of course, take part in this 'turn *to* life', which could just as well be interpreted as a 'turn *on* life'. It would have to study its effects, its transformational potential, its dangers and promises. But, first and foremost, it would see the 'life turn' in theory and science, as a symptom of wider contexts and change. It would take the turn to life as a symptom of these underlying changes (a combination of economy, society, culture; globalization and posthumanization; technoculture and technoscientific capitalism, etc.) and would thus ask: Why this current frenzy about thinking of 'life' or 'life-thinking' in the humanities, the social sciences and the biosciences? It seems that the renewed centring of thinking on 'life' has raised the stakes, so to speak, by moving from language and culture as main battlegrounds (cf. the 'language wars', and the 'culture wars') to science ('science wars'), ultimately, to 'life' ('life wars'?). Where life is at stake, death, of course, threatens: the death of the 'humanities', the death of 'humanism', the death of the 'human' – which remains an undeniable aspect of posthumanism, of the posthuman and of visions of posthumanity. One of the recent key sources in the turn to life (and death) is Giorgio Agamben's reinterpretation of Foucault's biopower, biopolitics in terms of a modern 'thanatopolitics'. Agamben is concerned with the resurfacing of the question of sovereignty over life and death, governmentality and politics in the age of neoliberalism, biotechnology and global terror. A great number of recent publications focus on the implications of Agamben's radicalization of Foucault's notion of biopower and biopolitics in terms of a critique of contemporary democracy. Agamben's rather pessimistic prognosis for contemporary biopolitics, veering ever more frantically into thanatopolitics, has recently been countered by attempts to think a more 'affirmative biopolitics' (cf. Campbell 2012). Instead of the seemingly inevitable thanatopolitical drift at work in modern biopolitics, Campbell's *Improper Life: Technology and Biopolitics from Heidegger to Foucault* (2012) returns to Foucault and an analysis of the role of *technē* (or 'the technical') in biopolitical thought. He asks:

> [I]s there something about the nature of biopolitical thought today that makes it impossible to deploy affirmatively? Does biopolitical thought do the dirty, intellectual work of neoliberalism, offering little opposition to local threats, while focusing exclusively on matters of life and death at the level of species? What is it about *technē* that calls forth *thanatos* in a context of life?
>
> (Campbell 2012: vii, viii)

At stake is, thus, on the one hand, an analysis of the potential for resistance within contemporary biopolitical thinking to current global techno-thanato-political developments. On the other hand, Campbell criticizes some of the main protagonists of contemporary biopolitical thinking – Heidegger, Agamben and Sloterdijk – in terms of their respective positioning vis-à-vis technology and technological determinism. Cambell's main starting point in his analysis of the reason why technology might cause biopolitics to drift into thanatopolitics is Heidegger's differentiation between 'proper' and 'improper writing' and the loss of 'authenticity' that this distinction causes. According to Heidegger, technology is that which 'enframes' modern man (and, arguably, even more so, contemporary (post)humans). It produces the forgetting of and withdrawal from (authentic) Being. Heidegger's example is the typewriter, which instrumentalizes the human hand: in other words, that which, for Heidegger, is most essentially human. The typewriter turns 'proper' (or organic) writing into inauthentic or 'improper' writing. It is Campbell's claim that this model of proper/authentic and improper/inauthentic or 'expropriated' becomes the main binary opposition that informs all modern biopolitical thinking and is both the reason and the explanation why biopolitics almost inevitably turns into thanatopolitics. Technology is seen as that which provokes the forgetting of Being while, at the same time, it 'reveals', exposes and challenges the essence of the human. It is the supposed 'inhumanity' of this technological challenge that produces the focus on death in modern biopolitics in the forms of 'danger' and 'risk'. The opposition between proper and improper writing (or the use of technology in general), accordingly, maps onto a division between 'proper' and 'improper life' in the sense of authentic humanity *versus* dehumanized, or mere 'animal-being', which of course opens the route taken by twentieth century totalitarianism (Nazism and Communism), and which, ideologically speaking at least, continues to shape contemporary biopolitical thinking under the conditions of neoliberal globalization. Campbell summarizes the role Heidegger's bio-thanato-logical thinking and its continued influence on contemporary (posthumanist) thinking thus:

> the Heideggerian ontology of Being presupposes the lesser form of the human, in a division that today, thanks to Agamben, we refer to as *zoē* and *bíos*. If today the thanatopolitical seems to dominate contemporary perspectives on biopolitics as well as our understanding of neoliberalism and globalization, it is because of this deep ambiguity concerning man and technology and the dehumanizing effects the latter has for man ...
>
> (2012: 28)

The problematic notions of 'authenticity', 'anthropocentrism' and 'technological determinism' that underlie Heidegger's 'bio-thanato-politics' return in Agamben's work. In his model, *bíos* is reserved for the 'proper' social life of the individual human being, while *zoē* is the 'improper' dehumanized, animalized and depoliticized form of 'bare life', which Agamben sees at work in the generalized trend towards the *homo sacer* (the silent, desubjectified, singular human life 'at the disposal' or mercy of bio/thanatopolitics, across the ages, but increasingly so, today) (cf. Agamben 1998). What characterizes the pro*life*ration of bare and exposed forms of life under the neoliberal, globalized, contemporary condition is the accumulation of *dispositifs* (apparatuses, devices, stratagems, mechanisms ...) – originally a Foucauldian term used to explain how modern society uses political 'mechanisms' in response to perceived emergencies (most famously, the 'panopticon' as a surveillance *dispositif*). Campbell, in his critical reading of Agamben and Roberto Esposito's work, shows how, by implication, in all contemporary approaches to biopolitics something like the *dispositif* appears as the main (technological) force which sends biopolitics onto the slippery slope towards the disposal over life, desubjectification, depoliticization and, hence, thanatopolitics.

A different approach to the notion of the *dispositif*, however, might be thinkable. While for Agamben the *dispositif* is clearly a – arguably the main – thanatological device, the role it plays in Esposito, who instead follows Deleuze (and also the 'later' Foucault), can also be enabling – maybe even life-affirming. This is connected to the ambiguity of the very process of subjectification that every *dispositif* necessarily presupposes. Being a subject is a prerequisite for agency, but being subjected also means being at the receiving end of (bio)power. In the ambiguity of subjective agency are thus forces and 'lines of flight' (Deleuze and Guattari's term) at work, which prevent any *dispositif* from being completely determined in terms of subjectification or desubjectification. There is, therefore, also the potential for an 'affirming' *dispositif*, and thus a harnessing of its 'impersonal' power for a renewal of community, according to Esposito (2008).

However, an affirmative (posthumanist) biopolitics, following Campbell, does not only need to overcome the opposition between proper and improper, authentic and inauthentic life, but needs to deconstruct or reposition the relationship between biology or life and politics in general. One attempt at doing so lies in Peter Sloterdijk's recent work (2013; further developing ideas in Sloterdijk 2001 and 2009). Sloterdijk reads globalization as an ongoing process of interiorization and immunization – both are anthropotechnics of humanization which create habitable spaces for humans, but which, at the same time, have adverse '(auto)immunitarian' effects. Humans, and in particular modern humans, use technology to create spaces (or protective 'spheres' or 'bubbles') through which to explore and control their environments, by separation and 'interiorization'. Sloterdijk uses the analogy of the astronaut and the space suit:

> Modernity essentially consists of the struggle to create these metaphorical space suits, immunitary regimes, he will call them, that will protect Europeans from dangerous and life-threatening contact with the outside ...
>
> (cf. Campbell 2012: 88)

Where the proper and improper distinction reoccurs in Sloterdijk's writing, however, is in the notion of the loss of authentic community in modern societies. The (auto)immunitarian drift within human history is being exploited by neoliberal globalization and governmentality to insulate the individual within their respective little spheres through the use of the *dispositifs* designed to create security and protection against terrorism. For Sloterdijk, there is thus a dangerous link between contemporary biopolitics and the discourse on terrorist threats, security and immunity, which leads to thanatopolitical forms of governmentality. The problematic aspect is that, for Sloterdijk, biotechnology and bioengineering seem to form possibilities for (at least some) humans to wrest biopolitics back from the claws of thanatology, by 'administering [their] own zoological features', or by 'administer[ing their] own life through death' (cf. Campbell 2012: 117; an argument already made, in a different form, by Fukuyama and Habermas within the debate on 'liberal' eugenics, discussed above).

In order to reevaluate and rethink the role of technology for thanatopolitics, Campbell, proposes to return to the 'final' Foucault and his 'affirmative' biopolitics based on the idea of the 'care for the self'. Cambell is motivated by the question: '[I]s the drift toward *thanatos* the only possibility for contemporary forms of technologized existence?' (Campbell 2012: 119). Given the need for a positive or affirmative biopolitics in the face of the exponential growth of neoliberal *dispositifs* aimed at controlling and securing populations, on the one hand, and promoting marketized forms of exchange to more and more generalized areas of life, on the other hand, we believe Campbell is absolutely right to ask: 'Is securing populations the only possibility for biopolitics in a technologized milieu, its increasing inscription as only biopower, with only a toxic mix of *dispositifs* and media to look forward to?' (126). Instead, Campbell emphasizes the aesthetic dimension of Foucauldian biopower and biopolitics as a starting point for a care for the self that would simply remove the negative and destructive inscription of *technē*, by 'attending' to the object and to the 'immanence' of life forms. He envisages forms of life that are not from the start captured by or for a self, and which would '[help] us create a breach between care and mastery, between a care for the self felt first in terms of forms of *bíos* and known only after in terms of mastery' (156).

It thus seems almost inevitable that an 'affirmative (posthuman or at least posthumanist) biopolitics' would have to embrace some form of (neo)vitalism, for example *à la* Deleuze, if not *à la* Nietzsche. Equally, there are a number of 'new materialisms' that seek to reposition the notion of 'life' outside propriety or impropriety, namely by 'de-athropo-centring' and 'de-ontologizng' it. These attempts, predominantly found in 'feminist' materialist thinkers like Rosi Braidotti, Vicki Kirby, Karen Barad and others, might, in fact, be called 'the other side' of the current critique of thanatopolitics. These feminist thinkers, who, through a critical rereading of Deleuze and the vitalist tradition, also argue for a more affirmative and inclusive notion of life, insist on the experience of a materialist notion of difference, however. The difference between the two approaches – both of which would have to be engaged with by a critical posthumanism – might be illustrated briefly with reference to the intense 'life-long conversation' between Jacques Derrida and Hélène Cixous. In Derrida's later works, in his exchange with Cixous, the theme of life (and death) becomes more openly addressed, especially in his late interviews and in *H.C. for Life, That Is to Say* ... (2006). Here Derrida, we believe, engages with precisely this feminist materialist, life-affirming tradition, which Cixous might helped to create, without, however, 'being on her or its side'. However, at the same time, he also feels compelled to reposition himself somewhat, by no longer arguing, at least not entirely so, from the 'thanatological' side of (patriarchal, Western) metaphysics (or carno-phallo-logo-thanato...--centrism (cf. Derrida, 1991)), or the 'side of death'. In fact, he describes the very impossibility of being able to 'choose'' sides in this context. A certain awareness of the problematic (or the aporia) of this necessity *and* impossibility at work in the choice 'for life' from the side of death (death, as Derrida explains, of course not being a side you can *be* on) demonstrates not only the continued indebtedness of Agamben, Sloterdijk and the entire contemporary bio-thanato-political tradition of thinking, to Heidegger's problematic notion of propriety and impropriety, authenticity and inauthenticity in technological humanity; but it would also have to address the male-centredness of this entire tradition, including what might be called its 'techno-phallo-centrism'. This is another reason why a critical approach to the broad issue of posthumanist subjectivity needs to resist the current tendency to foreground the importance of technology in discussions of human/social evolution. Rather, to return to our notion of a critical posthumanism 'without technology', the ubiquitous technological determinism in contemporary perspectives on bio-thanato-politics will have to be met with radical scepticism. The impossibility of 'choosing' between life and death –

> the *Belebtheit* of livingness [*vivance*] or of liveliness [*vivacité*], the live-ance of being in life [*le* vivement *de l'être en vie*] ..., this reviviscence of life would be the element, the only one, a universal element, since it has no limits or no limits or no other side: there is no side for nonlife
>
> (Derrida 2006: 112–13)

– or, in other words, the question of the other, impossible, side of life (which is not death) probably represents the main challenge for a critical posthumanism and the formation of posthumanist subjectivities.

Bibliography

Agamben, Giorgio (1998) *Homo Sacer: Sovereign Power and Bare Life*, trans. D. Heller-Roazen, Stanford: Stanford University Press.
Althusser, Louis (1971 [1970]) 'Ideology and Ideological State Apparatuses (Notes towards and Investigation', trans. Ben Brewster, *Lenin and Philosophy and Other Essays*, London: NLB, 121–73.
Anders, Günther (1956 [1992a]) *Die Antiquiertheit des Menschen 1: Über die Seele im Zeitalter der zweiten industriellen Revolution*, Munich: Beck.
—(1980 [1992b]) *Die Antiquiertheit des Menschen 2: Über die Zerstörung des Lebens im Zeitalter der dritten industriellen Revolution*, Munich: Beck.
Anker, Suzanne and Dorothy Nelkin (2004) *The Molecular Gaze: Art in the Genetic Age*, New York: Cold Spring Harbor Laboratory Press.
Armageddon (2001 [1998]) Dir. Michael Bay, Touchstone, DVD.
Aronowitz, Stanley (1988) *Science as Power: Discourse and Ideology in Modern Society*, Basingstoke: Macmillan Press.
Aronowitz, Stanley, Michael Menser, et al. (eds) (1996) *Technoscience and Cyberculture*, London: Routledge.
Artificial Intelligence: AI (2002 [2001]) Dir. Steven Spielberg, Warner Bros. and DreamWorks, DVD.
Ashman, Keith M. and Philip S. Baringer (eds) (2001) *After the Science Wars*, London: Routledge.
Atlan, Monique and Roger-Pol Droit (eds) (2012) *Humain – Une enquête philosophique sur ces révolutions qui changent nos vies*, Paris: Flammarion.
Babin, Dominique (2004) *PH1 – Manuel d'usage et d'entretien du posthumain*, Paris: Flammarion.
Badiou, Alain (1991) 'On a Finally Objectless Subject', in Eduardo Cadava *et al.* (eds) *Who Comes After the Subject?* London: Routledge: 24–32.
—(2013) *Theory of the Subject*, trans. Bruno Bosteels, London: Continuum.
Badmington, Neil (2000) 'Introduction: Approaching Posthumanism', in Badmington (ed.) *Posthumanism: Readers in Cultural Criticism*, Basingstoke: Palgrave: 1–10.
—(2001) 'Pod Alighty!; Or, Humanism, Posthumanism, and the Strange Case of Invasion of the Body Snatchers', *Textual Practice* 15.1: 5–22.
—(2003) 'Theorizing Posthumanism', *Cultural Critique* 53 (Winter): 10–27.

—(2004a) *Alien Chic: Posthumanism and the Other Within*, London: Routledge.
—(2004b) 'Post, Oblique, Human', *Theology and Sexuality* 10.2: 56–64.
—(2006a) 'Cultural Studies and the Posthumanities', Gary Hall and Claire Birchall, (eds) *New Cultural Studies: Adventures in Theory*, Edinburgh: Edinburgh University Press: 260–72.
— (2006b) 'Posthumanism', in Simon Malpas and Paul Wake, (eds), *The Routledge Companion to Critical Theory*, London: Routledge: 240–1.
Barad, Karen (2007) *Meeting the Universe Half-Way: Quantum Physics and the Entanglement of Matter and Meaning*, Durham, NC: Duke University Press.
Baudrillard, Jean (1988) *Selected Writings*, (ed.) Mark Poster, trans. Jacques Mourrain, Stanford: Stanford University Press.
—(1994) *Simulacra and Simulation*, trans. Sheila P. Glaser, Ann Arbor, MI: University of Michigan Press.
—(2004) *The Gulf War Did Not Take Place*, trans. Paul Patton, Sydney: Power Institute of Fine Arts.
—(2012) *Impossible Exchange*, London: Verso.
Beck, Ulrich (1992) *Risk Society: Towards a New Modernity*, London: Sage.
—(1998) *Democracy without Enemies*, trans. Mark Ritter, Oxford: Blackwell.
Belsey, Catherine (1980) *Critical Practice*, London: Methuen.
—(2007) *Why Shakespeare?* Basingstoke: Palgrave.
Best, Steven and Douglas Kellner (2001) *The Postmodern Adventure: Science, Technology, and Cultural Studies at the Third Millennium*, London: Routledge.
Bicentennial Man (2001 [1999]) dir. Chris Columbus, Sony Home Entertainment, DVD.
Blackmore, Tim (2005) *War X: Human Extensions in Battlespace*, Toronto: University of Toronto Press.
Blade Runner. The Director's Cut (1992 [1982]) Dirs. Ridley Scott and Michael Deeley, Warner Bros., DVD.
Bloom, Harold (1999) *Shakespeare: The Invention of the Human*, London: Fourth Estate.
Bolter, Jay and Richard Grusin (1999) *Remediation: Understanding New Media*, Cambridge: MIT Press.
Braidotti, Rosi (2000) 'Teratologies', in Ian Buchanan and Claire Colebrook, (eds) *Deleuze and Feminist Theory*, Edinburgh: Edinburgh University Press: 156–72.
—(2002) *Metamorphoses: Towards a Materialist Theory of Becoming*, Cambridge: Polity.
—(2006) *Transpositions: On Nomadic Ethics*, Cambridge: Polity.

Brake, Mark L. and Neil Hook (2008) *Different Engines: How Science Drives Fiction and Fiction Drives Science*, London: Macmillan.
Brewster, Scott, et al. (eds) (2000) *Inhuman Reflections: Thinking the Limits of the Human*, Manchester: Manchester University Press.
Bukatman, Scott (1993) *Terminal Identity: The Virtual Subject in Postmodern Science Fiction*, Durham, NC: Duke University Press.
Butler, Judith (1993) *Bodies That Matter: On the Discursive Limits of "Sex"*, London: Routledge.
Cadava, Eduardo (ed.) (1991) *Who Comes after the Subject?* New York: Routledge.
Campbell, Timothy (2002) *Improper Life: Technology and Biopolitics from Heidegger to Foucault*, Minneapolis: University of Minnesota Press.
Castells, Manuel (1996) *The Rise of the Network Society*, Oxford: Blackwell.
Chambers, Iain (2001) *Culture after Humanism: History, Culture, Subjectivity*, London: Routledge.
Cheah, Pheng (2006) *Inhuman Conditions: On Cosmopolitanism and Human Rights*, Cambridge, MA: Harvard University Press.
Clarke, Bruce (2008) *Posthuman Metamorphosis: Narrative and Systems*, New York: Fordham University Press.
Clarke, Bruce and Mark B. N. Hansen (eds) (2009) *Emergence and Embodiment: New Essays on Second-Order Systems Theory*, Durham, NC: Duke University Press.
Cohen, Jeffrey Jerome (ed.) (1996) *Monster Theory: Reading Culture*, Minneapolis: University of Minnesota Press.
Cohen, Tom (1994) *Anti-Mimesis from Plato to Hitchcock*, Cambridge: Cambridge University Press.
Coker, Christopher (2004) *The Future of War: The Re-Enchantment of War in the Twenty-First Century*, Oxford: Blackwell.
Colebrook, Clare (2012) 'Introduction: Extinction. Framing the End of the Species', in Colebrook (ed.) *Extinction – Living Books About Life*, Open Humanities Press & JISC, http://www.livingbooksaboutlife.org/books/Extinction [accessed 17 February 2013].
Cooper, Simon (2002) *Technoculture and Critical Theory: In the Service of the Machine?* London: Routledge.
Cottom, Daniel (2006) *Unhuman Culture*, Philadelphia: University of Pennsylvania Press.
Croissant, Jennifer L. (1998) 'Growing Up Cyborg: Developmental Stories for Postmodern Children', in Robbie Davis-Floyd and Joseph Dumit, (eds) *Cyborg Babies from Techno-sex to Techno-tots*, London: Routledge: 285–300.
Crook, Stephen, Jan Pakulski and Malcolm Waters (1992) *Postmodernization: Change in Advanced Society*, London: Sage.

Csicsery-Ronay Jr., Istvan (1991) 'The SF of Theory: Baudrillard and Haraway', *Science Fiction Studies* 18: 387–404.
Curtis, Neal (2006) 'Inhuman', *Theory, Culture & Society* 23.2–3: 434–6.
Cusset, François (2008) *French Theory*, trans. Jeff Fort, Minneapolis: Universtiy of Minnesota Press.
Davies, Tony (2008) *Humanism*, 2nd edn, London: Routledge.
Davis, Erik (1998) *Techgnosis: Myth, Magic and Mysticism in the Age of Information*, London: Serpent's Tail.
Dawkins, Richard (1976) *The Selfish Gene*, Oxford: Oxford University Press.
Deleuze, Gilles (1992) 'What is a Dispositif?', in T. J. Armstrong, (ed.) *Michel Foucault: Philosopher: Essays Translated from the French and German*, Hemel Hempstead: Harvester Wheatsheaf: 159–68.
—(1994) *Difference and Repetition*, trans. Paul Patton, London: Athlone Press.
—(2001) *Pure Immanence: Essays on a Life*, trans. Anne Boyman, New York: Zone Books.
Deleuze, Gilles and Felix Guattari (1987) *A Thousand Plateaus: Capitalism and Schizophrenia I*, Minneapolis: University of Minnesota Press.
Dennett, Daniel (1993) *Consciousness Explained*, London: Penguin.
Der Derian, James (2001) *Virtuous War: Mapping the Military-Industrial-Media-Entertainment Network*, Boulder, CO: Westview Press.
Derrida, Jacques (1989a) 'Psyche: Interventions of the Other', trans. Catherine Porter, in Lindsay Waters and Wlad Godzich, (eds) *Reading de Man Reading*, Minneapolis: University of Minnesota Press: 25–65.
—(1989b) 'Some Statements and Truisms about Neo-Logisms, Newisms, Postisms, Parasitisms, and Other Small Seismisms', in David Carroll (ed.), *The States of 'Theory': History, Art and Critical Discourse*, New York: Columbia University Press: 63–94.
—(1990) *Margins of Philosophy*, trans. Alan Bass, Chicago: University of Chicago Press.
—(1991) '"Eating Well", or the Calculation of the Subject: An Interview with Jacques Derrida', in Cadava (1991): 96–119.
—(1992) '"This Strange Institution Called Literature": An Interview with Jacques Derrida', in Derek Attridge, (ed.) *Jacques Derrida: Acts of Literature*, New York: Routledge: 33–75.
—(1994a) 'The Deconstruction of Actuality', *Radical Philosophy* 68: 28–41.
—(1994b) *Specters of Marx: The State of Debt, the Work of Mourning, and the New International*, trans. Peggy Kamuf, London: Routledge.
—(1995) 'Archive Fever: A Freudian Impression', trans. Eric Prenowitz, *Diacritics* 25.2: 9–63.

—(1997 [1967]) *Of Grammatology*, trans. Gayatri C. Spivak, Baltimore, MD: Johns Hopkins University Press.
—(1998) *Monolingualism of the Other; Or, the Prosthesis of Origin*, trans. Patrick Mensah, Stanford: Stanford University Press.
—(2001a) 'The Future of the Profession or the University without Condition (Thanks to the "Humanities", What Could Take Place Tomorrow)', in Tom Cohen (ed.), *Jacques Derrida and the Humanities: A Critical Reader*, Cambridge: Cambridge University Press: 24–57.
—(2001b) 'What is a Relevant Translation?' Trans. Laurence Venuti, *Critical Inquiry* 27.1: 174–200.
—(2002a) 'The Aforementioned So-Called Human Genome', in *Negotiations: Interventions and Interviews 1971–2001* (ed. and trans.) Elizabeth Rottenberg, Stanford, CT: Stanford University Press: 199–214.
—(2002b [1967]) *Writing and Difference*, trans. Alan Bass, London: Routledge.
—(2003) 'And Say the Animal Responded?' trans. David Wills, in Cary Wolfe (ed.), *Zoontologies: The Question of the Animal*, Minneapolis: University of Minnesota Press: 121–46.
—(2006) *H.C. for Life, That Is to Say ...*, trans. Laurent Milesi and Stefan Herbrechter, Stanford: Stanford University Press.
—(2007) 'A Certain Impossible Possibility of Saying the Event', trans. Gila Walker *Critical Inquiry* 33.2: 441–61.
—(2008) *The Animal that Therefore I Am*, trans. David Wills, New York: Fordham University Press.
Descombes, Vincent (1980) *Modern French Philosophy*, Cambridge: Cambridge University Press.
Diocaretz, Miriam and Stefan Herbrechter (eds) (2006) *The Matrix in Theory*, *Critical Studies* 29, Amsterdam: Rodopi.
Dollimore, Jonathan (1985) 'Introduction: Shakespeare, Cultural Materialism and New Historicism', in Jonathan Dollimore and Alan Sinfield (eds), *Political Shakespeare: New Essays in Cultural Materialism*, Manchester: Manchester University Press, pp. 2–17.
—(1998) 'Shakespeare and Theory', in Ania Loomba and Martin Orkin (eds), *Post-colonial Shakespeares*, London: Routledge, pp. 259–76.
—(2004) *Radical Tragedy: Religion, Ideology and Power in the Drama of Shakespeare and His Contemporaries*, 3rd (ed.), Basingstoke: Palgrave Macmillan.
Dunayer, Joan (2004) *Speciecism*, Derwood, MD: Ryce Publishing.
Dyens, Ollivier (2001) *Metal and Flesh: The Evolution of Man – Technology Takes Over*, Cambridge, MA: MIT Press.
—(2008) *La Condition inhumaine: essai sur l'effroi technologique*, Paris: Flammarion.

Easthope, Antony (1988) *British Post-Structuralism since 1968*, London: Routledge.
Ellul, Jacques (2004 [1977]) *Le Système technicien*, Paris: Le Cherche midi.
Esposito, Roberto (2008) *Bios: Biopolitics and Philosophy*, trans. T. Campbell, Minneapolis: University of Minnesota Press.
Foucault, Michel (1970) *The Order of Things: An Archaeology of the Human Sciences* (ed.) R. D. Laing, New York: Pantheon.
—(1990) *The History of Sexuality, 3: The Care for the Self*, trans. R. Hurley, Harmondsworth: Penguin.
—(1991) *Discipline and Punish: The Birth of the Prison*, trans. A. Sheridan, Harmondsworth: Penguin.
—(2008) *The Birth of Biopolitics: Lectures at the Collège de France 1978–1979*, trans. Graham Burchall, Basingstoke: Palgrave.
Franklin, Adrian (2007) 'Posthumanism', in George Ritzer (ed.), *The Blackwell Encyclopedia of Sociology*, Vol. VII (N–P), Oxford: Blackwell: 3548–50.
Fraser, Mariam, Sara Kember and Celia Lury (eds) (2006) *Inventing Life: Approaches to the New Vitalism*, London: Sage.
Fudge, Erica (2000) *Perceiving Animals: Humans and Beasts in Early Modern English Culture*, Basingstoke: Macmillan.
—(ed.) (2004) *Renaissance Beasts: Of Animals, Humans and Other Wonderful Creatures*, Urbana: University of Illinois Press.
Fudge, Erica, Ruth Gilbert and Susan Wiseman (eds) (2002) *At the Borders of the Human: Beasts, Bodies and Natural Philosophy in the Early Modern Period*, Basingstoke: Palgrave Macmillan.
Fuery, Patrick and Nick Mansfield (1997) *Cultural Studies and the New Humanities: Concepts and Controversies*, Oxford: Oxford University Press.
Fukuyama, Francis (1999) *Our Posthuman Future: Consequences of the Biotechnology Revolution*, London: Profile Books.
Gaggi, Silvio (1989) *Modern/Postmodern: A Study in Twentieth-Century Arts and Ideas*, Philadelphia: University of Pennsylvania Press.
Gane, Nicholas (2006) 'Posthuman', *Theory, Culture & Society* 23. 2–3: 431–4.
Garber, Marjorie (2003) *Quotation Marks*, London: Routledge.
Garrard, Greg (2004) *Ecocriticism*, London: Routledge.
Gattaca (2004 [1997]) Dir. Andrew Niccol, Columbia Pictures, DVD.
Graham, Elaine (2002) *Representations of the Post/Human: Monsters, Aliens and Others in Popular Culture*, Manchester: Manchester University Press.
—(2004) 'Post/Human Conditions', *Theology & Sexuality* 10. 2: 10–32.
Grau, Oliver (2003) *Virtual Art: From Illusion to Immersion*, Cambridge, MA: MIT Press.

Gray, Chris Hables (2001) *Cyborg Citizen: Politics in the Posthuman Age*, London: Routledge.
Gross, Paul R. and Norman Levitt (1998) *Higher Superstition: The Academic Left and Its Quarrels with Science*, Baltimore, MD: Johns Hopkins University Press.
Habermas, Jürgen (1979) *Technik und Wissenschaft als 'Ideologie'*, Frankfurt: Suhrkamp.
—(2003) *The Future of Human Nature*, Cambridge: Polity Press.
Halberstam, Judith and Ira Livingston (eds) (1995) *Posthuman Bodies*, Bloomington: Indiana University Press.
Hall, Stuart (ed.) (1997) *Representation: Cultural Representations and Signifying Practices*, London: Sage.
Halliwell, Martin and Andy Mousley (2003) *Critical Humanisms: Humanist/Anti-Humanist Dialogues*, Edinburgh: Edinburgh University Press.
Hansen, Mark (2000) *Embodying Technesis: Technology beyond Writing*, Ann Arbor: University of Michigan Press.
Haraway, Donna (1991 [1985]) *Simians, Cyborgs, and Women: The Reinvention of Nature*, New York: Routledge.
—(1992) *Primate Visions: Gender, Race, and Nature in the World of Modern Science*, London: Verso.
—(1997) *Modest_Witness@Second_Millennium. FemaleMan_Meets_OncoMouse: Feminism and Technoscience*, London: Routledge.
—(2003) *The Companion Species: Dogs, People, and Significant Otherness*, Chicago: Prickly Paradigm Press.
—(2008) *When Species Meet*, Minneapolis: University of Minnesota Press.
Harry Potter and the Philosopher's Stone (2009 [2001]) Dir. Chris Columbus, Warner Home Video, DVD.
Harvey, David (1989) *The Condition of Postmodernity*, Oxford: Blackwell.
Hassan, Ihab (1977) 'Prometheus as Performer: Toward a Posthumanist Culture? A University Masque in Five Scenes', *The Georgia Review* 21.4: 830–50.
—(1987) *The Postmodern Turn: Essays in Postmodern Culture*, Columbus: Ohio State University.
Hayles, N. Katherine (1998) 'How Does It Feel to Be Posthuman?', www.v2.nl/archive/articles/how-does-it-feel-to-be-posthuman [accessed 17 February 2013].
—(1999) *How We Became Posthuman: Virtual Bodies in Cybernetics, Literature, and Informatics*, Chicago: University of Chicago Press.
—(2005) *My Mother Was a Computer: Digital Subjects and Literary Texts*, Chicago: University of Chicago Press.
Heidegger, Martin (1949) *Über den Humanismus*, Frankfurt: Klostermann.

—(1962) *Die Technik und die Kehre*, Pfullingen: Neske.
—(1967) *Wegmarken*, Frankfurt: Klostermann.
—(1978 [1947]) *Basic Writings from Being and Time (1927) to The Task of Thinking (1964)* (ed.) D. Farrell Krell, London: Routledge & Kegan Paul.
—(1993 [1966]) '"Only a God Can Save Us": *Der Spiegel*'s Interview with Martin Heidegger', in Richard Wolin (ed.) *The Heidegger Controversy: A Critical Reader*, Cambridge, MA: MIT Press: 91–116.
—(2000) *Reden und andere Zeugnisse eines Lebenswegs, 1910–1976, Gesamtausgabe Bd. 16*, Frankfurt: Klostermann.
Herbrechter, Stefan (2004) 'Preface: Alterities – Politics of In(ter)vention', in Jacques Derrida, Pierre-Jean Labarrière et al. 'Alterities', (trans. and ed.) Stefan Herbrechter, *Parallax* 33: 1–16.
—(2005) 'Badiou, Derrida and *The Matrix*: Cultural Criticism between Objectless Subjects and Subjectless Objects', *Polygraph* 16: 205–20.
Herbrechter, Stefan and Ivan Callus (2004) 'The Latecoming of the Posthuman, or, Why "We" Do the Apocalypse Differently, "Now"', *Reconstruction* 4.3, http://reconstruction.eserver.org/043/callus.htm [accessed 17 February 2013].
—(eds) (2004) *Discipline and Practice: The (Ir)resistibility of Theory*, Lewisburg: Bucknell University Press.
—(2007) 'Critical Posthumanism or, the *inventio* of a posthumanism without technology', *Subject Matters* 3.2/4.1: 15–29.
—(2008) 'What Is a Posthumanist Reading?', *Angelaki* 13.1: 95–111.
—(eds) (2009) *Cy-Borges: Posthumanism, Memory and Subjectivity in the Work of Jorge Luis Borges*, Lewisburg, PA: Bucknell University Press.
—(2013) *Critical Posthumanism, Critical Posthumanisms 1*, Amsterdam: Rodopi.
Hollow Man (2001 [2000]) Dir. Paul Verhoeven, Sony Pictures, DVD.
Hutcheon, Linda (1988) *The Poetics of Postmodernism: History, Theory, Fiction*, New York: Routledge.
I, Robot (2004 [1995]) Dir. Alex Proyas, Twentieth Century Fox.
Invasion of the Body Snatchers (1956) Dir. Don Siegel, Allied Artist Pictures.
—(2000 [1978]) Dir. Philip Kaufman, MGM Home Entertainment, DVD.
Jameson, Fredric (1972) *The Prison-House of Language: A Critical Account of Structuralism and Russian Formalism*, Princeton, NJ: Princeton University Press.
—(2005) *Archaeologies of the Future: The Desire Called Utopia and Other Science Fictions*, London: Virgin.
Jardine, Alice (1986) *Gynesis: Configurations of Woman and Modernity*, Ithaca, NY: Cornell University Press.
Jeanneret, Yves (1998) *L'Affaire Sokal ou la querelle des impostures*, Paris: PUF.

Jourdant, Baudouin (ed.) (1998) *Impostures scientifiques – Les malentendus de l'affaire Sokal*, Paris: Éditions de la Découverte.
Joy, Bill (2000) 'Why the Future Doesn't Need Us', *Wired* 8 April 2000, www.wired.com/wired/archive/8.04/joy_pr.html [accessed 17 February 2013].
Kac, Eduardo (2005) *Telepresence and Bioart: Networking, Humans, Rabbits and Robots*, Ann Arbor: University of Michigan Press.
Kellner, Douglas (1994) *Media Culture: Cultural Studies Identity and Politics between the Modern and the Postmodern*, London: Routledge.
Kirby, Vicki (2011) *Quantum Anthropologies: Life at Large*, Durham, NC: Duke University Press.
Kittler, Friedrich (1999) *Grammophone, Film, Typewriter*, trans. Geoffrey Winthrop-Young, Stanford, CA: Stanford University Press.
Kroker, Arthur and Marilouise Kroker (1996) *Hacking the Future: Stories for the Flesh-Eating 90s*, London: St. Martin's Press.
Krüger, Oliver (2004) Virtualität und Unsterblichkeit: Die Visionen des Posthumanismus, Freiburg: Rombach.
Kurzweil, Ray (1999) *The Age of Spiritual Machines: When Computers Exceed Human Intelligence.* New York: Viking.
Laclau, Ernesto (1988) 'Politics and the Limits of Modernity', in Andrew Ross, (ed.) *Universal Abandon? The Politics of Postmodernism*, Minneapolis: University of Minnesota Press: 63–82.
Laclau, Ernesto and Chantal Mouffe (1985) *Hegemony and Socialist Strategy*, New York: Schocken.
Lafontaine, Céline (2004) *L'Empire cybernétique – Des machines à penser à la pensée machine*, Paris: Éditions du Seuil.
Lash, Christopher (2002) *Critique of Information*, London: Sage.
Latour, Bruno (1991) 'Technology is Society Made Durable', in John Law (ed.), *A Sociology of Monsters: Essays on Power, Technology and Domination*, London: Routledge: 103–31.
—(1993) *We Have Never Been Modern*, trans. Catherine Porter, Cambridge, MA: Harvard University Press.
—(2005) *Reassembling the Social: An Introduction to Actor-Network-Theory*, Oxford: Oxford University Press.
de Lauretis, Teresa (1987) *Technologies of Gender: Essays on Theory, Film, and Fiction*, Bloomington: Indiana University Press.
—(2003) 'Becoming Inorganic', *Critical Inquiry* 29.4: 547–70.
Lawton, Graham (2006) 'The Incredibles', *New Scientist* (13 May): 32–8.
Le Breton, David (1999) *L'Adieu au corps*, Paris: Métaillé.
Lecourt, Dominique (2003) *Humain Posthumain*, Paris: PUF.
Leitch, Vincent B. (2003) *Theory Matters*, London: Routledge.
Leroi-Gourhan, André (1945) *Milieu et techniques*, Paris: Albin Michel.
—(1964–5) *Le geste et la parole*, 2 vols., Paris: Albin Michel.

Lestel, Dominique (2004) *L'Animal singulier*, Paris: Seuil.
Lévy, Pierre (1998) *Qu'est-ce que le virtuel?* Paris: La Découverte.
Lingua Franca, Hgg. (2000) *The Sokal Hoax: The Sham that Shook the Academy*, Lincoln: University of Nebraska Press.
Luhmann, Niklas (1995) *Social Systems*, trans. J. Bednarz, Jr., with D. Baecker, Stanford, CA: Stanford University Press.
Lyotard, Jean-François (1984 [1979]) *The Postmodern Condition: A Report on Knowledge*, trans. Geoff Bennington and Brian Massumi, Minneapolis: University of Minnesota Press.
—(1991) *The Inhuman: Reflections on Time*, trans. Geoffrey Bennington and Rachel Bowlby, Cambridge: Polity Press.
—(1992) *The Postmodern Explained to Children*, London: Turnaround.
—(2001) 'A Postmodern Fable' [1993], trans. Georges Van Den Abeele, in Simon Malpas, (ed.) *Postmodern Debates*, Basingstoke: Palgrave: 12–21.
Malabou, Catherine (2008) *What Should We Do with Our Brain?* trans. Sebastian Rand, New York: Fordham University Press.
Matrix (2001 [1999]) Dirs. Larry and Andy Wachowski, Warner Bros., DVD.
Mauss, Marcel (1934) 'Les techniques du corps', *Journal de Psychologie*, XXXII: 3–4.
McHale, Brian (1987) *Postmodernist Fiction*, New York: Methuen.
McLuhan, Marshall (2001) *Understanding Media*, London: Routledge.
Menzel, Peter and MA Faith D'Aluisio (eds) (2001) *Robo Sapiens: Evolution of a New Species*, Cambridge: MIT Press.
Merrin, William (2005) *Baudrillard and the Media*, Cambridge: Polity.
Miami Theory Collective and Verena Andermatt Conley (1994) *Rethinking Technologies*, Minneapolis: University of Minnesota Press.
Michael, Mike (2006) *Technoscience and Everyday Life*, Maidenhead: Open University Press.
Michaud, Yves (2002) *Humain, inhumain, trop humain*, Paris: Micro-Climats.
Milburn, Colin (2002) 'Nanotechnology in the Age of Posthuman Engineering: Science Fiction as Science', *Configurations* 10.2: 261–96.
—(2003) 'Monsters in Eden: Derrida and Darwin', Modern Language Notes 118.3: 603–21.
Milon, Alain (2005) *La Réalité virtuelle: avec ou sans corps?* Paris: Autrement.
Minority Report (2003 [2002]) Dir. Steven Spielberg, Twentieth Century Fox, DVD.
Minsky, Marvin (1997) 'Will Robots Inherit the Earth?' web.media. mit.edu/~minsky/ papers/sciam.inherit.html [accessed 17 February 2013].

Moravec, Hans (1988) *Mind Children: The Future of Robot and Human Intelligence*, Cambridge, MA: Harvard University Press.
—(1999) *The Age of the Spiritual Machines: When Computers Exceed Human Intelligence*, Harmondsworth: Penguin.
More, Max (2003) 'Extropian Principles 3.0: A Transhumanist Declaration', Extropy Institute, http://www.maxmore.com/extprn3.htm [accessed 17 February 2013].
Nakamura, Lisa (2002) *Cybertypes: Race, Ethnicity and Identity on the Internet*, London: Routledge.
Nancy, Jean-Luc and Philippe Lacoue-Labarthe (eds) (1981) *Les Fins de l'homme – à partir du travail de Jacques Derrida*, Paris: Galilée.
Nietzsche, Friedrich (1918) *The Genealogy of Morals* [1887], trans. Horace B. Samuel, New York: Boni and Liveright.
—(1982) 'On Truth and Lie in an Extra-Moral Sense' [1873], trans. Walter Kaufmann, *The Portable Nietzsche*, London: Viking Penguin: 42–6.
Nowotny, Helga (1999) *Es ist so. Es könnte auch anders sein. Über das veränderte Verhältnis von Wissenschaft und Gesellschaft*, Frankfurt: Suhrkamp.
Parker, Ian (1992) *Discourse Dynamics*, London: Routledge.
Patterson, Charles (2002) *Eternal Treblinka: Our Treatment of Animals and the Holocaust*, New York: Lantern Books.
Pepperell, Robert (2003) *The Posthuman Condition: Consciousness beyond the Brain*, Bristol: Intellect.
—(2005) 'The Posthuman Manifesto', *Kritikos* 2, http://intertheory.org/pepperell.htm [accessed 17 February 2013].
Planet of the Apes (1968) Dir. Franklin J. Schaffner, Twentieth Century Fox.
—(2002 [2001]) Dir. Tim Burton, Twentieth Century Fox, DVD.
Poster, Mark (1995) *The Second Media Age*, Cambridge: Polity Press.
—(2001a) *The Information Subject: Essays*, Amsterdam: G + B Arts International.
—(2001b) *What's the Matter with the Internet?* Minneapolis: University of Minnesota Press.
—(2006) *Information Please: Culture and Politics in the Age of Digital Machines*, Durham, NC: Duke University Press.
Postman, Neil (1983) *The Disappearance of Childhood*, London: Virgin.
—(1993) *Technopoly: The Surrender of Culture to Technology*, New York: Vintage Books.
Readings, Bill (1996) *The University in Ruins*, Cambridge, MA: Harvard University Press.
Rees, Martin (2003) *Our Final Century: Will the Human Race Survive the Twenty-First Century?* New York: Heinemann.
Reichle, Ingeborg (2005) *Kunst aus dem Labor: Zum Verhältnis von Kunst und Wissenschaft im Zeitalter der Technoscience*, Vienna: Springer.

Rhodes, Neil and Jonathan Sawday (eds) (2000) *The Renaissance Computer: Knowledge Technology in the First Age of Print*, London: Routledge.
Ridley, Matt (2003) *Nature Via Nuture: Genes, Experience, and What Makes Us Human*, New York: Harper Collins.
Roco, Mihail C. and Williman Sims Bainbridge (eds) (2002) *Converging Technologies for Improving Human Performance: Nanotechnology, Biotechnology, Information Technology and Cognitive Science*, http://www.wtec.org/ConvergingTechnologies/Reprt/NBIC_report.pdf [accessed 17 February 2013].
Rose, Margaret A. (1991) *The Post-Modern and the Post-Industrial: A Critical Analysis*, Cambridge: Cambridge University Press.
Rosenau, Pauline Marie (1992) *Post-Modernism and the Social Sciences: Insights, Inroads, and Intrusions*, Princeton, NJ: Princeton University Press.
Rossini, Manuela (2006) 'To the Dogs: Companion Speciesism and the New Feminist Materialism', *Kritikos* 3, http://intertheory.org/rossini [accessed 17 February 2013].
Ruby, Christian (1989) *Les Archipels de la différence: Foucault, Derrida, Deleuze, Lyotard*, Paris: Editions du Félin.
Rutsky, R. L. (1999) *High Technë: Art and Technology from the Machine Aesthetic to the Posthuman*, Minneapolis: University of Minnesota Press.
Sanbonmatsu, John (2004) *The Postmodern Prince: Critical Theory, Left Strategy, and the Making of a New Political Subject*, New York: Monthly Review Press.
Sarasin, Philipp (2001) *Reizbare Maschinen: Eine Geschichte des Körpers 1765–1914*, Frankfurt: Suhrkamp.
Shakespeare, William ([1600] 1987) *The Merchant of Venice* (ed.) M. M. Mahood, The New Cambridge Shakespeare, Cambridge: Cambridge University Press.
Simondon, Gilbert (1964) *L'Individu et sa genèse psycho-biologique*, Paris: PUF.
Sloterdijk, Peter (2001) *Das Menschentreibhaus – Stichworte zur historischen und prophetischen Anthropologie*, Weimar: Verlag und Datenbank für Geisteswissenschaften.
—(2009 [1999]) 'Rules for the Human Zoo: A Response to the Letter on Humanism', trans. Mary V. Rorty, *Environment and Planning D: Society and Space* 27: 12–28.
—(2013) *You Must Change Your Life*, trans. Wieland Hoban, Cambridge: Polity.
Smith, Barbara Herrnstein (2005) *Scandalous Knowledge: Science, Truth and the Human*, Durham, NC: Duke University Press.
Sokal, Alan (2005) *Pseudosciences et postmodernisme – Adversaires ou compagnons de route?* Paris: Odile Jacob.

—(2008) *Beyond the Hoax: Science, Philosophy and Culture*, Oxford: Oxford University Press.
Sokal, Alan and Jean Bricmont (1997) *Impostures intellectuelles*, Paris: Odile Jacob.
—(1999) *Eleganter Unsinn: Wie die Denker der Postmoderne die Wissenschaften missbrauchen*, Munich: Beck.
Soper, Kate (2003) 'Humans, Animals, Machines', *New Formations* 43: 99–109.
Steeves, H. Peter (ed.) (1999) *Animal Others: On Ethics, Ontology, and Animal Life*, New York: SUNY Press.
Stepford Wives (2004 [1975]) Dir. Bryan Forbes, Anchor Bay, DVD.
Stiegler, Bernard (1998) *Technics and Time, 1: The Fault of Epimetheus*, trans. Richard Beardsworth and Georges Collins, Stanford, NC: Stanford University Press.
Stock, Gregory (1993) *Metaman: Humans, Machines, and the Birth of a Global Super-organism*, London: Bantam Press.
Stocker, Gerfried and Christine Schöpf (eds) (1999) *LifeScience*, Linz: Ars Electronica Center.
Teilhard de Chardin, Pierre (1955) *Le Phénomène humain*, Paris: Seuil.
Terminator (1984) Dir. James Cameron, Orion Pictures.
Terminator 2: Judgment Day (1991) Dir. James Cameron, Tristar Pictures.
Terminator 3: Rise of the Machines (2003) Dir. Jonathan Mostow, Warner Bros.
Terranova, Tiziana (2004) *Network Culture: Politics for the Information Age*, London: Pluto Press.
Thacker, Eugene (2003) 'What Is Biomedia?' *Configurations* 11.1: 47–79.
—(2004) *Biomedia*, Minneapolis: University of Minnesota Press.
Truong, Jean-Michel (2001) *Totalement inhumaine*, Paris: Les Empêcheurs de penser en rond.
Universal Soldier (2008 [1992]) Dir. Roland Emmerich, Optimum Home Entertainment, DVD.
Venter, Craig (2007) 'The Richard Dimbleby Lecture 2007: A DNA Driven World', http://www.bbc.co.uk/pressoffice/pressreleases/stories/2007/12_december/05/dimbleby.shtml [accessed 17 February 2013].
Vinge, Vernor (1993) 'Singularity', http://mindstalk.net/vinge/vinge-sing.html [accessed 17 February 2013].
Virilio, Paul (2005) *The Information Bomb*, London: Verso.
—(2009) *War and Cinema: The Logistics of Perception*, London: Verso.
Vita-More, Natasha (2003) 'Entropic Art Manifesto of Transhumanist Arts', www.transhumanist.biz/extropic.htm [accessed 17 February 2013].

Warwick, Kevin (1997) *March of the Machines*, London: Century.
—(2002) *I, Cyborg*, London: Century.
Weizenbaum, Joseph (1993) *Computer Power and Human Reason*, Harmondsworth: Penguin.
Wells, Robin Headlam (2005) *Shakespeare's Humanism*, Cambridge: Cambridge University Press.
Welsch, Wolfgang (1991) *Unsere postmoderne Moderne*, Weinheim: Acta humaniora.
Wiener, Norbert (1954) *The Human Use of Human Beings: Cybernetics and Society,* Boston: Da Capo Press.
—(1961) *Cybernetics, or Control and Communication in the Animal and the Machine*, 2nd edn, New York: MIT Press & John Wiley & Sons.
—(1964) *God and Golem: A Comment on Certain Points where Cybernetics Impinges on Religion*, Cambridge, MA: MIT Press.
Williams, Raymond (1989) *Politics of Modernism: Against the New Conformists*, London: Verso.
Wolfe, Cary (1995) 'In Search of Post-Humanist Theory: The Second-Order Cybernetics of Maturana and Varela', *Cultural Critique* (Spring): 33–70.
—(1998) *Critical Environments: Postmodern Theory and the Pragmatics of the Outside*, Minneapolis: University of Minnesota Press.
—(2003) *Animal Rites: American Culture, the Discourse of Species, and Posthumanist Thought*, Chicago: University of Chicago Press.
—(ed.) (2003) *Zoontologies: The Question of the Animal*, Minneapolis: University of Minnesota Press.
—(2010) *What is Posthumanism?* Minneapolis: University of Minnesota Press.
Žižek, Slavoj (1989) *The Sublime Object of Ideology*, London: Verso.
—(1992) *Enjoy Your Symptom! Jacques Lacan in Hollywood and Out*, New York: Routledge.
—(2002) 'Cultural Studies versus the "'Third Culture"', *South Atlantic Quarterly* 101.1: 19–32.
Zons, Raimund (2001) *Die Zeit des Menschen: Zur Kritik des Posthumanismus*, Frankfurt: Suhrkamp.
Zylinska, Joanna (ed.) (2002) *The Cyborg Experiments: The Extensions of the Body in the Media Age*, London: Continuum.

Index

actor network theory 41, 159, 173
Adam 54
Adorno, Theodor 180–1
affect 7, 99
Agamben, Giorgio 208–10, 213
agency 12–13, 41, 183–4, 189–90, 195, 199, 205, 210
alien 90, 107, 121, 123, 125
all-too-human 37, 55, 64–5, 70
alterhumanism 70
alterity 86–7
Althusser, Louis 11, 238, 44, 54, 83, 143
anamnesis 9
anamorphism 98, 120–2
Anders, Günther 170
android 35, 107, 122
animal 9, 21, 85, 131, 152
animal rationale 46
animality 56, 132, 166, 188
animalization 131, 133
anthropocene 48
anthropocentrism 2, 6–7, 15, 29, 32, 48–50, 58, 62, 70–1, 76, 78, 123, 132, 197, 199, 209
anthropodicy 166
anthropomorphism 173
anthropotechnics 166, 211
anthropotechnology 167–8
anti-semitism 64
antihumanism 3, 32, 41, 44–5, 58, 60–1, 70, 72, 97, 107, 126, 164, 174, 199, 202
apocalypse 3, 10, 13, 49, 87, 97, 101, 104, 114, 156, 171–2, 179
aporia 67, 213
apparatus 210 see also *dispositif*

archi-écriture 159
Aronowitz, Stanley 19–21, 149, 160
arrivant 87
art as inhuman practice 177–8
artificial intelligence 13, 20, 28, 35, 46–7, 51–2, 77, 79, 92, 104, 109, 115, 131, 151, 12, 184, 188
Artificial Intelligence: AI 129–31
artificial life 50
as if 175
Asimov, Isaac 101
Atlan, Monique 26
augmentation 55, 176 see also enhancement
Augustine 6, 58
auto-domestication 168
autoimmunity 76, 211 see also immunitarian
autopoiesis 20, 28, 198, 201–2, 205
avatar 19, 91, 183

Badiou, Alain 196
Badmington, Neil vii, 33, 44–6, 48–9, 60, 123–6, 174
Balibar, Etienne 196
Barad, Karen 212
bare life 210 see also life
Barthes, Roland 11, 23, 70, 123
Bataille, Georges 196
Baudrillard, Jean 24, 70, 96, 113, 115–6, 182–3, 189
Beck, Ulrich 80
becoming animal 105
becoming code 133
becoming human 149, 206
becoming machine 69, 105, 129

INDEX

becoming minoritarian 105
becoming other 105
becoming posthuman 130
becoming woman 105
before humanity 10
Belsey, Catherine 11–12, 58, 66–7, 70, 72
Benjamin, Walter 157, 178, 182
Bennington, Geoffrey 70
Best, Steven 49–55
Bhabha, Homi 86
Bicentennial Man 115
bioart 177
biocentrism 53
bioinformatics 171, 191
biomedia 191–2
bionic kids 111
biopolitics 53, 100, 188, 191, 198, 208, 211, 213
biopower 21, 90, 97, 188, 190, 208, 210
bios 43, 151, 209
biotechnology vii, 2, 20, 26, 91, 117, 131, 135, 151, 154, 157, 161, 163, 165, 168, 176, 188–9, 191, 197, 208
bioterrorism 27
Blackmore, Tim 189
Blade Runner 129–31
Blanchot, Maurice 196
Blavatsky, H. P. 33
blog 184
Bloom, Harold 57, 58, 64–8
Bourdieu, Pierre 114, 180
Braidotti, Rosi 86, 105, 120, 212
breeding 161, 166
Brewster, Scott 69
Bukatman, Scott 107, 116–17
Butler, Judith 86, 98

Cadava, Eduardo 195–7
Campbell, Timothy 208, 210, 212
Canguilhem, Georges 86
canon 39, 57

capitalism viii, 20, 25, 50, 79–80, 100, 115, 120, 136–7, 149, 154, 183, 186, 207
Capra, Fritjof 17
care for the self 211
carno-phallogocentrism 197, 213
Cartesianism 46, 93, 96–7, 188
Chambers, Iain 49
chatrooms 110
childhood 110–11
chimera 35, 90–1
Cixous, Hélène 212
Clarke, Bruce 198
cognitive science 8, 17, 25–6, 28, 61, 95, 112, 157, 201
cognitive turn 60
Cohen, Jeffrey Jerome 57, 87–9
Cohen, Tom 119–23
Coker, Christopher 189
colonialism 72, 160
common sense 11, 45, 72, 111
community 140–1, 210
constructivism 202
convergence 79, 176, 191
Copernicus, Nicolaus 115
Coriolanus 62
corporeality 186 *see also* embodiment
cosmopolitanism 71
Cottom, Daniel 10, 73, 119, 177–8
crimes against humanity 72
critical posthumanist reading 88, 118–34, 175
critical realism 82, 200
critical science studies 19, 22, 79, 149, 158, 160–1
Croissant, Jennifer L. 110–11, 113
cryonics 103, 115
Csicsery-Ronay, Istvan 116
cultural difference 68 *see also* difference
cultural imaginary 48, 110
cultural imperialism 160
cultural materialism 9, 58, 60, 119

cultural pessimism 18
cultural studies 17, 20, 84, 138, 140, 142, 144, 174
culture wars 142–3, 207
Curtis, Neil 55–6
cyberculture 20, 187–8
cyberdemocracy 183
cybernetics 6, 41, 48, 50, 52–3, 93, 95, 103–4, 111, 131, 138, 157–8, 171–2, 180, 186, 201, 203
cyberpunk 53, 97, 187, 192
cyberspace 104
cyberwar 188 *see also* infowar
cyborg 5, 13, 35, 38, 42–3, 48, 53, 61, 77, 83, 85, 90, 92–3, 99–103, 106, 109–11, 113, 120, 129, 131, 173, 189–92
Cyborg Bill of Rights 190
cyborgization 20, 27–8, 35, 40, 51, 63, 69, 84–5, 95, 97–8, 100, 105–7, 110, 118, 129, 131, 133, 150, 155, 176, 183, 189–90, 198, 200, 207
cynicism 97

Dante 58
Darwin, Charles 7, 27, 40, 48, 70
Dasein 14, 71
Davis, Erik 79, 103
Dawkins, Richard 17, 29, 45, 201
De Lauretis, Teresa 99
deconstruction 3, 9, 18, 22, 24, 32, 45, 48–9, 53, 55, 60, 69, 72, 77, 79, 86, 90, 71, 119, 14, 126, 132, 175, 195, 197–8, 202, 204 *see also* Derrida, Jacques
deep time 48
dehumanization 47, 69, 72, 78, 95, 124, 162, 170, 189, 191
Deleuze, Gilles 70, 85, 87, 105, 196–7, 210, 212

dematerialization 34, 95, 179, 183, 185, 188, 191
democracy, democratization 4, 55, 182, 190, 200
demystification 23, 90, 164
demythologization 123
Dennett, Daniel 17, 201
Der Derian, James 189–90
Derrida, Jacques 11, 14–15, 29, 32, 48, 66–7, 70, 85–8, 132, 143, 158–9, 161, 174–5, 179, 195, 197–8, 202–3, 212–13 *see also* deconstruction
Descartes, René 42, 48, 52, 62, 151 *see also* Cartesian
Descombes, Vincent 86, 196
desire 125
destinerrance 197
Dick, Philip K. 114
différance 11, 158, 197, 202 *see also* deconstruction
difference 12, 46–7, 65, 88–9, 125, 130, 134, 147, 202, 212
digital vii, 91, 104, 150–1
digital code 151, 179
digital culture 187–8
digital effigies 190
digital embodiment 133 *see also* embodiment
digital future 134
digital humanities 146, 179 *see also* posthumanities
digital revolution 25
digital subject 184
digitalization 25, 28, 107, 118, 133, 137, 177–93
discourse 11, 16–17, 38–9, 40–1, 83–5, 92, 99, 102, 159–60, 179, 207
disembodiment 95, 97, 101 *see also* embodiment
Disney, Walt 115
dispositif 210 *see also* apparatus

INDEX

distributed cognition 186–7, 205
Dollimore, Jonathan 58–60, 119
Dyens, Ollivier 99, 109, 151, 171
dystopia, dystopian 18, 102, 118, 27 *see also* apocalypse

e-learning 19
early modernity 59, 62, 64
Earth First! 53
eBay 84
ecology 9, 53, 193, 200
electricity 150
Eliasson, Olafur 177
Ellul, Jacques 155, 170
embodiment 4–5, 12, 19, 21, 25, 38, 42–3, 54, 62, 87, 89, 92–3, 96, 98–9, 100, 105–6, 112, 133, 177, 186–8, 201
emergence 37, 50, 79, 95, 161, 186, 201, 204, 206
empiricism 11, 175
end of man vii, 3, 13–14
enhancement 53, 96 *see also* augmentation
Enlightenment 6, 22–3, 32, 52–5, 72, 77, 93, 136, 180, 199
entropy 4–6, 9, 171
episteme 10
eschatology, eschatological 6
Esposito, Roberto 210
eugenics vii, 27, 161, 188 *see also* liberal eugenics
event 87
evolution 9, 49, 72, 101–2, 104, 172, 206
evolutionary psychology 201
evolutionary successor 51
excellence 138
existentialism 14, 15, 72
extrapolation 113
extropian, extropianism 37, 40, 53, 97, 103–4, 192 *see also* transhumanism

Facebook 84, 91, 110, 183
feminism 212
fetish, fetishization 57, 87, 89
Feyerabend, Paul 79
fictional, fictionality 175–6, 187
fictionalization of science 112
filmculture 115
Flusser, Vilém 78
Foucault, Michel 10–11, 13, 14, 21, 32, 36, 39–40, 44, 53, 70, 82, 85–6, 90, 97, 99, 137, 143, 153, 160, 188, 199, 208, 210–11
Frankenstein 27, 54, 87, 89, 114
Frankfurt School 180
Franklin, Adrian 41
free will 126–7, 132
French theory 145, 196 *see also* poststructuralism
Freud, Sigmund 7, 70, 82, 87–8
Fudge, Erica 62
Fukuyama, Francis vii, 27, 43, 62, 161–3, 165, 168, 211
future 35, 87, 90, 102
Futurism 34, 103, 177
futurology 17, 43, 103, 107

Gaggi, Silvio 75
Gaia 53
Galilei, Galileo 7
games, gaming 110, 191
Gane, Nicholas 41–2
Garber, Marjorie 135, 168–70
Gattaca 131–2, 161
Ge-stell 156
gender 93–4, 99
genetic art 177
genetic augmentation 43 *see also* enhancement
genetic determinism, genoism 131, 163
genetic engineering 27 *see also* eugenics
genetics 53, 89, 112, 168

genomics 28
ghost 9, 48, 88
Gibson, William 104
Girard, René 89
globalization 19, 23, 26, 72, 77, 79–80, 138, 142, 154, 164, 196, 207, 209–11
glocalization 79
gnosticism 96–7, 103 *see also* neognosticism
Google 84
Gould, Stephen Jay 17
governmentality 97, 160, 191, 208, 211
Graham, Elaine L. vii, 9, 60, 85, 88, 90–1, 103–4
grand narrative 6, 11, 23, 44, 49, 77, 137, 148 *see also* metanarrative
Granel, Gérard 196
Grau, Oliver 177
Gray, Chris Hables 43, 106, 189–90
Greenblatt, Stephen 58
Guattari, Félix 70, 105, 210
gynesis 160

Habermas, Jürgen 24, 27, 43, 162, 164, 168, 180, 211
haecceitas 197
Halberstam, Judith 98
Hall, Stuart 81
Halliwell, Martin 70
Hamlet 58
Hansen, Mark 99, 198
Haraway, Donna 41–2, 52, 61, 63, 86, 89, 95, 98–101, 105–6, 116, 129, 131, 173, 189–90, 198, 200, 207
hardware 184
Harry Potter 115
Hassan, Ihab 34–6, 79
haunting 86, 88, 151
hauntology 29, 88, 131

Hawkes, Terence 58, 70
Hawking, Stephen 17
Hayles, N. Katherine vii, 36, 41–3, 93–5, 151, 185–7, 195, 205–6
Hegel, G. W. F. 34, 43, 86, 163
Heidegger, Martin 14, 35, 106, 152, 155–8, 166–7, 178, 196–7, 209, 213
heteronormativity 98
Hillis Miller, J. 70
Hine, Thomas 49
Hollow Man 115
homeotechnology 168
Homer 58
hominization 44, 54, 79, 149, 158, 167–8 *see also* humanization
homo faber 170
homo inhumanus 166
homo sacer 210
Horkheimer, Max 180
humachine 181
human and animal 41, 61, 79, 101, 141, 200
human and environment 141, 185
human and machine 41–3, 61, 79, 99, 101, 181
human and nonhuman 21, 117, 129, 199, 201
human and system 71
human and technics viii, 105
human and technology 117
human cloning 161
human exceptionalism 29, 47, 162
human genome 151
Human Genome Project 91
human integrity 108
human nature vii, viii, 7, 11–12, 17, 23, 25–6, 29, 39, 43, 48, 55, 60–2, 64, 66, 90, 135, 161, 164–5, 168–9, 176, 189
human zoo 167

humanism 2–3, 6, 11–12, 16, 35, 46–8, 51, 59, 62, 69, 73, 136
humanitarian, humanitarianism 8, 66–7, 70
humanitas 57
humanities viii, 7, 13, 17, 41, 60, 135, 174 *see also* digital humanities; posthumanities
humanity 16, 20, 47, 58, 79, 90
humanization 69, 77, 166 *see also* hominization
Humboldt, Wilhelm von 136
Husserl, Edmund 196
hyperreal, hyperreality 96, 113, 116

I, Robot 115, 129–30
idealism 11
identity 11, 13, 19, 25, 51, 84, 124, 148, 183
ideology 38–9, 47, 53, 57, 78, 83, 93, 144, 188
immanence 204
immunization 211 *see also* autoimmunitarian
individualism 55
individuation 153–4, 158
Industrial Revolution 150
informatics 47, 112
information 25, 36, 42, 77, 92–3, 95, 136, 166, 171–2, 185–6, 190–1, 199
information society 19–20, 24, 78, 81, 92–3, 179–80
information superhighway 184
information technology 154, 171
informatization 79, 92–3, 111, 137, 142, 168, 185, 192
infotechnology 20
infoterror 191
inhuman 14, 22, 37, 45, 47, 49, 54–7, 87, 97, 118, 132, 134, 141, 171–2, 204

inhumanity 7, 9, 61, 68–9, 72, 77, 209
intelligent machines 42, 51
interactive, interactivity 19, 25, 185
interdisciplinarity 20, 39, 41, 135–78
interface 38, 43, 53, 96, 99, 117, 183–5, 192
internationalization 146
internet 19, 84, 154, 180, 183–5
interpellation 38, 83, 198 *see also* ideology; subject
Invasion of the Body Snatchers 124–5
invention of the inhuman 63
Irigaray, Luce 196

Jameson, Fredric 24, 77, 121–2
Jardine, Alice 160

Kac, Eduardo 177
Kamuf, Peggy 70
Kant, Immanuel 10, 58, 71
Kellner, Douglas 49–55
Kepler, Johannes 115
Kirby, Vicki 212
Kittler, Friedrich 93
Knodt, Eva 202
Kofman, Sarah 196
Kojève, Alexandre 43
Kroker, Arthur and Marielouise 36, 79
Krüger, Oliver 33, 36, 103
Kubrick, Stanley 35
Kuhn, Thomas 78
Kurzweil, Ray 40, 49–50, 103

La Mettrie, Julien Offray de 103
lab art 177
Lacan, Jacques 32, 44, 70, 82, 85, 143
Laclau, Ernesto 205
Lacoue-Labarthe, Philippe 14–15, 48, 179, 196

Lafontaine, Céline 171–2
Latour, Bruno 20–1, 41, 77, 130, 144, 158–9, 173, 198, 200
Law, John 41
Lawton, Graham 112
Le Breton, David 96–7
Lecourt, Dominique 152–5
Leitch, Vincent B. 147
Leroi-Gourhan, André 158
Levinas, Emmanuel 85, 141, 196–7
liberal eugenics 43, 165
liberal humanism 58, 67, 70, 93, 95, 120
liberal humanist self 52
liberal humanist subject 81, 151, 154, 181, 183, 186
liberalism 6, 136
life 176, 197–8, 207–13 *see also* bare life
life science 26, 140, 149, 207
life turn 207
life wars 207
liminal figure 101
linguistic turn 146
Linkedin 183
literacy 166
literature 57, 175
Livingston, Ira 98
logocentrism 70, 159, 202
Luhmann, Niklas 201–4
Lundgren, Dolf 115
Lyotard, Jean-François 4–8, 11, 14, 22–4, 44, 48–9, 56, 63, 77–9, 85, 87, 133, 136–7, 142, 147–8, 196

machine 28, 51, 85, 158, 183
machinic other 130–2
Malabou, Catherine 8
man-machine 103 *see also* cyborg
Mandelbrot, Benoit 17
Marinetti, F. T. 34, 49, 103
Marion, Jean-Luc 196

Marlowe, Christopher 64
Marx, Karl 35, 52, 70, 196
Marxism 6, 18, 47–8, 54–5, 136, 180
materialism, materialist 9, 12, 25, 97, 105, 184, 186, 212
materiality 12, 25, 93, 186
Matrix 97, 103, 133–4, 188
Mauss, Marcel 158
McEwan, Ian 61
McGergor, Wayne 177
McLuhan, Marshall 21, 24, 50–1, 79
mechanization 62–3, 91, 95
mediaculture 115
mediascape 181
mediation 21, 69, 154, 191–2
mediatization 50, 79, 115, 118, 178, 180
medicalization 91, 154, 160, 176
melancholia 6
Menser, Patrick 19–21, 149
Merchant of Venice 64–9 *see also* Shylock
metaman 104
metanarrative 76, 136, 148 *see also* grand narrative
Milburn, Colin 86, 114
military-industrial-media-entertainment complex 190
Milon, Alain 97
mind and nature 79
mind-body dualism 93, 96 *see also* Cartesian; Descartes
Minority Report 114, 126–9
Minsky, Marvin 17, 103–4
misanthropy 10, 73, 119, 177
MIT lab 49, 83
mobile phone 110, 153
modernity 6, 8, 10, 16, 21–4, 55,, 72, 111, 150, 154, 159, 173, 180, 184, 211
monster, monsterization 9, 85–6, 88–9, 159

INDEX

monster culture 57, 87
monstrosity 86–7, 105
monstrous other 86
monstrous posthuman 88
Moore's Law 50
MOOs 183
Moravec, Hans viii, 49, 103, 133
Moravec Test 92
More, Max viii, 40, 103–4
Mousley, Andy 70
MUDs 183
MySpace 91, 183
myth, mythology 11, 123, 160, 163

Nakamura, Lisa 99
Nancy, Jean-Luc 14, 48, 179, 196
nano-surveillance 190
nanobot 27, 190
nanotechnology vii, 20, 36, 53, 109, 112, 117, 135, 176
nanowriting 114
neognostic, neognosticism 97, 152 see also gnosticism
neohumanist, neohumanism 40, 172
neoimperialism 172
neoliberalism 23, 55, 77, 136, 165, 208–11
neoliberalization 137–8
neoplatonism 6, 72
neotony 167
neovitalism 105, 212
net art 177
network 50, 55, 78–9, 150, 166, 173, 179, 186, 190–1, 199, 201, 205–6
neuro-informatics 188
neurology 112
neuromedicine 26
neuroscience 47, 60–1
New age 53
new historicism 58 see also cultural materialism

new media 79, 83, 106, 110, 154, 177, 179–93 see also social media
new media art 191
new posthuman realism 43
new subjectivities 83, 95, 100, 187
Nietzsche, Friedrich 1–2, 4, 7, 31–3, 70, 132, 196, 212
nihilism 2, 32, 82, 196
Noble, David 103
nonhuman 12, 15, 37, 41, 54, 56–7, 88, 90, 95, 106, 123, 125, 150, 157, 173–4, 197
nonhuman actors 198–9, 206
nonhuman culture 173, 174
nonhuman other 57, 85, 200
nonhumanity 48
noosphere 104
Norris, Christopher 70
nostalgia 18
Nowotny, Helga 161
nuclear age 156

obscenity 182–3
observer 201
OncoMouse 89
onto-anthropo-genesis 167
ontological hygiene 85, 90
ontological liminality 88–9
originary technicity 69
Orlan 34, 103, 176
Orwell, George 53
other, otherness 9, 47, 63, 88, 131 see also alterity
othering 124, 129
Ovid 49

panopticon 210
paralogic 23
Parker, Ian 37
pedomorphosis 167
Pepperell, Robert 104
performance art 176

performative, performativity 137–8, 176
perlaboration 61, 75 see also working through
phallocentrism 70
phenotype 51
phonocentrism 159, 203
Pickering, Andrew 41
Pistorius, Oscar 109
Planet of the Apes 131–3
plasticity 8, 25, 96, 112
Plato 58
plurality 76, 81
Pol-Droit, Roger 26
politics of in(ter)vention 161
politics of representation 47, 57, 76, 81, 84, 87, 95, 102, 105
politics of the inhuman 56
popular culture 48, 78, 108
popular science 36, 83, 89, 144, 177
popular science magazine 17, 25
post- 16, 48, 69, 76, 87
post-gender 98, 100–1
postanthropocentrism 3, 14, 72, 80, 106, 168, 207
postapocalyptic 24
postbiological 27, 95–7
postcolonial theory 71
Poster, Mark 93, 180–5, 187
posthistorical 138
posthuman 24, 36–7, 49, 57, 69, 76, 83, 88
posthuman bodies 98–9
posthuman condition 29, 189, 198
posthuman culture 173
posthuman forms 75–106
posthuman monster 105
posthuman subject 93, 95
posthuman zoo 98
posthumanism as discourse viii, 36–7
posthumanism without technology 44–5, 156–7

posthumanist definition of culture 124
posthumanist politics 205, 210
posthumanist subject 59, 106, 213
posthumanities 13, 20, 60, 135–78, 179, 202, 207 see also digital humanities
posthumanity 36–7, 48, 69, 81, 151, 195–206
postindustrial society 24, 137
Postman, Neil 110, 160
postmetaphysics 197
postmodern 5–6, 51–2, 75, 79, 137
postmodernism 12, 16, 22–3, 136, 145–6, 181
postmodernity 16, 34, 137
postmodernization 23, 80
postscience 80
poststructuralism 3, 11–12, 14, 21, 31, 41, 44, 52, 58, 66, 71, 82–4, 111, 143, 180, 196, 198, 202 see also deconstruction; French Theory
pragmatism 140
prehuman, prehumanism 51, 141 see also before humanity
Prometheus 34, 54, 160
prosthesis 2, 35, 42, 96, 115, 171, 176
prosthesization 20, 28, 50, 91, 98, 107, 178
prosthetics 192
prosumer 184
psychoanalysis 9, 18, 48, 55, 68, 72, 82, 125–6

queer 98

Rabinow, Paul 70
race 99
Rancière, Jacques 196

Readings, Bill 138–44, 148
realism 5, 10–11, 21
Rees, Martin 29
reflexive humanization 80
reflexivity 155
rehumanization 71–2
religion 103
rematerialization 186, 191
remediation 63, 186, 192
Renaissance 115
representation 10–11, 13, 57, 121–2, 182, 185, 193, 202 *see also* politics of representation
response-ability 198
Rhodes, Neil 63
Ridley, Matt 201
risk society 80
Ritzer, George 41
robo sapiens 13, 92, 177
robot 77
robot teleology 42
robotic art 177
robotics 47, 131
Rosenau, Paul Marie 23
Ruby, Christian 85
Rutsky, R. L. 178

Sacks, Oliver 17
Said, Edward 86
Sanbonmatsu, John 71
Sartre, Jean-Paul 14, 196
Saussure, Ferdinand de 70, 82
Sawday, Jonathan 62–3
Schwarzenegger, Arnold 27, 38, 115, 121
science faction 114, 116
science fiction 34, 38–9, 46, 48–9, 51, 87, 97, 100, 102–3, 107–34, 144, 151, 164, 177, 187, 192–3
science wars 136, 142, 144, 207
scientism 160, 162
second media age 180, 184

Shakespeare, William 57–8, 61–2, 64, 66 *see also Hamlet*; *Merchant of Venice*
Shannon, Claude 186
Shylock 58, 64–8, 158 *see also Merchant of Venice*
Simondon, Gilbert 153, 158
simulacrum 24
simulation 42, 95, 116, 178, 182–3, 188, 191
singularity 15, 33, 40, 47, 104, 112
Sloterdijk, Peter 151, 165–8, 170, 208, 210–11
smart 150, 184
Snow, C. P. 41, 144
social media vii, 25, 154 *see also* new media
software 134, 184
Sokal hoax 145–6
sovereignty 208
species anxiety 25
species boundaries 91
speciesism 14, 47, 123, 133, 174, 199
Star Wars 101
Stelarc 34, 38, 96, 103, 176
Stepford Wives 129–30
Stewart, Ian 17
Stiegler, Bernard 152, 158
Stock, Gregory 104
subculture 84
subject, subjectivity 5, 10, 12–13, 21, 25, 38–9, 59, 70, 78, 81, 83, 85, 102, 144, 180–1, 183, 185, 195–206
subjugated knowledge 39, 160
subversion and containment 119
succession, successor, successor species 28, 172, 176
supplement 22, 86
surveillance 19, 25, 80, 188, 190–1, 210
Swift, Jonathan 115
symptom 87

system, systems theory 4, 8–9, 78, 95, 138, 195–206

taming 151, 166
task of thinking 157
technics 9, 22, 50, 79, 95, 149–50, 152–5, 193
techno-dystopia 111
techno-euphoria 85
techno-idealism 96, 103–4
techno-ideology 104
techno-sceptics 155
techno-utopia 111
technoart 178
technocracy 160
technocultural condition 116
technocultural imaginary 100, 113
technoculture 3, 19, 20, 35, 78, 80, 84, 89, 99–100, 110, 134, 136, 149, 151–5, 179, 207
technofeminism 98, 100
technological determinism 18, 78, 103–4, 113, 152, 155, 160, 181, 192, 208
technological imaginary 116
technological sublime 104
technological unconscious 151
technologies of the self 53–4, 85, 90, 96, 98, 153, 160
technologization 15, 20, 23, 35, 45, 50, 55, 72, 76, 79, 81, 91, 110, 115, 149, 176, 186, 198
technology 7, 17, 90, 106, 149, 150, 155, 178
technology of sex 99
technophallocentrism 213
technophilia, technophile 53, 192
technophobia 192
technopolis 160
technoprophet 46, 49, 55, 104
technosceptic 53
technoscience 19, 20, 23, 55, 79–80, 108, 115, 136, 149, 154–5, 207

technoutopia 51, 95, 152
Teilhard de Chardin, Pierre 104
  see also noosphere
telekinetics 183
teratogenesis 88
teratology 29, 88, 105
terminal identity 116–17
Terminator 27, 103, 115, 126, 151
Terminator 2 119–23
Terranova, Tiziana 99
terrorism 191, 208, 211 *see also* infoterror
text messaging 110
Thacker, Eugene 191–2
thanatopolitics 208, 210–13
theory wars 143
thinking after the human 158
third culture 17
Thrift, Nigel 41
Tipler, Frank 103
trace 158, 203–4
transcoding 192
transduction 158, 191
transgenic 171
transhumanism viii, 15, 32, 37, 39–40, 44, 51, 53, 55, 72, 78, 92, 95–7, 101, 103–4, 130, 166, 170, 177 *see also* extropian
transhumanity 13, 29
transhumanization 35
transnationalization 175
transversal reason 23
trauma 151
trickster 101
Truong, Jean-Michel 151, 172
Turing, Alan 93
Turing Test 92, 106
two cultures 41, 144

uncanny 88
Universal Soldier 115
university 72, 138

vampire 88
Varela, Francisco 201
Velázquez, Diego 82
Venter, Craig 27–8
Vickers, Brian 58
Vinge, Vernor viii, 104, 112
Virilio, Paul 189
virtual art 177
virtual reality 91, 97, 133, 184, 186
Vita-More, Natasha 103, 177
vitalism 32 *see also* neovitalism
vivants 197–8

Warwick, Kevin 38, 101–2
Weber, Max 70
Weinberg, Steven 17
Wells, Robin Headlam 60
Welsch, Wolfgang 22–4, 75–9
Western metaphysics 34, 86, 156
wetware 53
Wiener, Norbert 41, 103–4, 186
wiki 184
Williams, Raymond 18, 84, 160
Wittgenstein, Ludwig 140, 196
Wolfe, Cary vii, 174, 198–200, 201
working through 16, 48, 69 *see also* perlaboration

xenotransplantation 171

YouTube 84, 91

Žižek, Slavoj 17–18, 32, 86
zoe 209 *see also* bare life; *bios*
zombie 88
Zons, Raimund 14

Printed in Great Britain
by Amazon